CAUGHT WITH MY PANTS DOWN

and Other Tales from a Life in Hollywood

BY JIM PIDDOCK

Printed in the United States of America

Print ISBN: 978-1-953910-98-1
Hardcover ISBN: 978-1-956019-67-4
eBook ISBN: 978-1-956019-00-1
Library of Congress Control Number: 2022900607

Published by DartFrog Blue, the traditional publishing imprint of DartFrog Books.

Publisher Information:
DartFrog Books
4697 Main Street
Manchester, VT 05255
www.DartFrogBooks.com

Join the discussion of this book on Bookclubz. Bookclubz is an online management
tool for book clubs, available now for Android and iOS and via Bookclubz.com.

"Jim's book gives the reader an opportunity to understand the peripatetic nature of a creative life in Hollywood and an interesting view into the British expat community in Los Angeles. There are truly hilarious stories (one involving a train toilet fiasco that I will recall on my deathbed to cheer myself up), tales of production with people you've always wondered about, and real insights into the way the 'industry' actually works from someone with a range of experiences and a clear eye. The book is never less than extremely funny, intriguing, and thoroughly charming—like the man himself."
- **Diedrich Bader**

"Jim Piddock's often hilarious, sometimes wicked, and occasionally heartbreaking memoir provides a deeply entertaining look at a life filled to the brim with...well...life."
- **Bob Balaban**

"Jim Piddock is as charming and hilarious on paper as he is in person. I'm a sucker for a good Hollywood story and *Caught with My Pants Down* is chock-full. It's the perfect ratio of funny, fascinating, and cringe. You don't have to be in showbiz to appreciate this book, but after reading it you might want to be."
- **Ike Barinholtz**

"I laughed till I wet myself, down on the floor, gasping for air! Okay, I don't remember laughing, but my caregiver tells me I did when I read Jim's book, and I know the rest is true because it's right there in my chart at the end of the bed. It is a joyous journey through a life well lived that has happily intersected with mine quite often."
- **Ed Begley, Jr.**

"From Facebook surveys about who is the biggest **** in the industry, to the poignancy of his daughter's arrival in the world, Jim Piddock's book is a hilarious, passionate, beautifully told, and memorably waspish account of an actor, writer, father, and besotted

soccer player/fan, who loves—and lives—the bonkers world of show business. A raw, rude, and very funny account of Jim's decades on the planet. And, no, that's not a speck of dust in your eye."
- Hugh Bonneville

"Jim has done that rare thing that perhaps only Michael Caine and David Niven have done before; conjured a funny, inclusive, whimsical, and magical tale about the peculiar interior of the world of film and film stars. As warm and immersive as fentanyl, without the social damage (one hopes)."
- Russell Brand

"*Caught with My Pants Down* is an absolute classic. I laughed out loud so many times I was more out of breath than after playing ninety minutes of football. A truly wonderful read!"
- Mark Bright

"This a great memoir. Anyone interested in or considering the life of an actor should pick it up. Also, I can't tell you how happy I was to find Jim didn't mention his working with me on *The Drew Carey Show* in the chapter called 'Rock Bottom.' So definitely get this book. Whether you buy it or steal it is up to you and your God."
- Drew Carey

"If I'm honest, the chance to be in the company of actors like Jim, and hearing stories like his, are why I decided to go into acting. What a great hang this book is!"
- John Cho

"Jim Piddock has written a book, good for him. Jim hangs around in Los Angeles and goes to parties at Eric Idle's house, where lots of famous folk ask him what he does for a living. I have always liked him, he makes me feel very famous. People feel sorry for him because he

supports Crystal Palace, who help to make up the numbers in the English Premier League."
- Sir Billy Connolly CBE

"A crackerjack beaut doozy hot dog stuff humdinger jim-dandy lollapalooza book."
- Frances Conroy

"*Caught with My Pants Down* bears all the hallmarks of being the 21st century's answer to David Niven's classic Hollywood memoir *The Moon's A Balloon*. Although there wasn't enough about the wonderful actor James Cosmo."
- James Cosmo MBE

"I must confess that I am more than slightly biased, when I say how much I loved reading this memoir. Jim Piddock and I, along with several wonderful actors, shared the stage in the original Broadway production of Michael Frayn's *Noises Off*. Aside from being a superb actor, he's had great success as a screen writer. This book reveals his personal story in such an honest, hilarious, and truly moving way, I feel cheated by the time I've missed being in his company. It's a glorious reflection of a complicated, fascinating artist."
- Victor Garber

"A great storyteller, Jim Piddock shares insight, reveals his humility, and dishes just the right amount of gossip to make this the perfect read."
- Jessalyn Gilsig

"Jim Piddock is a funny man with a trove of stories to tell."
- Christopher Guest

"Fred Willard's dog-show color commentator in *Best In Show* might be, joke for joke, the funniest character in any movie...but

it doesn't work unless you have Jim Piddock next to him, playing it real and nuanced...and he does it so well that it makes Willard a billion times better. When I watch those scenes now, I just watch Piddock. He's a genius."
- Bill Hader

"Jim Piddock is a sharp, witty, and erudite man. Head to head with Shakespeare, most critics have said Jim would win in a knife fight. I like his style."
- Eddie Izzard

"A brilliant and colorful ride and romp through Hollywood from one of the business's funniest men. Honest, witty, and quite simply a great read."
- Ross King MBE

"This book is so much fun! Laugh out loud funny, warm, self deprecating, and hugely entertaining."
- Jane Leeves

"This funny, heartwarming, and delightful book is a lot like the author himself. Witty, dry, self deprecating, and utterly lovable in a British salty style. I love a good Hollywood yarn and this book is packed with them. I can't remember the last time I read a book in just two sittings, but it's a testament to Jim's charm and likability. I can think of no greater accolade than to say I will be buying several copies of this and sending them to friends, some of whom are mentioned in the book. I will also think twice about any significant bowel movements whilst traveling on British rail. Buy or steal this book from a friend. You'll be glad you did."
- Sean Maguire

"Filled with name dropping, gossip, and irreverence, you won't find a more delicious, funny, and often very moving ride through the world

of show business. It's crystal clear why Jim Piddock is one of the most beloved, enduring, and talented British actor-writers in Hollywood."
- Camryn Manheim

"When I wasn't gasping or laughing my head off, I was wondering why my life is so boring compared to Jim Piddock's. If you're ever wondering what it takes to be an actor, read this book."
- Elizabeth McGovern

"Just as Jim Piddock is a delightful addition to any film, TV show or play that he is in, so will this book be a delightful addition to your library, briefcase, or beach bag. Genial, cheeky, often hilarious, and grounded with a warm heart."
- Douglas McGrath

"Dry as a bone, lethal as a rapier. Couldn't put it down. Great read."
- Ian McShane

"Jim has a big heart and a sharp wit and both are on display in the pages of this book. So f*cking read it."
- Seth Meyers

"Jim has been responsible for too many comedic peaks to catalog them all here, in a quote. But he probably mentions them in this book."
- Chris O'Dowd

"Being in a sidecar of Jim Piddock's journey was an incredibly fun ride! So funny and vulnerable that I found myself rooting for him to win, whether on the field, in his career, or in life. You don't have to be an actor to relate. His win was my win."
- Cheri Oteri

"Jim is in his element as he takes the reader on a glorious adventure in acting (and football), peppered with wisdom, cautionary tales, and endless good humour."
- **Susanna Reid**

"If you ever wondered why anyone would cast their fate to the wind and become an actor (or if you just want to read something wildly entertaining), you will find that this laugh-out-loud book answers that question and much more. Jim's early stories of working the most bizarre, sometimes demeaning—and usually hilarious—jobs on his path to success will keep you turning the pages of this incredibly witty and often very personal memoir. His encounters with the great and near-great will make you guffaw, while his incredibly insightful take on his life, and life in general, will bring a tear to your eye as you nod knowingly. From briefly selling dildos for a living and filming in a pit of snakes to sparring with Sharon Stone, Jim Piddock entertains endlessly and most wisely."
- **Jean Smart**

"I've had the great fortune to work with Jim on two different films. On camera he's hysterical and exudes intelligence, warmth, and charisma. Off camera he is none of those things. That's why he's a great actor! Seriously though, he's the best and this book makes for a wonderful read!"
- **Nicholas Stoller**

"A hilarious and occasionally tear-jerking read. A fascinating insight into an actor/writer's life. I loved it."
- **Geoff Thomas MBE**

"As a fellow second-tier character actor, Jim Piddock's book provides hope that one day my own remembrances and celebrity-adjacent bon mots will add up to a memoir half as entertaining as this. It makes me realise that I should have treated him with much more

respect when we were working together."
- Alan Tudyk

"By turns philosophical and witty, and then delightfully vulgar, also chock-full of delicious gossip, this hilariously entertaining opus will have you laughing one moment, and surprisingly moved to tears the next, by some unexpectedly moving revelations. . . . My only misgiving is that Lord Jim Piddock was never caught with his pants down in my immediate vicinity, (though he did once audibly break wind during a scene we were filming together, but, ever professional, I resisted giggling, as I thought it might be have been mine)."
- Jacki Weaver

"*Caught with My Pants Down* is crazy entertaining. Jim Piddock has met everybody and pulls no punches."
- Chris Weitz

"Wow. This is a glorious, very funny, very tender and addictive book. Jim is a real actor (not a pampered star on Planet Mental) and his insider's view on working constantly as an open-minded, big-hearted Englishman in LA is just wonderful. The bits on his daughter and Sharon Stone (not the same bits FYI) will stay with me forever!"
- Sophie Winkleman

"I think I just went to a long, late night supper with Jim Piddock and his friends, and I had a few drinks and laughed a lot. Reading his book is like that. Wining and dining with someone who you hope will keep talking, regaling you with their stories and making you laugh."
- Mare Winningham

For Ally and Annie

CONTENTS

FOREPLAY

I have had the pleasure of knowing Jim Piddock for twenty-five years, ever since we met in 1996 on the set of one of the worst pictures ever made. He is the nicest funny man, and the funniest nice man I know. He is a frequent visitor to our house and has been to our secret European hideaway on many occasions, often with his lovely daughter Ally, and more recently with the amazing Annie, so I ought to recuse myself, but I'm not going to. Why? Because this is a foreword, not a bloody law court. I'm not shouting. I'm simply trying to explain to the casual reader why they should buy this book. No, I don't know the name of the casual reader. It's a metaphor. Alright, not a metaphor: litotes or something. I'm just trying to say that I am hopelessly tainted as an independent witness, because I have adored Jim from the day I met him in a psych ward with Naomi Campbell.

No, it wasn't a real one. It was on a movie set. We were acting: something Jim does effortlessly, and I reluctantly. We spent some days on a hospital set, with me gaga, Naomi adorable, and Jim very funny in a deadly but discreet way. He was a subtle subversive whom I liked at once. Modest, quiet, hilarious—I could be describing myself. What do you mean, no I couldn't? Yes, I know Jim is *nice*. I already said that. Yes, I do know nobody could accuse me of that. Yes, I agree he takes modesty to extremes and no one could charge me with—look, do you mind? I'm trying to finish this. There is a deadline. When? Yesterday. Yes, I know I'd better get on with it then...

Jim Piddock is what they call in Hollywood a hyphenate, or a multi, which means he's good at many things. He writes and produces movies and he also acts extremely well, or did in the days when you were allowed to pretend to be other people. I have exploited his comedic talents on many occasions, most memorably in *What About Dick?*

where he made me laugh my ass off. I discovered he was a fellow football freak, like me, addicted to English soccer. Back then, it was in its infancy on American TV, and you could watch it only by going down to the pub before dawn to a packed saloon filled with sweaty English footie fans in team shirts, shouting abuse, singing team songs, consuming a full English breakfast, and swallowing pints of beer at dawn while smoking heavily…

It was vile. I always came home sputtering and sick. Fortunately, it soon moved on to cable.

This book is more than a memoir; it's an intimate behind-the-scenes look at a young man from his early beginnings in weekly rep in the UK, to his escape to San Francisco, where he found success in the theatre, thence to Broadway and then Hollywood, and a home in the Hollywood Hills. Here in California, he is my brother from the same planet. I am the Jules to his Jim, the Long John Silver to his Hawkins. We share a love of English literature, football, cricket, irony, humor, humour, and relaxing in secret European hideouts. He's been my pal for a quarter of a century, and I love him dearly. I know that when you have read his book, you will see why.

ERIC IDLE

A note from the author about the spelling:

I debated whether to use British or American English when writing this book and, even though I've lived a lot more of my life in America, I decided that my British readers would be more likely to get upset by me using Americanisms than my American readers would be about any Britishisms.

I'm not sure what that says about each nationality, but I fully anticipate upsetting both sets of readers by using American expressions and British colloquialisms throughout.

And obviously the words "PANTS" in the title of the book means two slightly different things in each country. However, in this particular instance, it doesn't change the meaning or veracity of the incident in question!

INTRODUCTION

L et me start by saying I wrote this book somewhat by accident. In 2017, I was asked to appear in something the Screen Actors Guild organised called *Let's Talk About It: Inside the Industry*. Basically, it involved me being interviewed by a *Wall Street Journal* entertainment reporter named Erich Schwartzel in a 200-seat theatre in Los Angeles and then doing a Q & A with the audience after the interview. The whole thing lasted about ninety minutes, and the reaction seemed to be very positive, and I ended up really enjoying it. So much so that I began to think about breaking my long theatrical hiatus and putting together a one-man stage show, doing the same sort of thing as I'd done that evening: telling stories—irreverent, gossipy, and otherwise—about some of my professional and personal experiences over the years, along with a fair amount of shameless name-dropping.

So I started writing the show, but once I got going I was coming up with more and more material until it got to the point where it was going to be a one-man show that lasted at least ten hours. I figured that might test the attention span of even the most dedicated theatre-goer, so I decided to turn it into a book instead.

I knew while I was writing it that the quasi-memoir of someone who is *kind* of known but definitely not an A-list celebrity might be a tough sell. The simple truth is that if you were to mention my name to ten random people on the street, about one of them might recognise it. But if you then showed them a photo, about five or six might recognise me. And if you then showed them a list of all the things I've been in and/or written, about nine, or even all ten, might have seen one or more of them. However, this is by no means a scientific statistical analysis—mainly because I don't go around asking random people on the street such immodest questions—and I didn't let my lack of A-list celebrity status deter me from writing this book for two reasons: (1) I'd never written a book before and I'd always wanted to, and (2) I thought it would be something my daughter, Ally, may enjoy reading at some point.

While I was writing, I tried to make it something that would appeal to as wide a readership as possible, not just people who are already interested in—or maybe even involved in—the entertainment industry. But, more than anything, I wanted it to be a fun and colourful romp through some of the stories that have made up one man's life thus far, whatever field he happens to have worked in. If frequent brushes with well-known names and faces make the book more noteworthy or appealing, I'll take that. Although I also hope it can stand on its own, and in its own right. But if you think it doesn't, you can always re-gift it and give it to your worst enemy.

That all said, the *biggest* reason of all to buy the book (if you haven't already) is that a large percentage of any royalties I make from it will be split between two charities that are dear to my heart: BAFTA's US Access for All program in America and the Palace for Life Foundation in England (details of both of which can be found at the end of the book).

So please don't make me look bad by rendering me unable to give them each a handsome sum of money. If not for me, buy the book for all the kids and their futures!

JIM PIDDOCK
Los Angeles
February 2022

1

THE MOMENT OF TRUTH

I t all began in earnest when I was upside down. The year was 1977. I was twenty-one years old and it was my first day at drama school in London. And I was *very* nervous. I'd acted in plays at school and university, but this was the real deal. Time to prove myself among sixty other wannabe actors who had come here from all over the United Kingdom, Europe, and North America.

I wasn't used to beginning a day of classes so early, so by lunchtime I was starving. Most people had brought their own food in or gone to a nearby sandwich place. But I went down the street to a dingy little Chinese restaurant and ordered the three-course lunch special. After wolfing it down, I waddled back to the school and looked at my schedule for the rest of the day. And immediately wished I'd done that *before* I'd gone to lunch . . . because next up was a class called Movement. With my stomach distended with beef chop suey, egg fried rice, and kung pao chicken, I guessed it wasn't the same kind of movement I wanted at that moment.

I changed into the required attire for the class, which was leotards for women and black tights and roll-neck sweaters for men. And I felt particularly self-conscious, trying my best to look cool around all the young actresses in their flattering dance wear. The teacher was a small, bearded, and rather camp American man, and he announced that we'd start off with headstands. Two students stood at the end of a mat to act as spotters, and we all had to line up and take our turns at propelling ourselves into the headstand . . . at which point the spotters would grab our ankles and hold us in a perfectly perpendicular position for a few seconds before we'd roll out of it onto the mat. In theory, anyway.

After a few people had performed this feat—enviably well, in my opinion—I soon found myself upside down in the middle of the studio floor at one end of the mat. My headstand wasn't the best, I'll admit, but I hadn't disgraced myself so far. I held my position for the required number of seconds before the teacher commanded the two students holding me:

"And . . . *release!*"

And so I rolled out of the headstand and, as I landed, I *did* release . . . the loudest, hardest, sharpest fart you've ever heard in your life. It was so loud, hard, and sharp it almost sounded like the crack of a starting pistol.

I lay on the mat, mortified, in the stunned silence that now gripped the room . . . my eyes closed, counting the seconds before the inevitable explosion of laughter and derision that would surely follow. It was like those horrible few beats of anticipation when a child falls over and time stands still as its parents wait for the inevitable piercing scream and flood of tears. My whole *non*-future in show business flashed before my closed eyes in that moment. But that silence didn't end. For several seconds. And the laughter never came. And, finally, I very cautiously opened one eye and peered up at everyone gathered around and looking down at me as if they were peering into an open grave. Their faces were filled with a mixture of horror and confusion as I heard the Movement teacher gasp and exclaim:

"Omigod, are you *okay*? What *was* that?"

So I—recognising a potential lifeline when it was miraculously being thrown to me—winced as if in acute pain and said:

"It's my ankle again. An old football injury. It does that sometimes. Could someone help me up?"

And so a couple of very kind aspiring actresses helped me to my feet and, with great concern, supported me physically as I hobbled away to a nearby bench to "recover." After expressing their enormous sympathy and admiration for my stoic suffering, they went back to the headstand mat.

And I sat there for the remainder of the class, secure in the knowledge that I had *exactly* what it takes to be an actor.

Later on, when I was in the men's changing room, I received yet more concern and sympathy from all the guys in the class, who asked me if I'd be okay. And I responded:

"Yeah, I'll be fine. Couple of days, it should be better. Maybe less. In fact, to be honest, it feels pretty good right now."

As everyone started to filter out to the next class, one of the American students hung back.

"Can I ask you a question, Jim?" he said.

"Sure," I replied.

And then he said, as more of a statement than a question:

"You farted, didn't you."

Finally busted, I had to come clean and admitted that I had. His reaction was to high-five me and declare:

"Fuckin' A, man!"

Which goes to prove that you can fool most of the people most of the time.

But not *everyone*.

2

THE VALUE OF A MONOCLE

Acting wasn't my first career choice. Until I was fifteen, I wanted to be a professional footballer—or soccer player, if you're from America. And I was going to play for the team I'd supported passionately from an early age, Crystal Palace Football Club. There was only one thing that stopped me: I was rubbish at football. I don't mean I was too rubbish to captain my school team or play at a decent level at university, because I just about managed that. I mean I was too rubbish to even clean the boots of the teenage apprentices who clean the boots of the professional players at Crystal Palace.

I wanted to be a footballer because I loved playing and watching football and I thought it might be a good idea to spend my life doing things I liked. That always seemed to me like an obvious thing to do, given that in the grand roll call of history we're only here on this planet for the blink of an eye. But, on a less philosophical level, the truth is that, from a very young age, I got very bored very quickly when I did things that didn't interest me. So, choosing to do a job I wasn't interested in for forty odd years never seemed like a viable option.

My parents, Charles and Celia Piddock, provided a very stable and loving upbringing in our house in a tiny village called Bessels Green, located just outside Sevenoaks in Kent. And saying it was tiny is no exaggeration. There was a village green, one pub, two churches, and a post office in the front room of someone's terraced house. Being of good English middle class stock, ours wasn't a demonstrably affectionate or overtly emotional household, but I got along well with my (quite a bit) older brother, Peter, and my two sisters, Anne (slightly older) and Caroline (quite a bit younger). But, at the same time, I knew from a very young age that there was an itch that needed to be scratched. It wasn't a major source of angst or conflict, just more of an awareness that I didn't want to inhabit the world I was raised in for the rest of my life. I think there are a few people who are born into the exact circumstances they were destined for . . . and they end up living in the same place they were raised and remain part of a tight-knit family, working in the family business and marrying their childhood sweethearts. But I knew that wasn't going to be me. At the same time, human beings are tribal by nature, and, like most people, I wanted to belong to a clan.

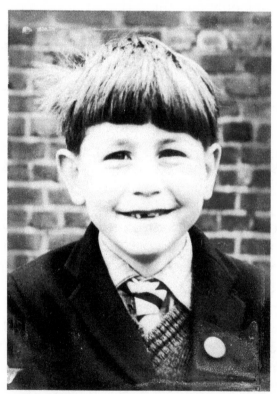

Clearly destined to become an international sex symbol.

This mild disassociation from my home life became a bit more complicated when, at the age of ten, I was packed off to a Catholic boarding school in Sussex called Worth Abbey, which was run by Benedictine monks. I was eager to experience new pastures and wanted to go there, but it was probably something I should have done two or three years later because I don't think I was ready to leave the nest and, for my whole first year, I was extremely homesick. So, for any parents reading this, packing your kids off to boarding school at age ten is an excellent thing to do if you want them to become independent when they're very young, but a bit less excellent if you don't want them to have a few minor abandonment issues later in life. The whole Catholic thing was another element, of course, but it left no lasting scars and can give one a fine appreciation of silly costumes and even sillier rituals—not to mention an arsenal of tricks when it comes to undermining them. Inventing "sins" for our weekly confession ritual was a particularly fun pastime. Although one creative classmate really pushed the boat out when he confessed to having had "red-hot monkey sex with Father Bruno." There was a rather long pause on the other side of the confessional screen before a voice quietly said:

"This is Father Bruno. And, no, you haven't."

Which reminded the rest of us to always check the name of the priest hearing confessions before going in.

I was above average on the intelligence scale but below average in having any enthusiasm for academic studies. I liked English and History, but not much else. Although, I didn't get off to the best of starts in English class in my first year. We were asked to write an essay, the subject of which I thought was quite strange: "What is your view on the value of a monocle?" But the whimsical nature of the assignment appealed to me, so I wrote a vigorous defence of the value of a single eyepiece as a great space-saving device, which I also considered to be rather stylish, albeit (although I'm sure I didn't use that word) in an old-fashioned way. It was the perfect implement, I argued, for someone with one bad eye and one good eye. And I could even speak from personal experience, because when I was a toddler I had acquired a serious squint after my developing eye muscles were repeatedly jarred from a bout of whooping cough. I had an operation when I was three years old, but one eye never got corrected properly, so I only had one functioning eye myself.

All in all, I reckoned I'd done a pretty decent job with my essay. But when it came back after being marked, I'd got an F. Hugely disappointed, I raised my hand to ask why I'd failed. The teacher smiled affably at me and said:

"Let me read a couple of sentences to the class and then I'll explain."

Which is what he did. And it got enormous laughs. Now I was even more confused. Why in the name of all things sacred was my passionate essay in defence of the monocle so bloody amusing? Well, finally, I was enlightened. It turned out the assignment of the essay had in fact been: "What is your view on the value of a *monarchy*?"

After the botched eye operation.

By the time I was fifteen, I'd managed to learn what the word "monarchy" meant, but I still felt like I didn't quite belong where I was currently situated in the world. I was a middle-class boy with an upper-class education and working-class interests. I was also really bored with school, so I decided, on a sudden whim, to audition for the annual school play—even though I was officially a year too young to be considered. But somehow I was considered, and somehow I got cast. And so I came to make my theatrical debut in The Worth School Dramatic Society's production of Jean Anouilh's *Ring Round the Moon*. The play even had an official program printed, which had an interesting disclaimer at the end. It declared:

> In the event of a power cut, the play will continue by candlelight, music being provided by Father Philip at the pianoforte and other sound effects by imagination.

That might sound like an oddly specific and pessimistic pronouncement, but between January 9th and February 28th of 1972, there was a widespread strike in England by the National Union of Mineworkers, so there were a number of power cuts during those weeks. I don't remember us ever being plunged into complete darkness, thanks to some disgruntled and underpaid coal diggers, but I do remember standing in the wings before my first entrance on opening night and feeling overwhelmingly nauseous and elated. I was absolutely terrified . . . and yet, at that same moment, I knew it was what I wanted to do for the rest of my life.

Although that was the first "aha!" moment about being a performer, there was probably an earlier clue about a decade earlier. At the age of five, I was taken to my first ever theatrical event, which was a Christmas pantomime at the Churchill Theatre in Bromley, Kent. I was a pretty timid and quiet child at that age, so, when the actors asked for some volunteers from the audience to come up on stage to participate in a scene, it was quite a surprise to my parents when my hand immediately shot up. I ended up being chosen, but while

I don't really remember what happened after I got on the stage, I don't believe I disgraced myself. When I try to recall what could have been going through my mind when my grubby little paw shot up so quickly, the only explanation I can come up with now is that I think it seemed like a much more magical and colourful world up there on the stage compared to the one I'd been living in up until then.

In my last year at school, we had a Careers Advisory Day. The careers advisor, a middle-aged bachelor who had taught me Latin and Greek, asked me what career I intended to pursue.

When I told him I wanted to be an actor, he replied:

"A highly unrealistic choice, Piddock. *Very* few people ever make a living doing that. What's your second choice?"

Coming up with a Plan B on the spot, I said that if I couldn't be an actor, I wanted to be a writer.

"Have you ever written a book?" he asked.

"No," I replied.

And his response to my Plan B was as definitive as it was to my Plan A:

"Then you'll never be a writer."

I think the moral of this particular little story is twofold:

1. Never let anyone tell you who or what you can or can't be because they're inevitably wrong.

2. Passing exams in Latin and Greek is as useful in life as a trapdoor on a submarine.

My seven years at boarding school certainly left an imprint on me. And I mean literally, because in those days, corporal punishment was still legal and it was used quite prevalently at schools like Worth Abbey. I wasn't a particularly subversive or disobedient kid but you couldn't help falling foul of some of the pettiest of the strict rules. So we'd all end up being regularly beaten on the backside with a cane— or a wooden spoon, in the early years—simply for talking to someone on the way from a classroom to the refectory or getting poor marks in an exam. Looking back at it now, the systematic cruelty and brutality of beating children seems appalling, but at the time we all just accepted it as the way things were. And it clearly didn't cause a lifelong resentment because, as well as keeping in touch with a number of my school friends, I've also maintained friendships with two or three monks and other teachers at Worth to this day. Also, to put another positive spin on it, I think it helped engender a feeling of togetherness and a "brothers in arms, united against a common foe" mentality among the students. In that sense, my boarding school compatriots became my new family and surrogate siblings. Which makes sense because I spent twenty-four hours a day with them for about eight months of every year. In other words, twice as long as I spent with my family at home. Not to mention the fact that, in order to maintain my sanity, I needed to find some kind of humour in the circumstances I found myself in, so, despite being more of an introvert by nature, I also became something of a class clown.

With my parents at a wedding, I believe
(I don't remember us dressing like this on an every day basis).

In addition to being easily bored, I've always been impatient. Except in the womb, where I must have been quite comfortable, because I didn't pop my head out until three weeks after my due date (and covered in sebaceous slime, according to my mother). But, once I entered the world, I've been consistently eager to make up for those lost three weeks. So it was no surprise that I wanted to become an actor the minute I left school. However, my father—though a firm believer himself in choosing a career you actually liked—persuaded me to at least get a degree in *something*, so I'd have a backup plan.

So I ended up going to London University to study for a degree in "English Literature and Language," which would offer me the least amount of career backup plans. And I chose London, rather than the fancier options of Oxford or Cambridge, because (a) I wouldn't have to live on a campus, which seemed far too much like the previous seven years at boarding school, and (b) I figured I could get by with just reading a few more books to supplement what I'd already read in school and spend the rest of the time doing stuff I actually wanted to do.

This resulted in me spending most of my time majoring in the subjects of acting and football. With a minor in drinking beer and getting laid which, as a heterosexual, had been a distinct challenge at an all-boys boarding school.

3

"F*CK OFF AND BE AN ACTOR!"

I never really felt particularly connected to university life, apart from joining two new surrogate families: a theatre troupe and a football team. But it was when I joined my college's drama society—which was rather grandly called The King's College, London, Theatre Workshop—that I really cut my teeth on stage. And I did a *lot* of acting at university.

Of all the many plays I acted in or directed at King's College, the one that perhaps stands out the most was a production of William Shakepeare's *The Winter's Tale*. I had a scene with an older postgraduate student who had a very unfortunate speech defect. He was halfway through one of his lines to me when a pair of false teeth suddenly flew out of his mouth and landed on the stage between us. I looked down at them in disbelief—they weren't quite chattering away, but they were sitting there as plain as day—before he stooped down without missing a beat, picked them up, shoved them back in his mouth, and continued his speech as if nothing had happened. And there wasn't a *peep* from the audience . . . not so much as a snigger or a titter. I was very confused by this, so after the show I asked a number of people in the audience what they thought about it . . . and *not one of them* was aware it had happened. It's possible the production was so interminably boring that they were all asleep by that point, but I interpreted it rather as a valuable lesson that it's actually possible to make an audience believe whatever you want them to, *if* you can do it with enough confidence and commitment. And it didn't even require inventing a fictitious football injury.

Speaking of football, I ended up playing for London University's 2nd XI. I was partnered as a striker with a tall Irish student called Mike Corcoran, who was a sociopath and a madman. Apart from eating four dozen eggs for breakfast once just because someone dared him to, he was also in the continual habit of "doing a runner" from restaurants. I went out to an Indian meal with him and a group of other guys on one occasion, but apparently I didn't get the memo because, at the end of the meal, he issued a command of "Now!" and everyone ran out before the bill arrived. Instant korma, rather than karma, you might say. Anyway, I certainly didn't have the money to cover the whole thing, so I negotiated with the owner to pay my portion while a kitchen staffer wielding a large machete gave chase to Big Mike and the others. Mike's morally questionable dining-out routine came to a sticky end, though, when karma— or maybe just blind stupidity—finally did catch up to him. He was on a ferry from Ireland back to England and he ate a meal in the boat's cafe, but he was in such a habit of "doing a runner" that he bolted out afterwards without paying. By the time he realised what he'd done, it was too late and he spent the next ten minutes being chased round and round the boat by some ferry officers before he was eventually caught.

While I was at university, I met two icons of the theatre world. The first was Marcel Marceau, the most famous mime in history. His goddaughter was a friend, and she invited me to see his show in the West End and have dinner with them afterwards. After the performance, I waited excitedly outside his dressing-room door while my friend went in to greet him.

I heard her saying that she'd brought along someone who wanted to be an actor, to which I heard him reply:

"*Merde!* Zere will be anozzer person at dinneyer zat I will have to pay for? I don't even know heem!"

I don't think he actually said *merde*—I just threw that in there for Gallic effect—but the point is I felt very humiliated and embarrassed as I was ushered in to meet him. Needless to say, the rest of the evening wasn't exactly a rip-roaring success. The legendary French mime turned out to be a relentlessly miserable, interminably boring, and deeply self-involved fellow. I much preferred him when he silently climbed imaginary ladders or pulled invisible elephants.

The other celebrity encounter I had while at university also took place at a West End theatre. At the interval ("intermission" in America) of a play I'd gone to, I found myself standing at the bar next to Quentin Crisp. If you don't know who he is, Quentin Crisp was a writer, raconteur, and actor who was kind of a twentieth-century version of Oscar Wilde . . . except a lot more outrageous, a lot more flamboyant, and a lot more gay. At that time, he'd recently become famous in England after ITV had made an award-winning television docudrama about him called *The Naked Civil Servant*, starring John Hurt. As we started talking, it soon became apparent that almost every word out of his mouth was a wonderful epigram or observation. And when it came up in our conversation that I was planning to be an actor, he said two things that I remember very clearly. The first was:

"Dear heart, I have been trying for sixty-six years to play the part of Quentin Crisp without *any* success whatsoever."

And the second was:

"Just remember that every theatre audience is a middle-aged woman with a broken heart, and you will *never* go wrong."

I loved those lines. They probably aren't entirely true, but who cares?

The English course at King's College, London, was highly academic and old-school. We had to study Old English, which is like another language entirely, and Chaucer, which is like half another language. However, much to my delight, the attendance requirements for the English department were minimal. There were a few compulsory lectures, and you had to turn in certain essays and papers by the end of each of the first two years, but mostly you were left to your own devices. Then, at the end of your last year—year three—you had eight exams covering all the subjects you'd chosen within the course, and your university degree was based solely on those eight exams. So I figured I'd keep my powder dry for a while—two and half years, to be exact—and save doing any real academic work until a few months before the end of my last year. However, I unfortunately neglected to read the small print, and I didn't turn in the requisite minimum of essays. And so, at the end of my first year, I was hauled in front of the dean and told that if I didn't fulfil these obligations before the end of the summer, I would not be welcome back the following year. So I immediately did whatever had to be done and was readmitted.

But I clearly hadn't been fully rehabilitated because, at the end of my second year, I received this letter from the subdean:

Dear Mr. Piddock,

At the staff meetings for Collections held on 25th June, the Department of English reported that they were not satisfied with your work and progress during the summer term and were concerned at your casual attitude. I was asked by the Faculty to warn you that we will not be able to re-enrol you in October unless we have received a satisfactory report from the Department of English. I look forward to hearing from you at your earliest convenience.

And so, once again, I did whatever was required to be granted a reprieve. But my cunning strategy eventually backfired very spectacularly at the end of February in my last year, when I had a meeting with my tutor. His name was Eric Mottram, and he was a genuine British eccentric: a middle-aged, socially liberal intellectual who swore a lot and had a very explosive and toothy laugh. He was deeply passionate about poetry and American literature, so much so that he hung out with the likes of William Burroughs and Allen Ginsberg and introduced the British public to the Beat Generation.

At our meeting, we quickly established that he didn't really know who I was because he hadn't actually seen me in the English department for two and a half years. He asked me what my eight exam subjects were, so I reeled them off. And when I got to the end, he nodded to himself thoughtfully a couple of times before declaring:

"I believe you have a problem."

"What's that?" I asked, thinking he probably—and quite rightfully—suspected that I was woefully underprepared for these eight exams.

"You only have *seven* subjects," he said.

I tried to hide my sudden panic with a lame joke about how I was never terribly good at mathematics before he outlined my predicament in very stark terms: I had just two months to do a crash course in a new subject within the course—as well as study for the other seven exams—or I was, in his words, "totally fucking fucked."

At this point, I assumed I was totally fucking fucked either way, but my eccentric tutor took pity on me and came up with a Hail Mary plan to try and avert the rare ignominy of a student graduating from London University without any kind of a degree at all. His plan was that I should do American Literature for my eighth paper. Why? Because *he set the exam!* And so I embarked on a highly selective crash course in American literature. A little bit of Nathaniel Hawthorne . . . a smidge of F. Scott Fitzgerald . . . a dip into Mark Twain . . . a touch of Edgar Allan Poe . . . and a rapid whistle-stop tour through the theatrical endeavours of Eugene O'Neill, Tennessee Williams, and Arthur Miller—because plays are *much* shorter than novels, and time was of the essence.

I'll never forget the day exam results were announced. I got out of the lift to the English department and saw a group of people huddled around a notice board where the results had been posted minutes before. Among them I could see my friend Rob—a teammate from my Sunday morning football team—and he was doubled up with laughter as he pointed at the results and then at me. Given the locker-room mentality of guys always finding other guys' misfortunes highly amusing, this was not a good sign. My spirits were sinking fast as I plucked up all my courage and looked at the results for myself. And I almost had a heart attack . . . because I'd got one of the highest-rated degrees anyone can get at a British university. Not that it's ever been of any use to me at any point in my life since.

I was still in shock when I went to see my tutor, Eric, a few days later, thinking either I was a latent genius or—far more likely—there had been a terrible mistake. He was chuckling as I entered his room, and when I sat down, he said:

"Well, you certainly confounded the examining board."

"What the hell happened?" I asked.

"You barely passed most of your papers," he replied. "But you got the highest mark in American Literature . . . not just at King's College, but the whole of London University."

I was stunned. London University was massive, so it was an extraordinary result. But, ignoring the obvious fact that without his help I'd never have got a degree at all, I then asked him with mind-numbing hubris:

"Do you think I should do a postgraduate course in American Literature?"

At which point the smile rapidly disappeared from his face, and he replied:

"No, I don't. Now fuck off and be an actor!"

After I left university, I aimed high—for the best way to fast-track my entrance into show business—by auditioning for RADA, the Royal Academy of Dramatic Art. RADA was where all the well-known actors of that era in England had trained: Albert Finney, Tom Courtenay, Timothy Dalton, the list was endless. The school's unofficial motto was: "If you want to act, forget it. If you have to act, we'll consider you." In Latin, presumably.

I prepared my two speeches—one Shakespeare and one contemporary—and went along to the Gower Street nursery of dramatic excellence for my audition. However, after a very bright opening, I made the rookie mistake of glancing down at the row of grim-faced adjudicators in front of me, and I immediately forgot all my lines. And so, unsurprisingly, I *didn't* get into RADA.

But the next time I auditioned, I got accepted at another London drama school called The Drama Studio, in Ealing, and that's where we came in at the beginning of this book.

4

IT WAS IN THE GENES

When you're a child, you mostly accept whatever your life is at face value. It's the only reality you know, so it all seems normal. My father, who was a chemical engineer, had been brought up not by his parents but by his aunt, who lived just down the road from our house in Kent. Her name was Gladys but she hated it, so we just called her "Aunt" even though she was actually our great-aunt. She used to come over for lunch every Sunday, and while the rest of us sat at the dining room table eating our Sunday roast, she would lie face-up beside us on the floor because she had a chronic back ailment. Which seemed like perfectly normal behaviour at the time.

My father used to visit his mother, whose name was Olive, once a week for lunch. Her house was about twenty miles from us, and she lived to be ninety-seven. But I have no idea if she also hated her name, because neither I nor any of my siblings nor even my mother ever met her. I don't know if that was my father's choice or his mother's, but I did find out much later on, when I was an adult, the reason why.

Harry Piddock, my father's father—and obviously my grandfather—was an actor and a comedian in music hall and farce. He married Olive and they had three children, all boys, in quick succession. But soon after the third was born, Harry decided he'd had enough of married life, and he left Olive for a chorus girl called Jane whom he'd met doing a show. My grandmother then decided she couldn't bring up three boys on her own, so she gave away the middle one—my dad—to her sister, Gladys, to raise.

Meanwhile, Harry married Jane, his chorus girl (almost certainly bigamously), and had a daughter with her, called Myra. Now, although I was completely unaware of any of my grandfather's history—theatrical or otherwise—when I was growing up, I *had* actually heard about Myra. While my father never talked about his mother or any family estrangements or abandonments, he did occasionally mention in passing that his half-sister, who was considerably younger than him, was an actress whenever her professional name—Myra Frances—popped up among the credits of some TV show we were watching. I didn't think anything of it at that early point in my life, but while I was at drama school I was reading a magazine article about a wonderful English actor called Peter Egan. And I discovered that not only was he married to my half-aunt Myra, but they also lived right around the corner from me in West London. So, after some hesitation, I summoned up my courage and wrote a letter to them. And I soon got a response saying they'd love to meet me. And so, in my early twenties, I met my half-aunt and uncle, Myra and Peter, for the first time.

I was quite nervous about meeting them, but I needn't have been because I was immediately and very warmly accepted into the bosom of this new branch of my family, which I felt an instant connection to. Myra had pretty much given up acting by then because, despite being very evidently talented, beautiful, and successful, she hated the business side of acting and wanted to dedicate her time to raising her young daughter from a prior marriage, Rebecca. However, before she chose an early retirement (which she never, for a second, regretted), she had already made screen history in a unique way in 1974 by sharing the first lesbian kiss ever seen on British television with Alison Steadman. Peter, on the other hand, had no such milestones in the annals of onscreen lesbianism, but was working as an actor a great deal at the time and was extremely generous in offering me advice about how to handle my career when it first started.

After we met, Myra started to fill me in on all the missing pieces of my ancestry jigsaw puzzle. This turned out to be a seminal time in my life, because I learned that almost *everybody* on my father's side of the family—except my father and his immediate siblings—was in show business and had been for generations. So it was literally in my blood. I wasn't the odd man out in my biological family after all—or, if I was, at least I was now in a majority.

Grandfather Harry Piddock.

The genesis of the family's skeletons in the closet began with my great-grandfather, John Charles Piddock, or J.C. Piddock, as he was known. Actually, he was originally known as J.C. Pid*cock* because that was the family name until someone obviously told him it sounded rather rude and he changed it. In actual fact, it wasn't really that rude because the name's origins were from France, where it was pronounced "Pidco." The "ck" at the end was silent, as in "Cockburn's port," but in England it wasn't pronounced quite so delicately. Anyway, J.C. Piddock—or Pidcock, if you prefer—was a singer and an actor who in 1902 went to perform in Australia, taking his wife, Fanny—I swear I'm not making these names up—and all their children with him. While he was there, he had a wild affair with an Australian woman called Mabel, which in itself might not have caused any long-lasting problems had he not decided to bring her back secretly to England on the same boat with his wife and children and set her up in a house—around the corner from his home in South London—and start a whole new family with her!

And so he proceeded to shuttle from house to house, and bed to bed, for ten years until the whole thing blew up in his face spectacularly when someone wrote an anonymous letter to his wife. And, from that moment on, there were two distinct tribes on my father's side of the family: the legitimates and the illegitimates. And, to their dying day, the descendants of the legitimates refused to acknowledge or speak to the descendants of the illegitimates. When they were mostly all still alive and semi-coherent, Myra and I went to visit some of them, and I can only say that the bastard side of the family were infinitely more agreeable. Which only goes to prove that good breeding is highly overrated.

Great-grandfather J.C. Piddock.

My newly found half-aunt Myra also told me that my grandfather Harry—her father—had a music hall act in his early career with a man called Charlie. Now there's nothing particularly remarkable about that, except that Charlie's last name was *Chaplin*. And he emigrated to America soon afterwards and went on to do quite well. But he would come back to England every now and then, and, on two occasions, he offered my grandfather the opportunity to join him and make films in Los Angeles. The first time it happened, Harry's father—my great-grandfather, J.C. Piddock (aka Pidcock)—advised him against it, telling his son there was no future in the movie business and that it was just a passing fad. Which suggests adultery might be more of a Piddock family trait than prescience. On the second occasion, a contract was actually drawn up on the back of a menu after dinner, and my grandfather was all set to head off to fame and fortune in California . . . until a friend got an underage girl pregnant and he coughed up the money he'd saved for the trip to bail the friend out. Anyhow, whether it's apocryphal or not, that's the story of how and why my grandfather Harry never made it to Hollywood. Despite the fact that he sounded like a pretty selfish and irresponsible sort of fellow, I still would have liked to have met him. But, unfortunately, he died in 1950, six years before I entered the world stage (three weeks late and covered in slime).

The night I first met Myra and Peter, I also met Harry's second wife—and Myra's mother—Jane Bayley, the chorus girl, who was a wonderful, carefree spirit and treated me like a long-lost grandson. I also met Jane's second husband, Nigel, who was certifiably insane. Nigel looked and dressed like the Major in the TV series *Fawlty Towers*, and was an "inventor" by profession. He had already tipped people off to his dubious mental condition several years before when he invited the entire family to a conference room in a Brighton hotel. He announced to the whole clan, whom he'd gathered with great urgency from all over the country, that he'd invented something that would change all of their lives forever. He then produced two pieces of paper and an inky black sheet.

He slipped the black sheet between the pieces of paper and wrote something on the top piece. Then he pulled the bottom piece of paper out and held it up for everyone to see.

"Look!" he exclaimed excitedly. "It's a perfect copy of what I just wrote on the first sheet!"

There was a long and very uncomfortable silence before one brave soul finally piped up:

"Nigel, that's carbon paper. It's been around for about a hundred years."

There was also one famous Christmas when Peter bought some pistachio nuts, which were quite a novelty at the time. Peter asked Nigel if he'd ever had them before, and Nigel, who always had to know everything about anything, said:

"Yes, of course, dear boy. Love pistachios."

He then proceeded to take a handful from the bowl and shove them in his mouth, shells and all. And for the next ten minutes, everyone almost burst a blood vessel trying not to laugh as he gamely attempted, while conversation continued, to eat all the pistachios—in their shells—that were nestled in his mouth.

Eventually, after several years of believing Nigel was just "eccentric," everybody came to the realisation that he needed to be evaluated psychiatrically. When the people from social services arrived, Nigel greeted them at the door, and they were surprised. Not because he was greeting them himself in person, but because he wasn't wearing any trousers or underpants and his entire tackle was on display.

"Come in, dear chaps, come in. Lovely to see you," he said to them. "This isn't my house, you know. It's my son-in-law, Peter's. Do you know him? Peter Egan. Lovely actor, but unfortunately he's in the habit of buggering me every night. Won't leave my arse alone."

At this point, Peter and Myra quickly interceded, sent Nigel upstairs to get dressed, and assured the evaluators from social services that Peter was *not* in the habit of sexually assaulting his father-in-law after hours. Apparently Nigel had developed quite an anal fixation, though, because when they all went upstairs half an hour later to see what had happened to him, they found him in the bathroom, very agitated, with the tube of his oxygen tank inserted into his rectum.

"Bloody thing won't work, Peter," he said. "I'm still having trouble breathing."

5

LEARNING THE ROPES AND SELLING DILDOS

When I reached my teens, I tried my hand at a number of temporary "vacation" jobs to earn a bit of extra cash. And, with the odd exception, they all emphatically proved that I was not cut out to hold a "normal" job.

At a cold storage warehouse one summer, I packed frozen turkeys for large companies to give their employees the following Christmas. It was mind-numbingly boring work, made only slightly less tedious by one of the regular workers there with the nickname "Brains," who was one of the stupidest people I've ever come across in my life. Some of his inane comments ("If you drive your car backwards, it reduces the miles on your odour meter.") provided a modicum of comic relief from the monotony of the job, but you had a better chance of having a meaningful conversation with one of the frozen turkeys. Working alongside Brains was a wizened older man called Alf, who smoked home-rolled cigarettes every single minute of every single day. They both used to head straight to the pub after work and, according to them, sink a minimum of fifteen pints of lager a night each. Though, to be fair, if I worked that job full time, I'd probably have done the same.

Another staggeringly dull job I had was on a farm, sorting picked hops on a conveyor belt. It was a ridiculously simple task, but I was somehow so bad at it that the farmer yanked me off the belt and sent me out to a field to watch cows. I can't for the life of me remember now why I had to watch them, but I suppose it must have been because some of them had recently escaped. I didn't mind the bovine sentry duty at all—because, as much as I like beer, the smell of cow shit in the open air is actually preferable to the intense smell of tons of hops in an enclosed barn. But, either way, my olfactory sensibilities became immaterial after a couple of days because I fell asleep in the field and ended up getting fired.

I also worked at Harrods one Christmas season. They assigned me to the hamper department, where I was one of a team of students assigned to pack luxury holiday gift hampers for the rich and famous. It was less dull than putting frozen turkeys into cardboard boxes, mainly because the foods were extremely impressive in range and quality. However, a few days before Christmas, the man in charge of the department—Mr. Culpepper was his name—summoned us all with a very grim expression. He explained in very sombre terms that Harrods Ltd. had been deeply shamed by our department. We all listened, intrigued, as he proceeded to tell us that a luxury hamper sent as a present to the Queen was found to have been sabotaged. Someone had put metal staples in her brandy butter. We didn't find out if Her Majesty had actually bitten into one of the staples, but the upshot was that none of us could be trusted any more and we were all to be punished by being transferred to other departments for the last few days before Christmas.

And this is where I hit the jackpot. Whereas some of my hamper department compadres were consigned to dull places such as Menswear or Haberdashery or Bedding, I ended up being sent to the wine cellar. When I arrived, I asked the two guys working there what they wanted me to do. They both chuckled knowingly and informed me that all the Christmas orders had already gone out. Since there were still three more days left until my employment ended, I was curious about what we were supposed to do. There was some more chuckling before one of them beckoned me over to a long aisle between two rows of wine racks filled with some of the best wines money can buy. Surveying them carefully, one of my new coworkers said:

"What do you fancy trying first?"

And that was that. I don't remember an awful lot about those last three days at Harrods because every one of them was spent drinking a marvellous assortment of fine wines—from the moment we clocked in in the morning until the time we clocked out at night. I do vaguely remember that we were so inebriated that none of us could be bothered (or perhaps manage) to make it to the toilets, and we ended up relieving ourselves in one of the aisles. Thinking back on it now, I'm not proud of this highly depraved and disorderly behaviour (the peeing, that is, not the drinking), but in my defence, let me just say that: (a) I was only eighteen years old, and (b) I wasn't the person who put the staples in the Queen's brandy butter.

During my time at drama school, I helped support myself by working on Sundays in a sex shop near Paddington Station that was rather quaintly called Lovejoys. The general salesman stuff I could handle fine. I quickly learned which inflatable dolls were two-hair/three-hole, one-hair/two-hole, one-hair/one-hole, two-hair/two-hole, and two-hair/one-hole. I knew which vibrators were two-speed/thrust-and-rotate, one-speed/thrust only, two-speed/rotate-only, and one-speed/thrust-and-tickle. I even became quite skilful at demonstrating the models on display, though not on myself or any customers, you'll be glad to know. But the part of the job I didn't much care for came at the end of the day. It took place at the back of the shop, where there was a row of coin-operated movie booths. And . . . yes . . . I'm afraid it was my job to swab the floors of the booths with a mop. However, when my very considerate employers learned that I had a degree in English literature, they thought I was much too well educated to be mopping up semen for a living, and they transferred me to their bookshop at Victoria bus station. So actually, now I come to think of it, maybe that English degree *did* come in handy after all.

The tiny little bookshop in Victoria was a store of two distinct halves. In the front you could find great works of literature such as Joseph Conrad's *Nostromo* and Thomas Hardy's *The Return of the Native*. And, in the back, you could find timeworn classics of a different type, such as *Bend Over Bunty* and *No Ifs or Ands, Just Butts*. Neither of which, for some reason, had been part of the English course at King's College, London.

One of the consequences of my job at Lovejoys was an event that made it into a book about football. Don't ask me how, but I managed to arrange a football match between Lovejoys and my drama school, with me playing one half for each team. I can't remember whether the pornographers or the poseurs won, but I'm fairly sure the fields of Hackney Marshes had never before, or have ever since, hosted such a historically silly sporting event. Incidentally, the writer of that book was my friend Rob from university who found my degree result so amusing. He was a very good goalkeeper and even played a few games for Millwall reserves. And on one occasion, when we were playing for our Sunday morning pub team, he incurred the best yellow card I've ever witnessed on a football field. There's a rule that goalkeepers can hold the ball for only a certain number of seconds, and in the referee's judgment, Rob had taken took too long to release it. So a free kick was awarded against him. Protesting indignantly, he said:

"Oh, come on, ref! That's a law more honoured in the breach than the observance."

To which the ref replied:

"That's dissent."

And Rob came back with:

"No. Shakespeare."

And was promptly booked.

Speaking of Shakespeare, the best role I had at drama school was playing the Scottish king in the play that nobody dares mention within the walls of a theatre for fear of a disaster of a supernatural kind. I had three weeks to learn the part while also doing other classes, so when performance time came, I was a little under-rehearsed, to say the least. The result was something of a disaster of a more natural kind. I remember having a sword fight in one of the battle scenes, which were rather crudely staged. I came on backwards, delivering a speech while engaging in combat with Macduff and declaring:

Thou losest labour.
As easy mayst thou the intrenchant air
With thy keen sword impress as make me bleed.
Let fall thy blade on vulnerable crests;
I bear a charmed life, which must not yield
To one of woman born.

And then Macduff and I, still banging swords, exited on the other side of the stage. At which point, we ran round the back of the set and came back on, continuing the scene—don't ask me why, I didn't direct it—but unfortunately I was so flustered from trying to remember all my lines, I didn't actually *continue* the scene. Instead I made my entrance again, fighting Macduff with my sword and declaring for a second time:

Thou losest labour.
As easy mayst thou the intrenchant air
With thy keen sword impress as make me bleed.
Let fall thy blade on vulnerable crests;
I bear a charmed life, which must not yield
To one of woman born.

And then we exited again, in perfect déjà vu symmetry, on the other side of the stage. Backstage, I kind of knew what had happened, but my mind had also gone blank and I had a dreadful feeling that we were going to be stuck in this horrifying loop forever because I couldn't for the life of me remember what came next. Luckily, either Macduff or I eventually managed to get us back on track. Otherwise we'd probably still be there today, going round in a vortex of perpetual, ever-repeating act 5 battle scene circles.

Our end-of-year production at drama school provided one of the most unsettling incidents I've ever experienced on a stage. We performed Dylan Thomas's *Under Milk Wood* in a small London theatre, and agents, producers, directors, etc. were all invited. In the cast was a rather—to put it politely—oversized young actress who had been under a lot of stress during the year and after several absences from classes was teetering on the brink of getting kicked out. But I don't think anybody knew quite how bad her mental state was, because on opening night she had an actual, very real, full-on nervous break-down live on stage. The first inkling I had of a problem was when I was doing a speech about her character and I noticed she was staring off into space instead of responding, as we'd rehearsed. Soon after-wards, she began fidgeting, and then—just as everybody was becoming aware that something was wrong and all eyes were on her—she started to lick her hands, very slowly and methodically . . . and then her arms . . . and then she pushed her hands down inside her blouse and started massaging and licking her very sizeable breasts. By this point, "Under Milk Wood" was fast gathering a new meaning. Luckily it was near the end of the show, and we somehow got to the end without her committing any more acts of gross indecency. But it was an extremely alarming and uncomfortable few minutes.

I heard, many years later, from a fellow drama school alumnus that he'd since seen the actress in question on a London under-ground train "serenading a dog." I've no idea if that was a euphemism or not, but he also told me she's had a pretty decent career doing voice-overs, so I guess all that was unwell didn't end entirely unwell.

Before leaving drama school, each graduate had a final assessment meeting with several members of the staff in which they asked some questions and told you where you stood in the vast historical regis-ter of aspiring actors wishing to carve out a career in show business. It was a bit more helpful than the Careers Advisory Day I'd endured at school, but it wasn't substantially any more influential. When my turn came and I sat down in front of the row of staff members, I was asked by a particularly smug and patronizing teacher-director whether I'd considered changing my name. I knew he was deliber-ately trying to throw me, because it was (a) so out of left field and (b) an unsubtle insinuation that my last name might induce mockery because it sounds like *pillock*, which is a British slang term for both a simpleton and a penis (something my great-grandfather had clearly not been aware of when changing the family name from "Pidcock" to "Piddock"). But the question blew up in his face somewhat because I replied that I had indeed considered changing it and thought that "*Laurence* Piddock, like Laurence Olivier, might be better than *Jim*." When this got a laugh from the rest of the staff, I stuck the knife in a bit deeper by adding an alternative suggestion of "Jim Buttock" as a potential stage name.

After the stupid question had received its even more stupid answers, we moved on. The consensus among the staff was that I was a decent character actor with a wide range, but I was warned that most producers, directors, and casting directors want to typecast and pigeonhole actors, so "you can't sell versatility, Jim." In terms of entering the show business world at that time—and even more so now—this was actually very sound counsel. But, just as with the advice from my Careers Advisor at school, I completely ignored it and spent the next four decades trying to prove them wrong.

6

SHIT GETS REAL

I was very fortunate when I graduated from drama school. One of the teacher-directors there became the artistic director of a children's touring company called Spectrum Theatre, and he offered me a job in the five-person troupe. Our first production, geared towards five- to eight-year-olds, was called *The Case of the Missing Carrots*, and my first professional acting role was that of Norman, a garden gnome who falls in love with a mermaid. Not quite Hamlet or Henry V, but definitely funnier. However, let me tell you here and now that when people say how adorable young children are, they've clearly never been in the shoes of a love-stricken gnome who wants to be reunited with the fishy-tailed object of his desire. In order for that to happen, I had to recruit all the angelic children in the audience to help me find a place to hide from two rather nasty dog characters called Slobber and Fang (I didn't write this, okay). The cherubic kids excitedly pointed to a gap in their ranks on the floor of the classroom and ushered me there to seek refuge. I gratefully accepted their assistance, but once I got there they all started giggling, and I began to feel my hands and knees getting *very* wet . . . because they'd knowingly steered me into a large puddle of kiddie wee on the floor, which was why there was a gap there in the first place. The devious little bastards.

Another part of my duties for Spectrum Theatre was driving the company van from venue to venue, so all in all it was a pretty gruelling slog. A few weeks before the end of my contract, I ended up getting sick and went back home to my parents' house for a couple of days. I had some blood tests done, and the general discussion around the family home was about what my father was going to do after he took an early retirement in a couple of weeks' time. Before I got the results of the blood tests back, I started feeling a bit better, so I rejoined the cast of *The Case of the Missing Carrots* on tour. A couple of days later, we arrived at a school in Essex to do our first show of the day, and as we were unloading the set from the van, the headmistress of the school came up and asked which one of us was Jim Piddock. I owned up, and she told me that my mother was on the phone. So I followed her to her office, picked up the phone, and heard my mother's voice:

"Jim?" she said.

"Yeah, hi, what's up?"

"Thank goodness I've reached you, I've been trying to find you since yesterday. I'm afraid I've got some bad news."

And then I remembered my blood tests. I assumed the results must have revealed something serious.

"It's Dad," she said, swiftly cutting off that particular line of self-involved speculation. "He had a stroke."

In that moment, I remember thinking that, at the age of fifty-six, my father was still young so he'd recover fairly quickly. But then my mother said:

"And, actually . . . he died."

And, actually . . . he died. Those four words, separated by a slight pause, stayed with me for years. And, within minutes of my hearing them, the word *died* didn't make sense to me any more. It was a verb, an *active* word. My father had *done* something. But it didn't mean that at all. It meant he'd *stopped* doing things. Here one minute, gone the next. A headache after breakfast, dead before lunchtime.

I suppose the first sign I was in shock was that, in the immediate aftermath of learning about my father's unexpected death, I was obsessing over the grammatical ramifications of a verb. The second sign was that I wasn't crying. And the third sign was that I still wanted to do the show before catching a train home. Luckily no one shared my misguided belief in the old adage that the show must go on, and they forced me to go home immediately.

So I returned again to the house I'd lived in since I was two years old. My first memory in life is from the day we moved there: I remember my father pushing me down the driveway on my tiny tricycle. Back in the house, I saw a clear plastic bag on my dad's desk. Inside it were his watch and his keys . . . all that had come back from the hospital where he'd died. Now I felt angry. His stupid fucking watch and keys were still alive. His desk was still there. But *he* wasn't. I might have gained a new theatre family of sorts on tour, but now I'd prematurely lost a major part of my biological family. And then, finally, I did cry. A *lot*. Like I hadn't cried for years. Years of tears.

A few days later, during the funeral, I remembered something strange. The day I'd left the house, after I'd been at home sick, my dad had gone out somewhere and I'd found a note to my mother from him on the table by the front door. This in itself was unusual. But the contents of the note were even more so. During all the years I'd lived there, all the times I'd left for school, university, or work— probably thousands of times—he'd never written a note like this one. It was very short. All it said was: "Say goodbye to Jim for me."

Ever since then, I occasionally wonder if our subconscious or unconscious minds know more about our cosmic Fate—our past, present, and even our future—than our conscious minds do. But rather than disappear down this rabbit hole of speculation about the potential but probably unprovable predictive powers of the human brain, I prefer to think of it as him simply saying goodbye to me for the last time, whether intended or not.

After I left the children's theatre company, I did a few auditions and found myself getting into a company called Newpalm Productions that did weekly rep, mostly playing the leading man opposite the company producer-director's wife, who was more than twice my age. That aside, the entire concept of weekly rep is sheer madness. Most plays rehearse for a minimum of three weeks, usually four or five. In weekly rep, you're playing one show for a week while simultaneously rehearsing another show for the week after, and so on and so on. Here's how it works:

1. On Tuesday morning, you start the cycle when you get notes from the director on the previous night's opening of the current play. After that, you rehearse act 1 of the new play and perform the second night of the current play in the evening.

2. On Wednesday, you run act 1 of next week's play and start rehearsing act 2—but not for long, because there's a matinée of the current play in the afternoon followed by another performance in the evening.

3. On Thursday, you finish rehearsing act 2 of next week's play, do a run-through of that, and then rehearse act 3, before doing a performance of the current play in the evening.

4. On Friday, you run through act 3 of next week's play, then run the entire play off-book, having (hopefully) learned it all by then. And, of course, you do another performance of the current play in the evening.

5. On Saturday morning, you run through next week's play again, in costumes if they're ready. Then you do a matinée of the current play followed by the closing night of the current play, after which the crew strikes the set of that show.

6. On Sunday—the actors' "day off"—you brush up on your lines for the new show while the crew put up the new set, re-hang the lights, and set the new sound cues.

7. On Monday morning, there's a technical run of the new play, followed by a full dress rehearsal in the afternoon. Then the director gives the actors their notes, which they try to incorporate into that night's opening performance of the new play, which is sometimes followed by a party if anyone's still alive.

8. On Tuesday morning, the whole process starts again.

Like I said, it's utter madness. But in my early twenties I found it immensely exciting. Now when I think about it, I feel an urge to swallow a fistful of Valium.

The first play I did in weekly rep was directed by someone who was also in it. And he made no bones about taking every shortcut available. He had his lines pasted all over the set: on the backs of the furniture, inside fruit bowls, on table lamps, *everywhere*. And in rehearsals, he showed such a deft ability to get through his scenes that I was genuinely impressed. It was a shifty performance to be sure, his eyes never meeting yours, but it didn't seem to falter. However, on the opening night—in the middle of my very first scene in my very first play in repertory theatre—he was supposed to make an entrance halfway through it, only he didn't. It was clearly one task too much for him, so I was stuck on stage with another actor, improvising for a very long minute and a half—which felt like an hour and a half—until someone finally shoved the fucker on.

The baptism of fire continued for consecutive seasons at Tunbridge Wells, Torquay, and Chelmsford, although Chelmsford was fortnightly rep (one show every two weeks), which was luxury in comparison to weekly rep. Pretty much everything that could wrong *did* go wrong in all those productions. There was a performance of Noël Coward's *Hay Fever* during which my love interest got food poisoning, so we did the entire third act without her, editing the play on the fly as we went. And there was an actress in an Agatha Christie play set in the 1930s, who was so cold backstage that she put on a baseball cap to keep warm, but forgot about it and played her next scene with a distinctly anachronistic look. And there was a Christmas pantomime where we did three shows on Boxing Day (2:00 p.m., 5:00 p.m., and 8:00 p.m.) and the only time to eat was backstage during the show, which resulted in me making a hasty entrance and saying a line with a mouth full of food. My amused comedy partner responded with his punch line, then added:

"And don't talk with your bloody mouth full!"

The insanity wasn't just restricted to performances, either. I remember one rehearsal in which the entire cast tried to keep a straight face as the director came in from the rain outside and gave us notes while black streaks ran down his face from the shoe polish he'd put in his thinning, greying hair.

And, no, his name wasn't Rudy Giuliani—our hapless director wasn't *that* insane.

And so it went on—a frantic, frenetic whirlwind of lunacy. I even directed a couple of plays for the company for good measure. But, as dreadful and chaotic as it all was, I learned what being a professional actor meant. And I got the full picture soon afterwards . . . because the next thing that happened was that I was unemployed.

7

ROCK BOTTOM

After a few months of not getting any work, I embarked on a single-minded campaign to get into television acting by breaking into the BBC. I mean that literally . . . because I broke into the old BBC building in Shepherd's Bush. I slipped past security and walked down the main passageway where all the producers' offices were located. Armed with a stack of 8 × 10 headshots and résumés, I peeked in every door, and, if the office was empty, I went in and dropped my picture and résumé on the desk. Then I'd get hold of some BBC stationery and attach a note—"Outstanding young talent. Must see!"—which I then signed with an indecipherable squiggle. Ingenious, huh? I was certain the punch line to this highly enterprising scheme would be that a week later I'd get a call from someone at the BBC, the rest would be history, and I'd be telling stories about my ballsy breaking-and-entering escapade on chat shows for years to come. But I didn't get a call. Not a week later . . . or a month later . . . or even a year later. So the rest wasn't history, and the story had to wait a while to be told on chat shows or anywhere else.

In the course of working as an actor for a couple of years, I'd (nominally) found a place in which I felt I belonged in the world. But now that I wasn't working anymore, I felt unmoored and disconnected from everything and everyone. I remember drinking a bottle of cheap wine alone and feeling very sorry for myself as I watched the 1980 Academy Awards on my nine-inch black-and-white TV in my rented ten-by-eight-foot attic room in South East London. Dustin

Hoffman won Best Actor for his performance in *Kramer vs. Kramer*, and in his speech he said that he didn't beat anyone, he was simply one of the lucky few who gets to act for a living, and that he saw the statuette as a symbol representing all those who strive in obscurity for excellence. I was a disgusting, sobbing, self-pitying mess by the time he finished his speech with:

"None of you have ever lost and I'm proud to share this with you."

Desperate to escape the black cloud hanging over me and to breathe more freely again, I approached Peter Layton, the principal of the drama school I'd attended, about directing a play or two at the branch they were opening in Berkeley, California. He very kindly didn't tell me to fuck off, but instead asked me to direct something at the school in London first. I didn't screw that up too badly, so Peter even kindlier offered me a three-month job in Berkeley starting the following January. It wasn't *exactly* what I wanted to be doing with my life, but it allowed me to get away and take a welcome break from the unemployment line and from mourning my father's death.

However, right after I was presented with the chance to go to America—in one of those periodic fork-in-the-road moments that happen in life—the company who'd employed me in rep offered me the position of artistic director at their new theatre in Weston-super-Mare. It certainly wasn't the most glamorous of posts, but I believe it would have made me—at the tender age of twenty-four—the youngest artistic director of a theatre in England. Which seemed completely insane at the time . . . and even more so now, as I think back on it. However, the prospect of going to America for three months, although it offered me a lot less security, seemed the more exciting and less predictable path to follow. So I turned the artistic director job down.

Getting my visa sorted out was intimidating. I'd been warned about the case of an older British actor who, when filling out his application, responded to the question "Do You Intend to Do Any Harm To The President Of The United States?" with "Sole purpose of visit" and was promptly denied entry. So I answered that and the questions "Are you a practicing homosexual?" and "Have you ever been a prostitute?" with a firm "No," which also happened to be true. Fortunately, there were no questions about having worked in a sex shop.

At a train station shortly before I left England, I ran into someone I'd known at university. He was now employed in a low-level job at the BBC, and when I informed him what career I was pursuing, he said:

"I imagine it must be terribly disheartening being an actor. You'd never believe the lengths some of them will go to, trying to get a job at the BBC. They sometimes even drop off their pictures and résumés in our offices."

"Oh my god," I replied, doing my best to sound utterly shocked and appalled. "That is so pathetic!"

We quickly parted ways, and to this day, I have no idea if he was fucking with me or not.

He had to have been, right?

8

ANOTHER WORLD

I arrived in America at the age of twenty-four with the grand sum of $100 to my name. And I spent my first two days in the promised land puking and shitting . . . because I caught some virulent stomach bug that was going around.

However, I immediately fell in love with California, which felt so warm and bright and open (once I'd got out of the toilet). The first time I drove from Berkeley across the vast span of the Bay Bridge to San Francisco, the vision ahead of me took my breath away. The sight of the shining silver metropolis against a backdrop of deep blue sky, with the magnificent Golden Gate Bridge arcing out of the city towards the green expanse of Marin County, seemed to scream that there was a whole new world I knew nothing about. And America, in general, felt so much less rigid and predictable than Britain. It appeared, to my eyes at that time, to be a more fluid and vigorous country . . . socially, economically, and creatively. And that was very exciting.

I enjoyed my time in Berkeley, directing student actors who mostly weren't much younger than me. In fact, some were older. There were a couple of students whose acting abilities stood out. Their names were Forest Whitaker and Cynthia Stevenson, and little did I—or they—know that our paths would converge again in Los Angeles, professionally and socially, a few years later. But, most of all in those first few weeks, I enjoyed two things more than anything else. The first was the *newness* of everything I was experiencing. Often when you travel to a place you've never been before, you become like a child again as you notice all the things, big and small, that are different from what you've experienced before. And I was hyperaware of all of those different things, which felt liberating rather than alien. The other thing I started to experience was the fact that, being a young Englishman abroad in America, I was different from most other people without needing to try to be. As a fish out of water, I was suddenly more clearly defined—as a person, anyway—just by dint of my accent alone. And I wasn't judged or pigeonholed by the way I spoke, as you are (whether you like it or not) as soon as you open your mouth in Britain.

Also, in terms of my love life, by the law of averages, it didn't hurt being youthful, in reasonable shape, and heterosexual in a predominantly gay city. Except for the time I went into a bar I'd never frequented before and ordered a drink. I was minding my own business when I started to notice that I was getting a *lot* of very dirty looks from a *lot* of different women. Confused, I cast my eyes around the joint and very quickly realised I was the only male in there...mainly because it was an extremely hard-core lesbian bar. Needless to say, that drink went unfinished and if looks could kill, I would have died a dozen deaths during my faux casual, forced-smile exit to the safety of the outside world.

Meanwhile, more to test the waters than anything else, I started spending my spare time working on something I had in my back pocket. It was a one-man show I'd seen in London called *The Boy's Own Story* about a maverick former professional goalie playing in a pub-league football game in a park on a Sunday morning. I'd contacted the writer, Peter Flannery, before I left England and had somehow managed to get his permission to perform it in the US, if I could ever find anyone mad enough to produce it. I approached every legitimate (and illegitimate) theatre company in San Francisco and got rejected by them all. Which wasn't terribly surprising, since I was a completely unknown British actor with a very English play about a sport that very few people in America gave a screaming shit about at the time.

When my three months in Berkeley was up, the Drama Studio asked me stay on for another three months to direct and teach in their summer program. I had absolutely nothing to go back to in London work-wise, and I was enjoying hiding out from the real world in the Bay Area, so I agreed to stay on. The second three months flew by, and I was just gearing up to head home when I got a call from the artistic director of the Julian Theatre, a ninety-nine-seat theatre on Potrero Hill in San Francisco. He told me that their first play of the new season had fallen through and asked me if I could get my one-man show up in a month's time to replace it. I immediately said yes, cancelled my flight back to London (again), and began to rehearse *The Boy's Own Story* under the watchful eye of a very good expat British director I'd recently met called Richard Seyd.

I also began some very intense physical training because, although I knew the show was well written, I soon learned that what was likely to make it a *tour de force* was the fact that the actor performing it was still alive at the end. The play was ninety minutes of nonstop, rapid-fire talking, walking, running, jumping, diving, falling, laughing, crying, yelling, and—needless to say—sweating. I went to a gym for the first time ever. I ran up and down the steep hills in San Francisco. By the time the show opened, I was in the best shape of my life. And, because most of the students at The Drama Studio in Berkeley were very eager to see one of their directors fall flat on his face trying to be an actor himself, the opening night was sold out. On the second night, however, I had just four people in the audience, all of whom sat in the front row. It was an intimate experience, to say the least. The next day, the reviews for *The Boy's Own Story* came out, and they were an actor's wildest dream come true. After that it was almost impossible to get a ticket for the show, and the run at the Julian Theatre had to be extended twice. Before I knew it, a producer in New York had heard about it and wanted me to do it off-Broadway. So I agreed that, after the run in San Francisco was finished, I'd move to the East Coast.

Life comes at you very fast sometimes.

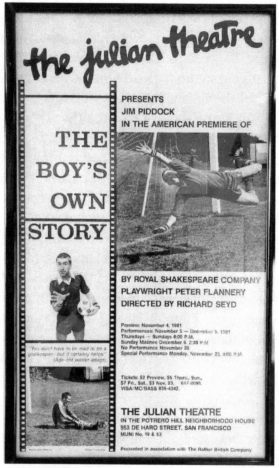

Poster for *The Boy's Own Story*, photo credit to Allen Nomura.

While I was living in San Francisco, I started seeing a woman called Tracey who was a year or so younger than me. She was smart, funny, and all-around adorable. But as our relationship progressed, she told me she was starting to have some really strange experiences. And I mean *really* strange. She believed that some evil force was around her—not me, I hasten to add—and she began having terrible nightmares. She even claimed she'd been levitated a couple of times at night out of her own bed. As soon as you've finished laughing, let me state for the record that I've always been a huge skeptic about stuff like that, but Tracey was a very down-to-earth person herself so I didn't know what to believe. Had I badly misjudged her? Was she in fact a complete psycho? Before I had time to answer these questions, I started having some very dark and scary dreams myself. I don't remember the specifics, but I do remember waking up one night and feeling distinctly as if something—or someone—very bad was trying to get into the little basement studio apartment I was renting. And, worse than that, it was somehow trying to get into *me*. I don't mean in a sexual way, I mean in a spinning, projectile vomiting, get-me-an-exorcist-pronto kind of way. Fortunately, the dreams stopped after a couple of nights and Tracey didn't have any more weird experiences, so we shrugged it off, rather spooked by it all but relatively unscathed.

A week later, we were having a relaxed after-dinner drink one night in my apartment when I needed to relieve myself. So I went into the little bathroom, had a quick pee, and was just about to flush when I heard Tracey screaming. And it was screaming like I'd never heard before in my life. I immediately grabbed the bathroom door handle and turned it . . . but the door wouldn't budge. Which was slightly alarming because I knew there was no lock on it. The screaming continued, and, getting considerably more concerned, I pushed on the door with all my weight . . . but it still wouldn't budge. So I stepped back and shouldered the door as hard as I could. Still nothing. By now I was in a state of some panic. The fact that this door—which had always opened and shut as easily as any normal, functioning door—wouldn't open for no explicable reason, *and* there was a woman screaming insanely on the other side of it, was—not to understate it—really starting to freak me out. But then, very suddenly, the screaming stopped. And I turned the door handle . . . and the door opened perfectly smoothly and easily. Standing in the kitchen doorway, about twenty feet away, was Tracey, shivering in terror.

"What the hell happened?" I asked her.

And when she finally calmed down, she told me.

Apparently, when I'd gone into the bathroom, she'd wandered

into the kitchen with some dirty dishes and glanced back at the closed bathroom door, which—rather oddly, as I think about it now—had a full-length mirror on the outside of it. She caught sight of her reflection in the mirror and was about to turn away again when the reflection of her face started to change. It became, in her words, "demonic and transformed into the grotesque features of a devil." Petrified, she tried to turn away . . . but couldn't. All she could do was scream. Then she heard me, trying to open the door and calling out to her, and became even more terrified when she realised that I couldn't get out. Finally she managed to turn away, and that was the moment when I was very suddenly and very mysteriously able to open the door. Now, even if I wasn't inclined to believe her story, there was no way on earth that she could have held the door shut herself, because she was much too far away when I opened it. And, judging from where her screams were coming, I knew she wasn't right outside the door anyway.

That night, I removed the mirror from the bathroom door, and soon afterwards I moved out of the apartment. Not surprisingly, our relationship cooled off a bit after that.

But there's also a footnote to this rather spooky story. After I left San Francisco, Tracey and I kept loosely in touch, and a year or so later, en route to a vacation in Hawaii, I decided to pay her a visit in Seattle where she was now living. Time had clearly dissipated the memory of that alarming night, and I think we were both feeling out the idea of possibly getting back together again. She picked me up at Seattle airport, and we were driving in her car on the freeway back to her apartment, reminiscing about old times, when there was a loud cracking sound and she completely lost control of the vehicle. It veered across two lanes at high speed, heading for an exit, then veered back towards the freeway, but not far enough; we were hurtling right towards the median barrier between the freeway and the exit. I honestly thought it was the final curtain and braced myself for a fatal impact. But it never came. The car stopped *an inch in front of the barrier*. We both stepped out of it and looked at each other knowingly. A discussion about whether we should get back together again never took place after that.

And that's the only tale of the supernatural you'll find in this book, because nothing like that has ever happened to me before or since. Whenever I've shared this story, I've heard all kind of theories about what might have happened: our past lives colliding (bit far-fetched) . . . the power of our imaginations (definitely not) . . . a temporary demonic possession (sure, if you believe in that kind of thing). I can't give you an explanation myself, simply because it was the most inexplicable thing I've ever experienced. But whenever anyone asks me if I believe in ghosts, rather than give them a straightforward yes or no answer, I tell them that story.

9

BROADWAY BUM

The day I arrived in New York, the producer who was going to stage my one-man show decided to put her money into a Broadway musical instead. So there I was, all dressed up in Manhattan with nowhere to go. However, a theatre in Minneapolis had also heard about my show and they booked it into their theatre for a three-week run. So, my original plan for a three-month stay in America was now going to stretch into the region of fifteen months.

After I'd done the show at the rather oddly named Mixed Blood Theatre in Minneapolis, I was invited back to San Francisco for the Bay Area Theatre Critics awards because the one-man show had been nominated for Best Play and I'd also received a nomination for Best Actor. I had no illusions about winning anything, but I went back because I knew it would be a fun reunion with every-one involved in the production of *The Boy's Own Story*. And it was. So much so that I was quite drunk by the time they announced the Best Actor winner and I was genuinely shocked to hear my name. Climbing the steps up to the stage without falling flat on my arse and then delivering a hastily improvised acceptance speech without slurring incoherently was a far more impressive piece of acting than whatever I got the award for.

When I got back to New York, I faced the same problem that I'd left London to escape: I was unemployed again, and I was facing the decision of whether to go back to England or see how things panned out in New York. But, at this point, I did have one new weapon in my armoury: a videotape of the play that had been filmed in San Francisco. Within a couple of weeks, that got me an American agent. A couple of weeks after that, my new agent sent me out to audition for a Broadway play, and, to my very pleasant surprise, I got the job. So, a couple of weeks later, I found myself rehearsing for a revival of Noël Coward's *Present Laughter* at Circle in the Square, directed by and starring George C. Scott. Life was definitely coming at me *very* fast.

Also making his Broadway debut in the show, and sharing a dressing room with me, was a very talented and funny young actor called Nathan Lane—who, despite going on to have a stellar career on Broadway and elsewhere, has maybe the worst actor's-humiliation story I've ever heard. A couple of years after we did the play together, he was cast in his first movie. It was a relatively small part, playing a hotel receptionist in a high-profile movie. He did his one-day shoot and waited for the film to open. When it did, he invited his family and a group of friends to celebrate his grand cinematic debut with him. Finally, his scene came up, and . . . I know, you're thinking, the part had been cut . . . but, no, worse than that. They'd reshot the scene with another actor and "forgotten" to tell him. Which only proves that the best among us can also get beaten down sometimes, and that, in turn, is a useful lesson about not giving up or getting too downhearted whenever it happens.

Nathan, Kate Burton, Dana Ivey, Christine Lahti, and I all made our Broadway debuts in *Present Laughter*. The play was stage-managed by Michael Ritchie, who went on to become the producer of the Williamstown Festival and then the artistic director of the Center Theatre Group in LA, and remains a great friend to this day. The play itself ended up being a hit, and it put my career on the map for the first time. I wasn't sure what map exactly, but it was all rather heady stuff and had all happened less than eighteen months since I'd come to America.

George C. Scott was the first major star I'd ever worked with, and he was every bit as gruff and intimidating as you'd imagine. As both director and leading man of the play, he didn't like to waste time, particularly if it kept him away from drinking and watching his beloved Detroit Tigers baseball team, so our rehearsals were brisk and to the point. Noël Coward's words don't need enormous analysis, and George had absolutely no interest in discussing anybody's "motivations" or "intentions." So when Christine Lahti, who was not really used to working that way, would stop in the middle of a scene and ask him a question, she'd inevitably get told in George's famously gravel-toned voice:

"Just enter, say your lines, then exit. And then we can all go home."

As it happens, he was a good director and excellent in the part. He wasn't an obvious choice to play Garry Essendine—whom Coward wrote as a preening, superficial light-comedy theatre actor—but the production turned out to be even funnier because George was cast against type. On the downside, however, he missed an average of one show a week during the run of the play through "illness." We all knew he was drinking heavily, but the absences were nevertheless surprising because he also had the constitution of an ox. The night before our final show, which was a Sunday matinee, he took the whole cast out to Gallaghers Steakhouse, and I've never seen a human being consume so much alcohol. When I arrived at the theatre the next day, George was sitting in his dressing room wearing nothing but his boxers and with the door wide open. He called me in and, as we chatted, it soon became clear that he hadn't gone to bed and had been drinking all through that Saturday night and Sunday morning. He could barely string two words together, and I was certain we'd have to cancel the show or put the understudy on. But I couldn't have been more wrong because we did the show and George didn't miss a beat, didn't slur a single word or put a foot wrong. It was uncanny but also terrifying.

After *Present Laughter* closed, I once again faced the decision of whether to head back to England and forge a career there, or to continue riding the wave I was on in New York. The decision was soon made for me when I was cast in another Broadway-bound play called *Make and Break*, written by Michael Frayn and starring Peter Falk. The play might have been Broadway bound, but it never arrived after out-of-town runs in Wilmington, Delaware, and at the Kennedy Center in Washington, DC. There are any number of reasons why plays intended for Broadway fall by the wayside. In this instance, the main reason was that production was rather like a donut with a sizable hole in the middle. Peter Falk was a genuine character, which was about half a degree removed from his famous Columbo role on TV—just without being ahead of everyone else or having the capability to solve anything. I liked him a lot, but he hadn't been onstage in years, and it showed. He didn't have the requisite energy to drive the play (which Leonard Rossiter had in spades in the prior London production) and I don't think he ever mastered his lines. Sometimes he'd just sit back on stage and enjoy scenes as if he wasn't actually in the play himself. He even said to me once, in front of an audience, "*That was very good!*" after I'd got a laugh on a line. And then there was the glass eye. I'm certainly not including it as a reason for the play's demise, but occasionally it would roll back and all you could see in one socket was a white orb. He'd usually notice you looking at him strangely and then wink at you with his good eye and adjust it. However, on one occasion, when everyone on stage was looking at him strangely and motioning with their heads, he didn't get that it wasn't the glass eye, but that he'd come onstage with his fly wide open.

Also in the cast of that production was a young actress who became the second girlfriend I ever lived with. Her name was Linda and our relationship kept me in America after *Make and Break* closed in Washington. We found an apartment on West 23rd Street in New York, half a block from the Chelsea Hotel and the Roundabout Theatre. That turned out to be very convenient when I was next cast in the Roundabout's revival of *The Knack*, a comedy which was first produced in the mid-1960s. The other actors in the four-person play were great: Daniel Gerroll (who'd recently been in *Chariots Of Fire*), J. Smith-Cameron (whom you'd probably now know from her role as the lawyer Gerri Kellman in *Succession*), and Robert Schenkkan (who went on to become a very successful Tony-winning playwright and screenwriter). But the play was horrifically dated and our audiences didn't know what to make of it. The theatre was run by an eccentrically gay, Brooklyn-born man in his sixties called Gene Feist. All of us were struggling in vain to get the clunky old play to come alive in previews, and finally we went to Gene for some suggestions. He looked at us thoughtfully for a moment and then said in his fey, laconic drawl:

"You need to play act 2 *before* act 1 at tomorrow's matinee. That should make it work."

We all laughed, but he stared us without a hint of a smile. It turned out he was deadly serious and we ended up having to do it. But performing act 2 before act 1 made absolutely no difference at all. The audience was just as confused by the play and laughed no more or less at the dated jokes than audiences who'd seen us perform it in the right order.

The Knack at the Roundabout Theatre, New York, with J. Smith Cameron, Robert Schenkkan, and Daniel Gerroll. Credit: Billy Rose Theatre Division, The New York Public Library. © 2022 The New York Public Library, Astor, Lenox, and Tilden Foundation.

After leaving audiences at the Roundabout Theatre in a state of confusion, I did a reading of a new Broadway-bound play called *The Slab Boys*—written by John Byrne—about a group of young Scottish men working in a carpet factory in a town near Glasgow in the 1950s. The play was to star three young, up-and-coming Hollywood actors: Sean Penn, Kevin Bacon, and Val Kilmer. My role was that of a slightly more senior worker, who is the constant butt of all their jokes and teasing. The reading wasn't terribly inspiring. Kevin Bacon and Val Kilmer were both fine, but Sean Penn mumbled and bumbled his way through the whole thing, barely able to string two words together, let alone put on any kind of performance. I was offered the role soon afterwards and, even though it didn't really excite me, I would have done it. However, that same week, Michael Blakemore, who'd directed *Make and Break*, offered me a part in another Michael Frayn play, which was to be the first Broadway production of *Noises Off*. Weighing my two options, I chose what I thought was a far better and more enjoyable play (and role) and accepted the latter.

I learned a valuable lesson when I attended the opening night of *The Slab Boys*. Brian Benben, who went on years later to star in the HBO series *Dream On*, ended up playing my part and he did it more than justice. But that had nothing to do with the lesson I learned. The real eye-opener for me was that Sean Penn's performance was by far and away the best thing about the whole production. He was terrific, and, for the first time, I became acutely aware that there are many ways of working as an actor. He was someone who obviously needed to find his way into a role and felt no pressure to give a finished performance at an early reading. Of course, it didn't hurt that he was already a movie star from *Fast Times at Ridgemont High*, so he could afford to be terrible in an early reading without the fear of being fired, but it was still a valuable lesson for me not to judge an actor so hastily in the rehearsal stages.

Broadway Show League softball game with John Malkovich.

Around the same time, Linda got cast in a Broadway production of Arthur Miller's *Death of a Salesman* starring Dustin Hoffman and John Malkovich. So, with me doing *Noises Off*, it meant we were working around the corner from each other on Broadway for several months. Every night after my show ended, I'd walk over to their theatre to meet her and, for whatever reason, Dustin Hoffman took an immediate liking to me. The first time I met him, he told me I had "a Jewish soul"—although I'm still not sure what that means—and whenever he'd see me he'd immediately launch into one of the worst English accents I've ever heard. He'd also often ask me, in a loud stage whisper that everybody could hear:

"So what's it like . . . you know . . . *doing* it with Linda?"

He was always making suggestive and questionable remarks, but, in my experience, they were always far more Benny Hill than Harvey Weinstein. It was silly and jocular more than anything . . . and he was like that with everybody. His wife, Lisa, would just shake her head and roll her eyes as if she was just mildly bored by his raunchy humour at that point in their relationship. The other thing I'll say about Dustin Hoffman is that he was extremely generous, both materially and of spirit. When the cast of *Noises Off* won a Drama Desk Award for best ensemble, he stood up at the ceremony when I received mine and began a standing ovation for me. Given that, only four years earlier, at one of the lowest points in my life, he'd reduced me to emotional rubble with his Oscar speech, it all felt *very* surreal and exhilarating. I didn't share the details of this coincidental turnaround in my life with Dustin—or anybody else, for that matter—because I was still having to pinch myself to believe it had all happened.

And also possibly because, to my developing writer's eye, it all seemed a bit too much like a cheesy rags-to-riches script.

Between my mid and late twenties, I lived the high life in New York City. The opening night of *Present Laughter* had been exciting enough, but *Noises Off* took things to a whole new level. There were celebrities from all walks of life in the audience and, to this day, I've never heard laughter that loud or prolonged in any theatre anywhere. But New York can be very snobby about crowd-pleasers, so we had no idea how the critics would respond. The opening night went as well as it could have, and I was delighted that my mother and my younger sister Caroline were able to fly over from England to be there. The party afterwards was at Sardi's, which is the stuff of dreams for any theatre actor. After the show, I met my mother and sister and we walked the few blocks to the famous restaurant. As we were entering, everyone—including some very well-known faces—got to their feet and started applauding. I immediately turned around to see what celebrity had come in behind us. It was only when people started laughing—because they thought I was doing a comic "bit"—that I realised the standing ovation was for me. It's probably just as well that I could deflect it with an unintentional joke, because I don't think I was equipped back then to deal with that kind of attention. But it's still a moment in my life I'll never forget.

The other thing I remember clearly about that night was when Bill Boggs—TV personality and husband of fellow cast member Linda Thorson—arrived with copies of *The New York Times*, hot off the press, in the early hours of the morning. The review was outstanding and we were destined to become a massive hit. Frank Rich, the *New York Times* critic, who could be extremely vicious (and once had a bowl of pasta thrown in his face by an actor he'd eviscerated), described it as "the funniest play written in my lifetime." The movie rights were soon bought by Steven Spielberg. I remember running into him on a number of occasions as I came out of the theatre after the show, because he'd want to discuss with anyone in the cast—or anyone who'd listen—how to adapt it for the screen. He was like an energetic and animated schoolteacher whose unbridled enthusiasm was infectious. Of course, none of us in that Broadway cast ended up in the film when it finally got made, but that's show business, baby.

I did over four hundred performances of *Noises Off* with a wonderful cast that included Dorothy Loudon, Victor Garber, Brian Murray, Deborah Rush, Paxton Whitehead, Linda Thorson (whom older readers will remember well from the TV show *The Avengers*), Douglas Seale, and Amy Wright. And there were quite a few shows that weren't without incident.

One midweek matinee, I was in the middle of a scene at the beginning of the second act with Paxton and Linda T., and we gradually became aware that a large man was walking down one of the aisles towards the stage. But he didn't stop at a row or a seat, he just kept walking. As he started climbing up the steps onto the stage, I saw a gun-like shape hanging by his side, and Paxton, Linda, and I—and the whole audience—collectively held our breath . . . until he breezed right past us and headed off into the wings. It was then that I realised the object hanging from his belt was not in fact a gun but a large *telephone*. He was from New York Telephone and was looking for the backstage pay phone, which hadn't been working for a couple of weeks. Not seeing a pay phone on the stage or behind the scenery, he soon re-emerged and walked past us *again* . . . down the stage steps . . . and back up the aisle and out of the theatre. I don't know if you're familiar with *Noises Off*, but the set for the second act is actually a theatre backstage area, which gives him a small hint of an excuse. But what the hell did he think an entire audience of people, the blinding stage lights, and three actors in costumes saying lines were all about?!

The scene in *Noises Off* that came to a rude halt. Credit: Billy Rose Theatre Division, The New York Public Library. © 2022 The New York Public Library, Astor, Lenox, and Tilden Foundation.

Noises Off was nominated for four Tony awards, but I didn't go to the ceremony. I decided instead to go to the Players club to join the *Death of a Salesman* cast, who were having a party there. It was going to be a dressy affair, but I couldn't be bothered to hire a tuxedo because one of my costumes in *Noises Off* was a far-too-small tux (for comedy purposes), so I thought I'd just wear that. So, after the Sunday matinée—the last performance of the week—I took a shower, went back to my dressing room, and changed into my ill-fitting comedy tux. I made my way to the stage door and was surprised to find it locked. And there was no sign of the guy who locked up. So I then went to the stage and discovered the whole theatre was in pitch darkness except for a naked lightbulb in front of the safety curtain. At this point, I realised—much to my horror—that I'd been locked in and the next show wasn't for *another two days*. And remember, this was a time before cellular phones, so my options were very limited. Which is why I then went to the lobby and started banging on the glass doors to get the attention of passers-by on the street, who—in typical New York fashion—either quickened their pace or didn't bat an eyelid at the sight of a crazed young man in an ill-fitting tux having an apparent nervous breakdown inside a Broadway theatre. So now I had to opt for the nuclear option; I called 911 from the backstage pay phone (which, thankfully, the intruding technician from New York Telephone had managed to fix). The fire department was clearly puzzled by my highly unusual emergency, but they told me to hang tough and wait onstage. So I obediently stood next to the lonely bulb in front of the safety curtain for a few minutes before I heard a loud crash up near one of the private balcony boxes. I craned my neck, and, beyond the open curtains at the back of the box, I could just make out an axe coming through a window. The glass shattered some more, a hand reached in and opened the window, and a New York City fireman climbed into the balcony box and looked down at the stage:

"Ready to go?" he called out cheerily.

I made my way to the back of the theatre, up the stairs, and to the box. He held the window open for me and I looked out at another fireman perched at the top of a fire-engine ladder that descended to . . . *a street filled with very curious spectators and members of the press!* So then—in my comedy tux, which came down to just below my elbows and knees, and with one fire-man below me and another above—I slowly descended the very long ladder to 47th Street as the crowd of people cheered and applauded. The next day, alongside coverage of the Tony awards, the New York tabloids had a sensational story about a dramatic Broadway theatre rescue, accompanied by a photo of me with my arse hanging out of an ill-fitting tuxedo as I was being carried down a fireman's ladder by two New York City firemen.

After a year in *Noises Off*, I took over a role in a revival of Noël Coward's *Design For Living* on Broadway—a part that had been originated by Frank Langella. It was near the end of the play's run and I had only about ten days to rehearse. But it was the first time I'd ever had my name above the title on a Broadway billboard, which was exciting, even for such a humble and modest actor as myself. On the other hand, it was also a mammoth part and very hard to pull off with so little preparation. Before my first night, I was in my dressing room, feeling really nervous, when Raúl Juliá—who'd been in the original cast with Langella and Jill Clayburgh—stuck his head in the doorway and said:

"Don't worry, my friend. You are *bound* to fuck up!"

Which was a superb piece of advice, both for the theatre and life in general. It was unrealistic to think I'd be flawless—I was bound to fuck up at some point—so I might just as well accept it and enjoy myself. And I did enjoy myself. And I did fuck up.

By the time *Design For Living* closed, Linda and I were no longer a couple, so I was out of work and out of a relationship. Incidentally, I should probably add here that Linda's last name was Kozlowski, and not long after we split up she got cast in *Crocodile Dundee* opposite Paul Hogan, with whom she had a rebound relationship, and soon after that she became the second Mrs. Hogan.

At this point, I was pretty exhausted from doing eight shows a week for the better part of three years, and I found myself at a crossroads in my life. In the four years since I'd arrived in America, all the signposts indicating which direction I should take had been hard to miss. But, when I finally paused to breathe, I wasn't sure that I wanted to be an exiled British thespian in New York for the rest of my days. I'd had a wonderful three years, mostly performing on Broadway, and every cast I was in became a temporary new family. I finally felt like I belonged to a vibrant and highly esteemed theatre community. But, despite the many things I loved about the city, it never quite felt like *home*.

Since I was also now harbouring a not-so-secret desire to work in films and TV, I found myself facing three separate paths that I suspected would probably determine more than just my immediate future. I had the choice of (a) going back to England, where I had no real professional track record, (b) staying in New York where my career was now established, or (c) heading out west to LA and throwing my hat into the Hollywood ring. I was so undecided that I even folded up three scraps of paper with the words "London," "NYC," and "LA" scribbled on them, then shuffled them around in my hands behind my back before opening one. Needless to say, I didn't accept the first result (whatever it was) and repeated this very silly charade dozens of times before I ended up even more confused than I was before! So then I sought some outside guidance. I mentioned my dilemma to a well-known veteran Broadway theatre director and he said to me:

"Dear god, you don't want to go to Hollywood. Everyone I know who's gone there . . . their brains completely turned to mush within a couple of years."

I also had the advice of Michael Blakemore, who directed me in *Make and Break* and *Noises Off*, ringing in my ears. He'd made it clear a year or two earlier that he thought I should return to England and pursue a serious theatre career there. I wasn't quite sure why he considered my career in the United States to be any less serious than it would be in England, but maybe it was because he'd emigrated to England from Australia and believed London to be the epicentre of the theatre world.

The truth is I think there are certain times in life when you can't just rely on sailing whichever way the wind is blowing, or allow someone else's opinion to sway you, and you have to make an unassisted choice about which direction to chart. So, ignoring all the insightful advice from my elders and betters, I finally made a decision. On Monday, January 28, 1985—at the ripe old age of twenty-eight—I moved to Los Angeles to try and become a screen actor.

10

FALLING OFF THE HORSE

I'd visited LA very briefly a couple of times before and liked it, even if it did seem a bit overwhelming. But this time, the warm weather and smell of jasmine and orange blossom made it seem all the more seductive, particularly after the noise and general abrasiveness of a cold New York winter.

It's different now, but in the mid-1980s, most people in Hollywood thought that saying "I was just on Broadway" meant you'd just driven down a street by that name in downtown LA. But, eventually, touting my recent New York credentials opened enough casting director's doors to earn me my first television part. It was a guest star role in a new Western drama series called *Wildside*, starring Howard Rollins Jr. I couldn't believe that my first appearance on screen was going to be in a Western—and it turns out I had good reason to be incredulous, because, of the one hundred and twenty-something parts I've played on screen since then, I've never done another Western. I got the role primarily because the director said he thought I had a "wide-eyed twinkle" in my audition, which in layman's terms means I was almost certainly overacting wildly, but I'd got away with it. I was also asked if I could ride a horse and I said yes, despite the fact I'd never sat on a horse in my life. The day after I was cast, I got a call from the production office, telling me they'd set up some riding lessons for me. When I asked why, they said the producers assumed I was lying about being able to ride. I was happy I got the part but even happier to know I'd already mastered the art of Hollywood bullshit.

The night before I was due to start the job, I was in my short-term studio apartment in Toluca Lake, flicking through TV channels, when I came across the last couple of minutes of a very bad sitcom called *Charles in Charge*, which I'd never seen before—or since, thank god. In the very last scene, an adorable young actress appeared for a couple of lines, and I was immediately struck how good she was, even from the tiny amount she had to do. The next day I showed up on the set of *Wildside* and was amazed to see the very same actress, who it turned out was a regular on the show. And I was right; she *was* very talented. As we chatted on the set, the coincidences multiplied as it turned out we had the same agent, she also had just moved out west from New York, and she also was staying at the same Oakwood apartments on Barham Boulevard. However, although we ran into each other a few times in the next couple of years, the similarities between our lives pretty much ended right there. Her name was Meg Ryan.

I soon found myself a small, one-bedroom apartment to rent in West Hollywood, in the basement of a building rather oddly called The "Fontainebluea"—a flagrant misspelling that, to my knowledge, still hasn't been corrected to this day. Even more oddly, I also found out that my neighbour in the building was the mega-famous singer in the 1960's, Dusty Springfield, and her de facto American actress wife. She was clearly down on her luck financially, and was physically unrecognisable from her glory days, and her domestic relationship seemed to be a highly contentious one. It was stark reminder, as I entered the jaws of Hollywood, of how fleeting and tenuous the world of show business and fame could be.

In terms of my own career, I had a tough time reinventing myself during my first year in LA. Apart from riding a horse (very badly) in that TV episode and playing Jean Smart's romantic partner in a TV pilot (quite amusingly), I had a *lot* of time on my hands. I hadn't intended to do any theatre in LA, but I was getting desperate to occupy myself with something. So when I was offered a part in a play called *The Common Pursuit*, written by the well-known British playwright Simon Gray, at a ninety-nine-seat "Equity waiver" theatre (which means the Actors Equity Association union allows the theatre to hire Equity members without paying them) in West Hollywood, I jumped at it. And here beginneth the lesson of this particular tale: never do anything in life out of desperation. *Especially* if you're not being paid for it!

One of the producers turned out to be one of the most neurotic people I'd ever met, and the director liked to preface his notes with the phrase, "Let me give you a basic acting lesson here," which is the most condescending thing I've ever heard come out of any director's mouth. And the writer, Simon Gray, was a profoundly disgruntled and bitter alcoholic. So that was pretty much hitting the misery trifecta right there.

It got worse. Cast members were hired and fired in rehearsals almost every day, which astounded me. How can you be fired from a job when *you're not being paid for it?!* It soon became clear that the tense, hostile atmosphere of the rehearsals wasn't something I—or anyone who's not addicted to extreme adversity and humiliation—needed to experience. Less than a year before, I'd had my name above the title on Broadway, and now I had people in a tiny fringe theatre in LA telling me they didn't think I could hack it as an actor. I'm not kidding. The neurotic producer actually came to my apartment three days into rehearsals and told me he just wasn't "seeing it up there on stage" and that he'd had only the word of a mutual acquaintance that I could act! Right then and there, I should have told him to shove the play up his arse and thrown him out on his ear. But I was way too British and polite (and desperate to work).

After that, my performance in rehearsals went from finding my way to not finding my way to flat-out dreadful. Finally, I went to see Simon Gray at the Magic Castle Hotel in Hollywood, where he was staying, and I told him I was miserable and I was hating the rehearsals and I was going to quit the show. He thanked me for my honesty and courage, then offered me a glass of already-opened champagne. It was nine o'clock in the morning, so I politely declined.

That whole production of *The Common Pursuit* was later

chronicled by Gray in an incredibly mean-spirited book which, even more incredibly, became a TV movie in the UK. In the unlikely event that anyone reading this has either read that book (which I did) or seen that TV movie (which I didn't), I can now reveal that I am Ted Larkins. Everybody in the book is referred to by their real names . . . except me. And I soon discovered why. Whether it was the alcoholism or his own natural malevolence, Mr. Gray—who had never once said an unpleasant word to my face—decided to trash me in the book *and*, with shameless dishonesty, claim that he'd fired me! To be fair, I was far from being the only person he trashed or lied shamelessly about in his book, but the whole thing seemed pointlessly vindictive and petty.

Speaking of vindictive and petty, I have to confess that I did get some measure of revenge. I had a friend in Northern California called Jeffrey—from my Drama Studio days up there—and he mailed a succession of letters for me. In these letters, I wrote to Simon Gray in England in the guise of a real person called Ted Larkins from Berkeley . . . who also happened to be an actor and whose career and health had taken a terrible nose-dive after the publication of Mr. Gray's libellous book. We continued this correspondence for quite a while, in which an increasingly unbalanced and psychotic Ted Larkins from Berkeley threatened an increasingly worried and paranoid Simon Gray in London with everything from lawsuits to dropping by to see him very soon, when next visiting London, for a "cozy little chat, if you know what I mean." I suspect—and certainly hope—Simon Gray spent a few months nervously looking over his shoulder as he went about his life. Whether he did or not, he didn't appear to learn anything from it because, a decade later, he did the exact same thing to the very delightful Stephen Fry, who'd been so unhappy in a West End play Gray had written and directed that, after three performances, he disappeared and went into hiding in another country! Only this time, Mr. Gray trashed Stephen—a person who he claimed had been a good friend—by name, calling him "cowardly, incapable, and inadequate" in the press. It's amazing how unrepentant alcoholics, rather like sociopaths, love to project their own shortcomings onto others.

Despite exacting some kind of revenge on the malevolent playwright, the whole unpleasant experience left me quite rattled. I'd also just suffered my first experience of professional jealousy when I saw my ex-girlfriend, Linda Kozlowski, on the front page of several tabloids, having become something of a celebrity after the success of *Crocodile Dundee*. Additionally, several other actors I'd known or been a peer of in New York were quickly making names for themselves in films or TV series. Jealousy is a truly horrible and insidious human emotion but, unless you happen to be a saint, it's more than likely you'll experience it at some point or another in your life. Even now, I still occasionally have to remind myself that every human journey is a very different one, filled with its own triumphs and tragedies, and the only person you should ever be competing with is yourself. With the benefit of hindsight, I'm also very aware that some of those people who I envied so much at that low point in my career have not had the charmed existence which I assumed was being bestowed upon them at the time. In fact, it's very sobering to reflect on how many of them have endured illness, or financial ruin, or a humbling slide into obscurity, or alcoholism, or drug addiction, or even a premature death.

I wish I could say it was with such philosophical reflection that I was able to shake myself out of my general state of discontent back then and get back on more of an even keel, but I'm afraid it was something considerably more superficial and less noble. As I was wandering around the Beverly Center mall a week or two after I quit *The Common Pursuit*, feeling like a complete and utter failure and trying to figure out what else I could do for a living, I stopped in a card shop to look for a birthday card for a friend. I got momentarily sidetracked in my original task when I saw a whole section of cards that told you which famous people had been born on each day of the year. My curiosity piqued, I found my own birthday and skimmed through the list inside the card. I was about halfway through it when

I did a double take . . . because I saw "1956: JIM PIDDOCK, Broadway actor" among the names. My first instinct was that it was some kind of an elaborate practical joke, but once I'd figured out I wasn't on an episode of *Candid Camera*, it slowly started to sink in that maybe I wasn't *quite* such a complete and utter failure after all and I might not have to find another career just yet.

After this serendipitous little ego salvation, I gradually started getting more TV roles, either guesting on shows or occasionally getting a shot at fame and fortune in the lottery that is pilot season. In those days, the networks would make dozens of TV pilots, but only a handful ever got picked up for a series. I soon learned that if you heard anyone on the set say that your pilot was the network's favourite, you knew it was doomed. And I *always* seemed to hear that. I was dying to hear someone say: "The network thinks this is an absolute piece of shit and destined for the trash can of television history." Then I'd know I would be on a hit show for several years.

I also "got back on the bicycle" and did some more theatre while I waited for my big break in TV or films. I was kindly asked to become an "artistic associate"—although I didn't really know what that meant—at the Los Angeles Theatre Center (LATC), in downtown LA. The first play I did there was called *Diary of a Hunger Strike* about the IRA hunger strikes in prison, written and directed by Peter Sheridan (brother of film director Jim Sheridan). I was playing a character who was the government negotiator with the two hunger strikers, who were played by Shaun ("Da Doo Ron Ron") Cassidy and Colm Meaney. Let me just say here that Colm is a wonderful actor, but he wasn't exactly the *slimmest* of fellows. So it was all I could do not to improvise a line referring to the fact that he looked in amazingly robust condition for someone who was supposedly dying of starvation. At least the play didn't dwell on the IRA dirty protests and have Shaun and Colm writing their names in shit on the prison walls.

Another production I did at LATC was the renowned 1960s revue *Beyond The Fringe*, in a revival of the show that had started at the Old Globe in San Diego. It was directed by my good friend from our

Noises Off days, Paxton Whitehead, who had taken over Jonathan Miller's role in the original Broadway production of *Fringe* in the '60s. He offered the job to me in person over dinner. A couple of days later, the managing director of the Old Globe called me up and told me that when he phoned my theatre agent at ICM to make the offer and do the deal, she said to him:

"Oh, I have another client who's better known; you should cast him instead."

Welcome to the shark-infested world of Hollywood agents! Being a man of integrity, the theatre's managing director declined her highly unethical counteroffer, saying that I was actually the actor Paxton wanted. After I hung up the phone, I made a call myself and, five minutes later, ICM were no longer my agents. I also told them I'd sooner eat my own testicles than pay them any commission for the job. Fortunately, they didn't take me up on that challenge.

The show ended up being a great success, and I persuaded the Los Angeles Theatre Center to bring it up to LA. I also, very cheekily, invited Dudley Moore—whom I didn't know and had never met—to come to the opening night. He, Peter Cook, Jonathan Miller, and Alan Bennett had been in the original production, and I'd been a fan of Dudley's since childhood. He'd also become a big movie star by this time, so I knew it was a massive long shot. But to my amazement he called me in person and said he'd be happy to come. And he did. And I'll never forget how extremely kind and supportive he was that night.

The last play I did at LATC was Oscar Wilde's classic *The Importance of Being Earnest*. I was cast as Jack Worthing, one of the two main characters, and it was directed by a man called Charles Marowitz, who was renowned for being a very *avant-garde* director in London in the 1960s and '70s. Unfortunately, he was more *après-garde* by this point and he decided to take a play that had worked perfectly for a century and put his own unfortunate spin on it. The spin was that Algy and Jack, the two friends who fall in love with Cecily and Gwendolin, are in fact gay . . . and Lady Bracknell is an alcoholic . . . and Miss Prism is a lesbian . . . and so on and so on.

By this point, I was so impervious to theatrical dumbfuckery in Los Angeles that I pretty much ignored every piece of direction he gave me. But when we got to tech week and I saw the set for the first time, I could ignore no more. The walls were covered in paintings of naked men sodomizing each other, and there were large dildos littered around everywhere amid the furniture.

Well, clearly I had far more qualms about acting with dildos than selling them because I went straight to LATC's artistic director, Bill Bushnell, and—bastardizing the line Oscar Wilde is reputed to have uttered on his deathbed—I said:

"Either that set goes or I do!"

Marowitz was then summoned and he screamed at me like a crazed banshee, saying I'd never work in the theatre again, he'd have me barred from Equity for life, and he'd eat all my unborn children (okay, that last one I made up). In the end, though, sanity prevailed, and the offending—albeit amusing in another context—parts of the set were removed. And, to Charles's credit, he clearly wasn't a man to hold a grudge because from that point on until his death nearly thirty years later he always greeted me like a long-lost friend.

The production itself was riddled with catastrophes, self-inflicted and otherwise. One night, the actress playing Lady Bracknell, who'd always had a bit of a problem remembering her lines, suddenly had a *lot* of a problem and couldn't remember anything at all. Not even the names of our characters. Or her own name. I tried helping her along by feeding her with her own lines, but she just kept saying:

"Oh dear . . . I don't know . . . I don't know . . . I don't know."

And then she walked off the stage.

The actor playing Algy—an amusing fellow called Jonathan Schmock who later came up with the idea for the TV series *Sabrina the Teenage Witch*—smiled at me mischievously, and then *he* walked off the stage, leaving me all on my own, which wasn't much fucking help.

The audience clearly knew something was wrong, and you could hear a pin drop as they waited to see what would happen next. Which ended up being this:

I walked over to a clock on the mantelpiece, looked at it, then took out my pocket watch and adjusted it with a shake of the head and a few tuts. Then I went over to the table where afternoon tea was laid out. I picked up the teapot, then, very slowly and deliberately, poured myself a cup of tea. Then I added some milk. And then some sugar, which I stirred in as I whistled tunelessly to myself. Then I picked up a finger sandwich and ate it with an approving nod. By now, a couple of minutes had passed and nobody had come back onstage, and the anticipation of the audience—who clearly knew by now that I was playing for time—was at a fever pitch. I could see the panicked stage manager in the wings shaking her head and drawing her finger across her throat, which I didn't take to be a good sign. So, finishing the sandwich, I picked up my saucer and cup of tea, strolled casually to the front of the stage, smiled at the audience as I took a sip of the tea, and said:

"Talk amongst yourselves."

The whole theatre immediately exploded with laughter and, as I finally sauntered off the stage myself, I received a hearty round of applause. It was by far the best reaction I ever got from any line in that show's entire run.

We continued with Lady Bracknell's understudy after a short break and managed to get through the rest of the play without any more major mishaps. But we weren't so lucky a couple of weeks later when, about half an hour into the show, the lower back pain I'd been feeling most of that day got radically worse . . . to the point that I thought I was going to pass out. When the scene ended and I was backstage, someone told me I looked green. And, as I sank to the floor, doubled up in pain, I knew I couldn't continue. I was immediately rushed to hospital, where I learned that I had a kidney stone. Unfortunately, my understudy had already gone home, so the show continued with the stage manager reading my part. But I'm absolutely certain—without any shadow of doubt—that this particular production of Oscar Wilde's classic didn't suffer one iota because of it.

"CHOOSE ME, PLEASE!"

I know a few actors who say they enjoy auditions, but I don't buy it. They might psyche themselves into *believing* they enjoy them, and they might enjoy them after the fact because they finally got a chance to do a bit of performing, but I don't think the vast majority of actors actually *enjoy* auditions. I certainly don't—and never have—apart from the satisfaction of having done myself justice if I didn't screw it up completely. As it happens, I'm actually not bad at auditions but I still *hate* having to go through all the preparation and stress and self-doubt to prove to someone I'm right for a role.

In the early 1990s, I auditioned for a guest role on *Seinfeld*, which was a hugely popular show at the time. I went in, very well prepared, and took my place in the waiting room with some other actors. Clearly they weren't sure what they were looking for, as the age range was vast. I was in my early thirties and there were some actors there much younger and some much older. One in particular was in his early sixties. When my turn came I walked into the room and there were about half a dozen people sitting there: Larry David, who'd created the show; some writer-producers; and Jerry Seinfeld himself. When I began the scene, reading with the casting director, a very strange and unnerving thing happened: Larry David yawned, put his feet up on his desk, and opened a newspaper so that I was completely obscured from his vision. I was thrown for a second but, because everyone else was paying attention and politely laughing now and then, I soldiered on to the end. But, as I headed to my car, I was fuming. I figured there could be only two explanations: (a) he was one of the biggest assholes on the planet, or (b) he was one of the biggest assholes on the planet.

When I reached my car, I saw the sixty-something actor emerge from the building and he was bright red in the face and almost in tears. I walked back and asked if everything was okay. Looking like he might combust with rage, he then explained the exact same thing had just happened to him.

In yet another odd coincidence in my life, I went to a wedding the following weekend and who should walk in and sit in the same row, a couple of seats away from me, but Larry David. But I took the high ground again and behaved impeccably . . . although refraining from breaking a fellow guest's nose right before the ceremony was probably the right call in terms of wedding etiquette.

One thing I will say, though, is that not all unsuccessful auditions are necessarily humiliating experiences. When I was in New York, I auditioned for a Broadway musical that Tommy Tune was directing. There were a couple of almighty pitfalls for me on that one. Although I believe I can act, my singing is substandard—and, by that, I mean sub anyone's standard—and my dancing abilities are even worse. For someone who's reasonably athletic, it defies logic how beyond useless I am when it comes to learning dance moves. So I read a scene for Tommy Tune at this audition and I sang a song and, for some reason, I wasn't asked to leave show business altogether. Instead, he asked me if I could tap dance. I replied that I couldn't (but I can ride a horse!) and added, in the interest of full disclosure, that I was not a dancer of any kind. At which point he jumped up onto the stage, all six foot six inches of him (yes, I looked it up on Wikipedia), and with immense charm and enthusiasm he said:

"Don't worry, I can teach anyone the basics of tap dancing in less than ten minutes."

"Are you sure?" I replied. "Because I might be the first you can't, and that would be kind of terrible for both of us."

He laughed and said: "Just wait and see!"

And then he threw himself with great energy into giving me a whirlwind ten-minute tap dance lesson. He was so patient and kind—and, of course, brilliant because he's one of the greatest tap dancers in American history. At the end of the ten minutes, he smiled benignly as he put his arm around my shoulder and said:

"Well, I guess I can't teach *anyone* to tap dance in under ten minutes after all."

We both laughed, and I left. I knew of course that I didn't have a chance in hell of getting the job, but I've loved Tommy Tune ever since because of that audition.

The most embarrassing audition I've ever done was at the Mayfair Theatre in Santa Monica in the first few months after I'd moved to LA. They were holding open calls for a new sketch comedy TV series that the producers of *Saturday Night Live* were going to do. It seemed right up my alley, except . . . they wanted people to come in with a "character" they'd created and improvise in that role. At that point in my life, I'd done a fair amount of sketch comedy but I hadn't created any "characters" and I didn't have any professional improvisation experience, so I was thinking about passing the audition up. But my friend Jeffrey from Berkeley was in town and he said:

"What about that Indian voice you do? It's hilarious."

So I started riffing in my faux East Indian voice and he fell about laughing and insisted I *had* to do it for the audition. In hindsight, let me just say there were three key problems with this, in addition to the very obvious fact that it was incredibly racist by today's criteria. Although back then, it really wasn't considered to be, I promise. Back then wasn't *that* long after Peter Sellers had been in *The Party*, in which he did that voice—the one I was essentially ripping off—*and* in brownface, and people loved it. Not to mention that Johnny Carson was still doing his turbaned "Carnac the Magnificent" character every night on television. However, before I dig an even deeper hole for myself with this questionable defence, the three *other* key problems with me doing this were:

1. A silly voice is *not* a character.
2. Never trust that what the friend who laughs at pretty much everything you do says is funny *is* actually funny.
3. *Definitely* don't listen to said friend when he suggests that the "icing on the cake" would be to paint a red dot on your forehead when you go to an audition as this character.

To further compound these three problems, I also decided I didn't need to prepare for the audition, as I had no idea what questions I'd be asked so I would improvise all my hilarious answers on the spot. There is one minuscule saving grace about this story, by the way: I *didn't* wear a costume. No turban, no Gandhi diaper, nothing as tasteless that. However, I *did* have a red dot on my forehead.

So I arrived at the audition and immediately got some weird looks from the people ahead of me. Finally, my turn came and I walked out onto the stage. A voice shouted out from the darkness:

"And who are you?"

And I replied, "Deepak," which was the staggeringly unoriginal name I'd come up with on the drive to the audition.

There was an uncomfortably long pause before the voice said:

"Okay then, Deepak, tell us about yourself."

And that was it. No specific questions, nobody to riff with, nothing. They just wanted me to do a monologue in my "character." And so I attempted, very sadly and very desperately, to do so. Within seconds I knew I was dying a thousand excruciatingly painful deaths. I came up with absolutely *nothing* that was even remotely funny. And the silence in the theatre was pin-droppingly quiet. Finally, after what felt like half an hour but was probably no more than five minutes, my face was redder than the dot on my forehead as I mumbled my way to a finish of sorts and virtually sprinted off the stage. To this day, I still cringe with embarrassment when I remember that audition. I only relate it now as an important cautionary tale for any aspiring young performers who might be reading this book.

The most "Hollywood" audition I've ever had happened many years later, when my career was in a very different place. It was for a guest role on a new comedy series called *Documentary Now!* starring Bill Hader and Fred Armisen. My first instinct was to tell my agent it should be an "offer only," which, in Hollywood parlance means you don't need to audition for the role because they just offer it to you. My agents dutifully relayed this to the casting office. But the next day, my schedule got freer, and I thought it might be fun to work with those two guys, so I decided to go in and read for it. The casting people were happy to see me and extremely enthusiastic when I finished the audition, which they put on tape. They said they thought it was "just *perfect!*"

As I walked out of the studio gates, a couple of actors in 1970s costumes and wigs were approaching a transportation van to head off to set. As I got closer, I realised it was Fred Armisen and Bill Hader. I'd never met either of them before, but their faces lit up when they saw me, and they hurried over, saying they were "huuuuuge" admirers of my work. Bill seemed particularly excited and said he'd recently written an article about comedy in which he'd mentioned me.

I was intrigued by this, but I didn't believe it for a second. So when I got home, I typed "Bill Hader and Jim Piddock" into Google Search, and the article, written just a few months earlier, immediately popped up. It was titled "10 Underrated Comic Actors You Should Know, by Bill Hader" and he'd rated me at number five and written:

Fred Willard's dog-show color commentator in *Best in Show* might be, joke for joke, the funniest character in any movie. Every line kills. But it doesn't work unless you have Jim Piddock next to him, playing it real and nuanced. He could easily milk that part to get himself a laugh, but he's smarter than that. To make the scene work, he's gotta be thrown and annoyed, and he does it so well that it makes Willard a billion times better. When I watch those scenes now, I just watch Piddock. He's a genius.

Okay, I'll admit that after I read that my hat size grew at least an inch or two. And I figured that getting the role on his new show was a mere formality. But it wasn't, because I never heard another word about it!

Which is *definitely* one of the most Hollywood things that's ever happened to me.

12

"BECAUSE YOU'RE BLACK."

Many years before I fooled the very kind Bill Hader into believing I was a comedy genius, I finally got my first recurring role on a TV series. Except it never did recur. I was cast as a villainous nemesis on the cult show *Max Headroom*. In my second episode, we were shooting on top of a skyscraper in downtown LA. The scene had me climbing out of a helicopter and delivering some kind of evil ultimatum to somebody or other. We did a couple of takes before the producers arrived and had a quick huddle with the director. After some serious head-shaking and anguished grimaces, they assembled the cast and crew and told us it was "a wrap." Since it was early in the day, everyone was confused, but clarification soon followed; it wasn't a wrap for the *day*, it was a wrap for*ever* because the series had been cancelled. They pulled the plug mid-episode—something I'd never heard of before or since—so the unfinished episode never aired and my recurring role ended up being a single guest star appearance.

Soon afterwards, though, I got cast in my first film, *Lethal Weapon 2*, which became the top-grossing movie the year it was released. It was directed by Richard Donner, who is the most (nontoxic) masculine man I've ever met. I met him socially a few times, years later, and once said to him, "I want to be you when I grow up." I only had one scene in the film, but one of my lines has amazingly managed to live on in folklore.

I played the South African envoy, and Danny Glover and Joe Pesci come into my embassy building in LA to cause a diversion . . . I believe so that Mel Gibson could then do something immensely heroic. Their whole cunning ploy is to say that Danny Glover wants to emigrate to South Africa. It was still the time of apartheid, so this scene necessitated me doing a lot of open-mouthed "shocked acting" as I fall for their cheeky little ruse. Finally, after delicately dancing around the subject, I tell Danny Glover straight up, in a heavy South African accent, that he can't emigrate there:

"Because you're black (pronounced *bleck*)."

For some reason, the line amused Joe Pesci every time we did a take, and, because he repeated it a few times later on in the movie, it became the film's unofficial catchphrase. To this day, more than three decades later, I still get total strangers hailing me with that line. And, more often than not, they are themselves "bleck."

Around this time, I think I made a subconscious decision about what kind of actor I was going to be. It was clear that I was getting cast in an assortment of British, Australian, or South African roles, which were all accents that came easily to me. When I was asked to audition for American roles, I never felt particularly comfortable— partly because I kept thinking I wouldn't hire me to play a part that hundreds if not thousands of American actors could do better, and partly because I was mostly auditioning for comedy roles, and doing an American accent threw my timing off. But, most of all, I just wasn't very good at it. In addition to my voice mysteriously dropping a couple of octaves, I sounded like an exaggerated cartoon character in an old Hanna-Barbera show. I definitely got a lot better at it as time went by (and with help from some dialect coaches), but I never set out to become an American actor. Nowadays, almost every British actor alive wants to be one and does so with varying degrees of success. And today I feel much more comfortable myself doing an American accent. Maybe, back then, my reluctance had something to do with establishing my identity as an Englishman abroad. Or perhaps I just didn't have the balls, earlier in my career, to "sell ice cream to Italians in Italy."

Soon after my first film, I did my first TV movie, called *A Mom For Christmas*, in which I played a mannequin that comes to life with another mannequin, played by Olivia Newton-John. Which I suppose is a cue for me to make some sort of a joke about how wooden my performance was, but I can't think of a good one, so I'll just say that I was very grateful for all the residual checks when it was broadcast ad nauseam at Christmas for the next couple of decades.

It wasn't long too before I also experienced being cut from a film, accompanied by a hefty dose of Hollywood bullshit. The film was directed by a major director—a person I still very much admire professionally and personally for a number of reasons—and my being cut from the film was quite unusual because it didn't involve ending up on the cutting room floor. While I was in my trailer, in costume, all made up, and ready to shoot my scene, there was a knock on the door. It was the director, who was profusely apologetic and said that he was just going through the script and he'd already figured out that whole sequence of the film would end up being cut, so he didn't want to waste his and my time by even shooting it. To be honest, it made perfect sense to me and, despite the inconvenience of wasting a day of my life, I'd still get paid so I wasn't too put out. Which makes what he told me next all the more unnecessary. He said:

"To make it up to you, I promise you'll be in another one of my movies."

I knew right then and there it was bullshit. And it turned out to be, because I never heard from him again. Although, to be fair, many years later I did actually end up in a film that his production company made. But that was because the director of the film cast me, rather than him.

Around this time, I also did a couple of episodes of the popular sitcom *Coach*. I didn't know a lot about its star Craig T. Nelson, and still don't, but all I can say is that both times I worked with him, the whole set had to be closed down and cleared because he had some very heated "creative differences" with the producers. Another thing I remember is that, on my second episode, neither he nor his co-star Jerry Van Dyke said a single word to me the entire week, which was quite an achievement since all my scenes were with them! Which means that during the read-though, a week of rehearsals, endless breaks in the greenroom, several run-throughs, and the whole taping of the show, they didn't talk to me once. But when we did a curtain call at the end, Craig pulled me into a very manly embrace in front of the studio audience. Which seemed like another example of egregious Hollywood bullshit. But, hey, what do I know? Maybe he's just very shy.

Things were a bit more congenial when I did a couple of episodes of *The Tracey Ullman Show*, which was where *The Simpsons* was born. The animation was originally a short segment, but it went on to outlive the series that spawned it by many decades. There were two actors, around the same age, on *The Tracey Ullman Show* who were regular supporting performers. Both were talented and funny. One of them ended up doing a voice in the animated shorts, and the other didn't. Dan Castellaneta (aka Homer Simpson) became a gazillionaire from it. Sam McMurray has had much more of an on-camera career than Dan, but I suspect his current bank balance is slightly less bloated. Ah, the fickle financial fortunes of the fantasy factory.

And that's quite enough alliteration for one chapter.

13

A BETTER PARKING SPACE

Outside of work, at a lesbian party (don't ask) in the Hollywood Hills, I met a woman called Margaret who had been a writer on *Saturday Night Live*, and we fell in love and started living together in Studio City. She could see that acting on its own wasn't keeping me sufficiently occupied or creatively fulfilled, so she encouraged me to write . . . which is something I'd always dabbled in. We had adopted an insane dog called Lucy, and we talked about chronicling the resulting disruption of our lives by writing a screenplay about it. I had a bit of spare time on my hands (okay, quite a lot), so I wrote a first draft. Margaret did a second draft and we tinkered together on a third. We then gave it to Margaret's agent, who sold it for a low- to mid-six-figure sum. And, boom . . . I suddenly had a second career.

It also meant that I added to my growing collection of agents. So far, I had accumulated an agent for acting in films and TV, an agent for commercials, and an agent for voice-overs. And now, Margaret's literary agent became my agent for writing. His name was Bob Wunsch and he was a veteran in Hollywood. Although, what I liked about him most was that he had much more of a New York literary agent's sensibility, in that he actually cared more about writers than "the deal." He also had a delightfully snarky and dry sense of humour. I remember Margaret and I being in a meeting with him in his office and an assistant coming in to tell him that some major studio had just paid a million plus dollars for a script about a ten-year-old boy who becomes the manager of a Major League Baseball team. He nodded for a moment as he absorbed this breaking news, then got to his feet and drolly exclaimed:

"Excuse me for a moment while I leave show business."

And then walked out of the office.

Becoming a professional writer bumped me up to being a second-class citizen in Hollywood, one who gets a designated parking space on a studio lot. It also introduced me to LaLa Land litigation (sorry, I'll try to keep this alliteration thing to a minimum). Before the company that ended up buying Dwayne (the name we chose for our fictitious dog and the movie) read the script, it had also been sent to a Major Studio—which shall remain nameless—which had passed on it. And before the company who bought our script were able to get it into production, the Major Studio made and released a similar film that became a massive hit. Now, the concept of similar projects being developed—or even made at the same time—happens all the time in Hollywood. I've heard this particular phenomenon explained in two ways. Either (a) there's a cosmic universal consciousness that creative people tap into at any given moment in time, or (b) nobody ever really has anything original to say. In our case, however, there was possibly a different explanation: a number of scenes in the Major Studio's big-hit film were very similar—and I mean very similar—to scenes we'd written. And there was clear evidence that our script had been seen by executives involved in the Major Studio's movie.

In the ensuing lawsuit, I had to give my first legal deposition, even though I wouldn't get a dime from the lawsuit because we'd already been paid in full when the script was bought. Eventually the case was settled out of court and the smaller company was awarded a substantial figure (far bigger than what they'd paid for our script) from the Major Studio.

Since then, I've also been involved on the other side of a legal dispute. I wrote an episode of a successful police procedural TV show in which a psychic goes to the cops to say she's had visions that will help them find a murdered body, and, because what she tells them turn out to be right, she becomes a prime suspect. As a not-so-clever play on words, I named the psychic character Faith and titled the episode "A Question of Faith." About a year after the episode aired, an unknown and never-produced writer sued the TV network, the studio, and me, claiming I'd stolen the episode from a TV movie script he'd written. It turned out his script was about a psychic whose name was also Faith—and there, I believe, the similarity ended. In addition, there was also not a shred of evidence that the studio, the network, or I had ever seen his script. In due course, I had to give another deposition—this time as a defendant—but the whole thing disappeared very quickly. However, you're not anyone in Hollywood until you've been involved in a lawsuit, and I'd been in *two* within the first couple of years of being a writer!

The next thing I wrote was a solo effort. It was a mystery-thriller, which were all the rage at the time. I think my childhood obsession with Agatha Christie novels stood me in good stead, and the script got some immediate interest. It ended up being optioned by The Samuel Goldwyn Company, which was run by Sam Goldwyn Jr., son of one of the first legendary Hollywood moguls, Sam Goldwyn. In the negotiations, I asked my agent to take a risk. They'd offered a $50,000 option, with a purchase price of $200,000 if the film got made. But, even though I knew the film ever getting made was a real crapshoot, I was keen to get my screenplay quote up to a higher figure. So I asked my agent to counter the offer with a much *lower* option sum of $15,000 but a much *higher* purchase price of $350,000. I think the business affairs department at the Goldwyn Company were so surprised that a writer would ask for less money up front that they immediately accepted it. And, fortunately, my gamble paid off, because the film did get made.

The script was originally called *Beyond Suspicion*, but the film was released with the title *Traces of Red*. We ended up with Jim Belushi, Loraine Bracco, and Tony Goldwyn in the lead roles (okay, nepotism isn't completely dead, but he *is* a good actor). I also played a small role in it myself, more as an afterthought than anything else. Most people assume actors turn to writing to create roles for themselves, but I never did. I wish it weren't so, but acting and writing occupy very different parts of my brain, so I never think in those terms. In the last few years I've consciously tried to create more roles for myself, but it's still not high on my list of priorities when I'm writing. (Note to self: work on that, you idiot.)

During preproduction, I went down to Florida with the director, Andy Wolk, and one of the producers, David Picker. David was a very gentlemanly, old-school Hollywood guy who had run United Artists at one time and who is credited with helping to launch the film careers of Sean Connery, Steve Martin, and various other people. One night, he took Andy and me to dinner at an Italian restaurant in Miami Beach. It had been there for decades and was once owned by someone who was reputed to be notorious gangster Meyer Lansky's front man in Miami, which makes it unsurprising that several scenes for Brian De Palma's remake of *Scarface*, starring Al Pacino, were shot there. It was also a favourite hangout of Sammy Davis Jr., Judy Garland, Jackie Gleason, Frank Sinatra, and Richard Nixon. We were treated like kings that night by a succession of waiters, who all looked like they were from the cast of *The Sopranos*, until finally the owner's son very kindly told us he wanted to give us a private tour of their wine cellar, which contained ten million dollars' worth of wine. So we went down to a basement beneath the restaurant that was cordoned off with steel bars and padlocked to the hilt. He showed us several of their best vintages and then pointed to a smaller cage that was protected with a security system. In that cage was a single bottle worth $75,000. All in all, it was a very pleasant and enlightening evening.

The next morning I picked up a newspaper, and the front-page story immediately caught my attention: the restaurant had burnt to the ground in the middle of the night, about three hours after we'd left. I've no idea if any of the wine survived, but I imagine there were some substantial "insurance claims."

After I got back from Florida, I had a meeting with Hollywood mega-producer Arnold Kopelson, who'd won an Oscar a few years before for *Platoon.* He asked me what I wanted to work on next, so I told him there was a book I loved called *Good Times, Bad Times,* written by James Kirkwood, that I'd always wanted to adapt because I thought it was funny, tragic, and very moving. Arnold asked me what studio owned it, and I told him: Warner Bros. I also mentioned they'd had a few screenplay drafts written over the years, but nothing had come of them and the project was now dormant.

"Warners is where my deal is," he said. "So let me give them a call." And he picked up the phone and called a young executive there whom I'll call "Dan." And, as it happened, Dan not only knew about the book, he'd also taken a pitch the week before from an up-and-coming young director who also wanted to revive the project. But he hadn't liked her "take" on it, so a meeting was set up for the following week for him to hear my vision of it.

The next week, I went in to Warners with Arnold, who immediately told Dan how much he *loved* the book—even though I knew he'd never read a single page of it—and I walked out of the meeting with a deal to adapt it. I was in hog heaven. And I remained in hog heaven while I wrote the first draft, because that, as any screenwriter will tell you, is the best of times. The first draft is *your* version of the film, with nobody else's input or meddling. But once you turn in your first draft, things almost always head downhill from there. And, in this case, things headed very rapidly downhill at a terrifying speed. With "speed" being the key word, because it turned out Dan was a very major, very out-of-control drug addict.

There was one script meeting where he was eating a massive bowl of popcorn and maniacally pacing the room as he told me his latest "brainwave." Just for context, the book is a nuanced story about two teenagers, students at a strict and repressive all-male boarding school in New England, whose friendship is sabotaged by their uptight headmaster who secretly has a crush on one of them, and it eventually leads to a tragic and heart-wrenching conclusion.

You get the picture . . . kind of an upmarket, but more tragic, *Dead Poets Society* kind of thing. However, Dan's "brainwave," which came to him as he paced the room and stuffed his face with so much pop-corn it was sometimes hard to understand him, was that the head-master is secretly *killing all the boys and burying them in the school grounds* until the two teenage friends, our heroes, finally thwart him.

As I was listening to this completely insane direction he wanted to take the script in, I gradually figured out what he was doing: he was trying to turn it into a (very bad) version of *Silence of the Lambs*, which just *happened* to be the number one film at the box office that week. When he finally finished his demented dissertation and turned to me with a flourish, awaiting my approval, all I could do was stare at him with a stunned expression. He could obviously tell I wasn't impressed because he let out a nervous laugh and said:

"Jeez, are you this much of a buzzkill with everyone, or is it only with me?"

To which I replied: "No, it's only with you."

And that was pretty much when my dream job came to an end.

A few months later, I heard Dan had been forcibly checked into a rehab facility, and I knew then it was definitely the final curtain for *Good Times, Bad Times*, which had so rapidly become *Bad Times, Bad Times*.

14

A COWARD AND AN IDIOT

After five years of living together, Margaret and I decided to get married, which marked the beginning of the creation of a new domestic family. My mother and sister-in-law came over from England to stay with us, and we all went out to a huge antique mall on Beverly Boulevard called Antiquarius so I could buy her a wedding ring.

It was a Monday afternoon and the place was deserted. We wandered from stall to stall until we found just the right ring. Well, *she* did . . . I have as much affinity and enthusiasm for jewellery as I do for getting a colonoscopy. As I handed over my credit card, I became aware that a woman had come into the store and was standing near us, browsing at things in the glass counter. She was the only other person, apart from our little family group, in the entire place. Out of the corner of my eye, I suddenly realised it was Linda Kozlowski . . . the last woman I'd lived with, whom I'd broken up with seven years before *because she wanted to get married and I didn't!* I had about a nanosecond to decide whether to acknowledge her or keep my back turned away and my face hidden. In other words: be a man or be a coward. I knew the chances of my escaping identification were slim because Linda had met both my mother and my sister-in-law on several occasions, but I chose the coward option anyway and angled myself further away. At which point the woman behind the counter said, in a *very* loud voice:

"This card is a bit worn, sir. Is the correct spelling of your last name P-I-D-D-O-C-K?"

I literally froze (well, not *literally* literally, as it was a very hot LA afternoon). The game *had* to be up now. Out of the corner of my one good eye (remember the botched eye operation I mentioned in chapter two?), I glimpsed Linda looking up. And then my sister-in-law said in an equally loud voice:

"So, Jim, who's keeping the ring until the big day?"

Well, if there had been any slither of doubt about what we were doing in that store until now, it flew right out the window. I mumbled something as I took the boxed ring, then hurriedly led my party of four out of the store, my head turned at an unnatural degree like a demented crab as I tried to avoid eye contact with my ex, who was still rooted to the spot at the counter. I finally made it out, without looking back, but I have no idea to this day what—if anything—that strange, billion-to-one odds-defying moment meant. It was so absurdly coincidental I can't help wondering sometimes if there might actually be some higher power in the universe pulling all the strings. If so, he, she, or it has a very questionable sense of humour, or is simply an unbridled sadist.

Another "please let the ground open up and swallow me whole" moment occurred earlier that same year when Margaret and I were traveling in Italy. We ended up, in early June, at a nice quiet resort overlooking the ocean a little way down the coast from Genoa. On Sunday morning, we went down to the dining room for breakfast and there were a few guys in tracksuits ahead of us in line for the buffet. I could hear the one in front of me—around my age—speaking English with an accent of some sort and I asked him if they were a football team. He said they were and, feeling sociable, I then said:

"Are you in a league or anything?"

He said they were, and I told him I also played in a Sunday league in Los Angeles. And he replied: "What position do you play?"

So I explained I'd always been be a forward, but now I played in midfield because I was getting too slow. He laughed and said he was a forward, too, and was also getting slow. I then asked him where their game was that morning and he told me it was actually in the afternoon and in Genoa.

"Sounds like fun," I commented, for want of anything else to say, before asking him what the name of his team was.

And he replied:

"Roma. We're playing in the final of the *Coppa Italia*."

And it was then that I finally realised this wasn't just another guy who meets up with his mates on a Sunday morning for breakfast, then goes and plays a game of football before collapsing wearily in the pub for a few pints. This was a man who was about to play in the Italian Cup Final in front of 40,000 people at the stadium itself and millions more watching on TV. In my (admittedly slim) defence, I was only half-awake on a Sunday morning, but I still felt like a complete idiot—especially being such a big football fan.

When I looked at him more closely, I thought he *did* look a bit familiar, and that's when he introduced himself. And then I felt even more like an idiot because I discovered I was talking to Rudi Völler, who was not only the captain of Roma but had also captained Germany to their World Cup Final win the previous summer against Argentina. I knew *exactly* who he was now . . . mainly because he was one of the most famous football players in the world at the time.

He was very gracious, and even amused, when I apologised profusely for mistaking him for a Sunday morning pub team player, but when I saw in all the papers the next day that Roma had won the final 1-0 and that Rudi Völler had scored the only goal of the game, I felt just that little bit more of an idiot.

15

ROYAL FLUSH

There's an unwritten understanding among out-of-work actors that the only surefire way to get a job is to book a vacation. After I'd auditioned for the role of Prince Charles in a CBS miniseries called *The Women of Windsor* and didn't hear anything back for a couple of weeks, Margaret and I decided to take a driving trip to Idaho and Montana, where I'd never been. But, by the time we reached Oregon, I got an urgent message from my agent saying I was now being *offered* the role of Prince Charles, but I needed to get to Toronto within forty-eight hours to start shooting. I was a little surprised, since I'd originally not even got a callback from my audition, but figured it was probably because someone had either dropped out, been fired, or died. Which are pretty much the three reasons most actors get any job.

Turning the car around and driving back to LA was the least of my problems. My bigger concern was that I'd just had a summer buzz cut and shaved off most of my hair. Obviously I didn't tell the producers that when I got the job, but I knew the hair and makeup departments were going to have a near-impossible task making me look less like Vinnie Jones and more like Prince Charles. But, miraculously, they did it—including putting wax behind my ears to make them stick out more—and I ended up having a very jolly time playing the part.

When I phoned my mother from Toronto to tell her that I was playing Prince Charles, her reaction was that of the quintessential middle-class English mum who eschews anything that might cause big-headedness in her children.

All she said was:

"Oh, for goodness sake, Jim."

When I related this to Robert Meadmore, the actor playing Prince Andrew, he immediately burst out laughing and told me that his mother had had an almost identical reaction. When he told her he was playing Andrew, her immediate response was to say, rather disapprovingly:

"Oh, you're *not*, are you?"

Of course Robert and I knew that both our mothers would be proudly telling all their friends what their sons were currently up to the minute they got off the phone, but they couldn't possibly let us know that!

The whole undertaking of playing Prince Charles was extremely silly, but at least I knew I could do a reasonable impersonation of the heir apparent to the throne. And in case you're wondering, or want to try it at home, here are the three basic steps:

1. Speak in a very clipped aristocratic accent, but also as if you have a severe case of lockjaw.
2. Maintain a slightly constipated expression at all times.
3. Fiddle with your shirt cuffs as much as possible.

Et voilà!

Prince Charles in *The Woman Of Windsor*, with Nicola Formby as Lady Di.

Entertainment Tonight came to the set while we were shooting. When they interviewed me, they asked how I was approaching the role. I'm sure they were expecting an elaborate explanation of how I transformed myself through some complex acting technique involving a deeply committed process of character immersion, but I'm afraid the answer they got was:

"I'm just trying not to get any laughs because I don't think it's a comedy."

Even now, I have no idea if I succeeded in achieving this very singular goal or whether it was unwittingly the funniest performance I've ever given. But one thing I know that I did get right was making him a relatively sympathetic character, which I genuinely believed he was. So I was delighted when the technical advisor on the series—a woman who'd worked for years as a personal assistant to Charles and Diana—came up to me on the set one day and told me I'd really captured how charming and kind Charles was, something which she thought a lot of the general public didn't really appreciate. I thanked her graciously and then asked her what she thought of Diana.

"Oh, she was a total bitch," she replied.

So there you go. I didn't ask her to elaborate, which is probably just as well, as I suspect she could have given Piers Morgan a run for his money when it comes to unbridled royal spouse bashing.

And I've still never got around to visiting Idaho or Montana.

16

INFERNO OF HELL

S oon after I moved to LA, I met a fellow Brit and film writer-director called Duncan Gibbins, who played in the same expat football team. Duncan was a cool customer off the football field and a homicidal maniac on it. He not only became a close friend, but he's also the only person I've had a fistfight with since I was thirteen years old. We were two ambitious and competitive peas in a pod, and that was never more evident than when we talked about whatever we were currently writing.

"I took it easy today," he'd say. "I only wrote for ten hours."

And I'd reply: "Yeah, me too. I can't have written more than fifteen pages at most."

We were fast heading towards a minimum of three screenplays a week, but what were unspoken challenges off the football field started to become very spoken *on* it. Duncan's fiery personality and passion for the game would lead him to say things in the heat of the moment that I didn't particularly appreciate. For several months I refused to rise to his bait, but eventually I got fed up with it and so I dealt with it in the most mature way possible. I didn't speak to him for about a year.

But the volcano finally erupted one Sunday morning at a high-school soccer field in Woodland Hills when Duncan, in the way only he knew how, pushed one button too many, and I saw red. Before anyone knew it, we were swinging away at each other and players from both sides were pulling us apart.

At half-time Duncan showed immense class and resilience when he came over and sat next to me. He held out his hand and said:

"We shouldn't be fighting like this, Jim. We're making the other team laugh, mate."

Not to be outdone, I responded with even more class and resilience and I didn't speak to him for another six months.

Eventually things turned around when I became the manager of our team and I had to phone all the players up every week. We were finally forced to start talking again, and he said to me:

"So are we friends again now, mate?"

Duncan in full director mode.

Once again he'd laid down the gauntlet, and this time I couldn't refuse it. And, after that, there was nothing that could shake our friendship. We were two battle horses approaching middle age—him a few years ahead of me, as I'd often remind him—who'd been through a whole lot of bullshit together and come out the other side.

Tuesday, November 2, 1993, was one of those very dry, blustery, late autumn days in Los Angeles when the light never quite fools you into thinking it's summer because the sun never gets high enough. I'd just got back to the house after a doctor's appointment when I heard there was a fire in Topanga Canyon. I turned on the TV and saw live shots of two men, one all wet and in tattered clothes, talking to some paramedics. A reporter's voice-over said they'd been caught in the fire, one of them had injuries, and there was a third person who'd also got caught in it. Seconds later, my phone rang. It was one of the guys on my football team.

"Are you watching this fire stuff on Channel 4?" he asked.

"No," I said. "Channel 9."

And that's when he informed me:

"They just gave the name of the third injured person. They said it was Duncan Gibbins."

My first thought was that I hoped he'd be okay for our game at the weekend because we were a bit short of players. I was also surprised because, though Duncan liked to be in the thick of things, if anyone knew how to look after himself it was him. After I hung up, I heard about someone being airlifted to Sherman Oaks Hospital. I doubted it was Duncan but called the hospital just in case. And they said that, yes, he *had* just been brought there by helicopter. I explained who I was, and I was told to hold before a hospital administrator then got on the line and asked me if I could get over there right away.

When Margaret and I arrived at the hospital, there was a crowd of press outside. We were whisked past the media into the lobby and greeted by someone whose title was victim-psychologist-some-thing-or-other, who led me into a small room.

"Since there are no relatives here," he said, "I'd like to ask you how well you know Mr. Gibbins."

Tactfully leaving out our infamous fistfight, I told him.

And, with that established, he said: "He has burns over ninety percent of his body."

"What does that mean exactly?" I replied.

And his answer was: "It means he's not going to make it. It's not a question of *if* he's going to die from his injuries, it's a question of *when*."

At that point, my brain slid into an alternate universe as I tried to process what I was hearing. Duncan sold scripts . . . he got to direct some of them . . . he was playing football at the age of forty-one after a serious knee injury. He *always* made it.

It was only when I was allowed to see him that the sudden new reality I was living in hit me. Duncan was lying on a gurney in a strange-smelling emergency room, wrapped from head to toe in bandages like an Egyptian mummy. There were holes for his mouth and nose, and he was breathing with the aid of a ventilator because his lungs had been so badly damaged from the smoke inhalation that they weren't functioning. And the reason his eyes were covered was because both his corneas had been burnt off. I was told he wasn't in any pain because of the drugs he'd been given and the brain monitor indicated he could hear what was being said to him. I sat down, alone, beside the mummified figure that they assured me was my friend, and I told him I was there for him. I said that, if he could hear me, this wasn't a final goodbye. Without any adherence to any particular religious belief, I found myself adding:

"See you next time, mate."

I tried to imagine what was he was going through and what he was thinking. Did he know he was about to die? Was he scared? Was it true what they said in all those books about life after death? Was he above his body right now, looking down at me sitting beside his destroyed body? I instinctively looked up, which made me laugh through my intense shock and my grief.

Finally, I told him I loved him and I left.

Later that day, I met the owner of the ranch where Duncan lived and realised he was one of the two men I'd seen on the TV news. He told me the fire had started across the street from his compound. It was a small section of burning brush at first, but, with the Santa Ana winds kicking up, it soon crossed the road. He, his other tenant, and Duncan had tried to water the roofs down but soon figured out it was time to get the hell out. But, as they were leaving, Duncan went back to have one last look for his cat, which was missing. At that point, the fire swept over the hill at seventy-five miles an hour, so it was like he was hit by a massive flamethrower. With his clothes on fire, Duncan jumped into their swimming pool, and that was where the firefighters found him when they arrived minutes later. He was still conscious and talking. I saw a horrific picture in a magazine a week later and there he was, looking bedraggled and charred, talking to firefighters as they pulled him out of the water. The accompanying report quoted him as saying two things to them: "Can you try and find my cat?" and "I don't want to die." Supposedly, his voice was distorted, squeaky and rasping, because of all the smoke damage.

The cat was later found, unharmed, and received offers of a new home from all over the world. But Duncan died the following evening. When I heard the news from the hospital, I thought about how he and I had stayed behind after our football game the Sunday before and the two of us had gone off to a hardware store together to find a better padlock to secure our goals and nets. I remember him saying how awful he thought the premature death of River Phoenix the night before in West Hollywood was, and now, just a few days later, Duncan was also gone.

Over the next week, I helped look after his inconsolable mother, who was in her seventies, widowed, and totally unable to comprehend the sudden loss of her only son. It was one of the hardest things I've ever had to do in my life, mostly because I couldn't begin to comprehend her loss myself.

For several years afterwards, I organised an annual memorial football tournament to honour my good friend and teammate, and the American Society for the Prevention of Cruelty to Animals (ASPCA) renamed its foremost award for people who perform heroic deeds for the cause of animal welfare to the Duncan Gibbins Award. I also still have his picture—the one you can see in this book—hanging in my office. The knowing but almost scolding expression on his face, and the raised finger—whether intended to alert or reprimand—capture him perfectly, and I know that what always followed that expression was a broad smile.

On his face and on mine.

17

TEARS OF A DIFFERENT KIND

The early 1990s were an unsettling time to be living in Los Angeles. There were the Rodney King riots in 1992, the fires and mudslides in 1993, and the Northridge earthquake in 1994. That earthquake was something everyone who lived through it will never forget. I remember being woken up in the middle of the night by a terrible, ominous rumbling and the feeling that our whole house was floating on water and being tossed around in a violent storm. I'd been through a few earthquakes before, and I knew right away this one was a *much* higher magnitude.

Apart from some cracks in the walls and ceilings, our house wasn't too badly damaged, but every room looked like a bomb had gone off in it. The kitchen was almost knee high in broken crockery and, because the fridge door had opened, there was food all over the place. But our dog Lucy was very happy about that.

When the earth beneath you literally starts to move—and powerfully enough to bring down large buildings—your whole sense of security is undermined. Margaret and I were as rattled by the quake as everybody else, but we were also preoccupied at that time by something that had taken up a lot of our emotional energy over the preceding couple of years. When we'd got married, we decided we wanted to have a baby. But after a couple of years of trying with no success, Margaret was put on a fertility drug, which I had to inject into her. I learnt something about myself during this time: I don't like *getting* injections, but I'm absolutely fine *giving* them. In fact, I rather enjoy doing it. Unfortunately, though, as I jabbed needles into her every day, I suffered the kind of verbal abuse that no medical person, amateur or otherwise, should ever have to hear. But, after several months of obscenities, she finally got pregnant.

Anyone who has gone through a pregnancy knows that every single day multiplies the excitement. We decided to play it safe and not tell anyone right away, but we couldn't help thinking about names, and how we'd convert the spare room into the baby's room, and debating whether we'd rather have a girl or a boy, etc., etc. We reached an important milestone when the doctor could hear a heartbeat and then we were given ultrasound pictures of the tiny foetus. And, once it became that real, we were more comfortable telling people about it. But then Margaret went for a routine prenatal checkup and suddenly there was no longer a heartbeat.

Having a miscarriage is a very peculiar and nebulous experience. It's hard to know exactly what or how you feel. There's the same kind of loss as if someone has died, but the grieving process isn't nearly as clear-cut. It's more like the loss of a future glorious promise than losing someone who'd been an integral part of your past. But, after licking our emotional wounds, we decided to go ahead and try the fertility injections again. And, soon afterwards, Margaret got pregnant again. And, this time, we were meticulously careful about making sure we didn't lose the baby. Which is why, if the first miscarriage had had us on the ropes, the second one had us on the canvas.

A few months later, we heard about a doctor who was being hailed as a fertility guru in LA. So we made an appointment with him and decided to try the item on the menu called "artificial insemination." For me, this simply involved masturbating into a test tube, which I'm very happy to say I managed with flying colours. Although driving in my car across Coldwater Canyon to deliver the results made me slightly nervous because I had no idea what I'd say if I got into an accident and the police asked me why there was semen all over the upholstery.

After a few failed attempts, our fertility doctor wanted my spermatozoa to be super-extra-and-immediately fresh, so we went to his office and I was ushered into their masturbatorium (my word, not theirs) by one of the nurses. She showed me a stack of magazines, as well as a pile of videos "if you should need it." Since the "if you should need it" was said with a little bit of an attitude, I was determined to make do with just the magazines. A lot of things raced through my mind during the next five minutes (okay, two), but I remember wondering: if we got a daughter from this, would she look like Miss July from Fort Wayne, Indiana? But I never found out, because artificial insemination didn't work either. Several times. And then we knew we had to stop. No more doctors, no more drugs, no more injections, no more waiting rooms filled with hope or despair. Which left us with one last alternative.

I only ever knew three adopted children when I was growing up, so the whole concept was very foreign territory to me. The thing was, while I'd pictured myself having children one day, in my mind they were always *my* children. It's amazing how much stock we put in biological traits, especially given that the genetic things we inherit from our parents are often the very things we dislike the most when we look in the mirror. So why, then, did I want my own biological children? After some introspective reflection, I finally concluded that it could only be because of one thing: *ego*. And, once I came to that realisation, it was like a heavy curtain had been lifted. I still wanted a child, but not for me . . . for *them*. Of course, if they did something wonderful to improve the world and I got some of the credit for it, that would be okay too. Conversely—and I'm not saying this was the absolute clincher in deciding to adopt—if the child grew up to be a psychotic mass-murderer, I had the perfect out: "Hey, not my genes!"

And so we met Doug, our adoption lawyer. But by the time he'd outlined all the various procedures of adoption, I was already having second thoughts. First off, we had to put together a letter, résumé, and photographic portfolio for prospective mothers to see, so I immediately got audition nerves. Then, if we were selected from all the other portfolios—and that was a *big* if—we'd be allowed to meet the mother. And then, if everyone hit it off, we'd need to agree to undertake all her medical expenses and living costs and become as close to her as she felt comfortable with. And *then*, after the pregnancy was over and we'd taken the baby home, she could change her mind at any time, as could the birth father, and either of them could legally reclaim the child for up to *six months* after the birth.

It seemed like an emotional and financial minefield. And I was completely overwhelmed and terrified by it all. So, naturally, I wrote the letter and résumé and picked out half a dozen photos, and the whole package was on Doug's desk by the end of the week.

Several months passed, in the middle of which was the Northridge earthquake, until one Monday morning Margaret and I were woken up very early by the phone ringing. It was Doug, talking very fast and with great urgency. His sister-in-law worked at a hospital a couple of hours outside LA, and a young woman had walked in the day before and announced she was having a baby and wanted to give the child up for adoption because she was already struggling to raise one child on her own and she knew she couldn't manage raising another. He'd sent over a selection of potential adoptive parents' résumés and she'd picked ours, but we needed to get over there right away if it was to happen. Oh, yeah, and one more thing . . . it was a girl!

On opening nights in front of two thousand people, I've experienced extraordinary rushes of adrenalin, but what I felt half an hour later as we were driving out of LA against the flow of morning traffic was in another league altogether. There's a good reason human pregnancies last nine months: you need that much time to prepare for having another person invade your life. Even with adoptions, you normally get at least four or five months. If this worked out today, we'd have four or five *hours*! So there we were, trying to stay within the speed limit, me driving and Margaret thumbing through one of those thick baby manual books and reading out passages:

"Newborns generally need to be fed every two hours."

Okay, got it.

"If they are crying, and you know they are not hungry, check to see if their diaper needs changing."

Got it.

"If you are not breast-feeding, all bottles and nipples must be highly sterilised. The following methods are recommended—"

"Oh my god!" I exclaimed as I drove. "NAME! If this happens, what are we going to *call* her?"

A couple of minutes later, that was settled. We'd already boiled it down to a half dozen we liked, and now, under pressure, we were unanimous on "Alexandra."

"What about a middle name?" Margaret asked.

And I blurted out: "Jane!"

I've no idea why, because we'd never once considered it when we'd gone through all those "names for your baby" books. But Margaret thought about it for a moment and agreed that Alexandra Jane sounded right somehow.

When we arrived at the hospital, we were met by two nurses who led us into the birth mother's room . . . *at the exact moment that she was seeing the baby for the first time.* Talk about a loaded emotional situation. We introduced ourselves, nobody daring to take more than a surreptitious peek at the tiny little form wrapped in blankets in a crib beside the bed, and within moments everybody in the room was talking, laughing, and crying openly. Whether it was the heightened circumstances or not I don't know, but it was as though we all knew that Fate had brought us to this particular time and place. She told us that the deciding factor in choosing us had been a photo accompanying our résumé that we'd originally decided not to include but then changed our minds about at the last minute. It was taken at a Christmas lunch at our house and, in true Brit fashion, I'd bought some Christmas crackers, so everyone was sitting round the table wearing silly paper hats on their heads and even sillier grins on their faces. It looked like Christmas in a mental institution, to be honest, but it turned out the birth mother's family always did the same thing, and that was what clinched it for her. Even if she couldn't raise her, she wanted her child to have lots of Christmases like that.

The nurses took the newborn baby back to the nursery, and Margaret and I went out into the hallway to talk. We took one look at each other and knew immediately what we were going to do. We went back into the birth mother's room and told her our decision and everybody cried and hugged and cried some more. We offered her the opportunity to maintain contact with us, but I think it was just too hard for her to imagine anything but a clean break after making what had to have been an incredibly heartbreaking, but ultimately monumentally selfless decision. Then, after some papers were signed, we said goodbye. She checked herself out of the hospital and we've never seen her, or heard from her, since.

After she'd gone, we went into the nurse's office and did the rest of the paperwork. It was only when I was telling the hospital administrator our choice of a name that I saw the form the birth mother had filled out right after the birth. By law, she'd had to choose a provisional name for the baby, so she chose her own middle name. Which, believe it or not, was . . . *Jane.*

In the billing department, I asked if I could pay her medical bills with a credit card because—I'm not going to lie to you—it would mean a *lot* of frequent flyer miles. So I put our new baby, Alexandra, on my Mastercard. At least I had the decency not to ask if she was tax-deductible.

We were then taken to the nursery, and the nurses brought out the bundle we'd glimpsed an hour before—and dreamed of and talked about and wanted and sacrificed ourselves at the altar of fertility for, for so many years. One of the nurses handed me the tiny little soft, warm, white bundle, and cradling the baby in my arms felt like the most natural thing in my life. I looked down and saw two little eyes squinting open at me, which is unusual for a newborn, and I heard a voice—I think it was one of the nurses but maybe it was just in my head—saying:

"This is your daughter."

I'm not a big crier, generally speaking, but tears were pouring down my cheeks as the two little eyes inside the bundle looked up at me and confirmed what the voice was saying: *Yes, I'm your daughter.*

It was then that I knew—in my gut, in my heart, in the deepest place inside me—that she *was* my daughter. And that I would do anything and everything to protect her, raise her, and love her forever.

And I finally had a family of my own.

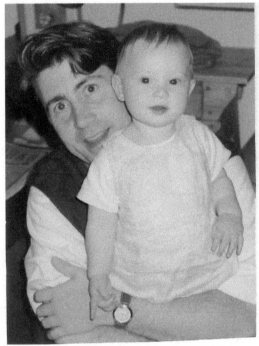

With Ally as a baby.

18

NAME-DROPPING FOR ENGLAND AND SAVING THE WORLD

After becoming insta-parents and the human contingent of our household having grown by fifty percent, I rented an outside office to write in. And the place I found was fantastic. It was on Ventura Boulevard in Studio City in a two-story 1930s building called the Andrews Building, which was owned by an elderly widow called Beverly Andrews who, for some extraordinary reason best known to herself, loved writers. So the second floor was a collection of eight offices, which she rented out to writers at ridiculously low rates. Each office door had a frosted glass pane in it, so the whole place felt like it was straight out of a Raymond Chandler novel.

Every so often, our dowager landlady would drop by and tell us all about how the building had been a brothel before her late husband bought it and she'd then regale us with lurid stories of what nefarious deeds used to take place there in those decadent days of yore.

Right below us was a high-end liquor store called The Flask, run by two middle-aged Jewish brothers called Marty and Chuck. Marty was smiley, chatty, and incredibly upbeat. And Chuck was gruff, dry, and incredibly sarcastic. I used to find any excuse I could to pop down there to buy something or just say hello, because they were both very funny, had great wines and beers for sale, and knew all the gossip on the street. The building was also half a block from the historic show business eatery Art's Deli. Zero Mostel was one of the many Hollywood luminaries who had frequented Art's in years past, and he was reputed to have once quipped that their pastrami sandwich had "killed more Jews than the Holocaust."

By the time Alexandra came into our lives, I'd been living and working in America for more than a dozen years, so it was fairly obvious that I'd probably reached a point of no return in terms of ever going back to England and trying to start my life and career all over again from scratch. With that in mind, I applied for my US citizenship. There's a myth that when you do this you have to give up the passport of the country you were born in. As far as the UK is concerned, this is nonsense, and I happily kept my British passport and added an American one to keep it company. The application process was fairly quick, but the day I went for my immigration interview in downtown LA, there were several helicopters circling above the building, and a massive police presence everywhere in addition to battalions of media lining the street. I soon discovered this wasn't to herald my arrival as a potential American citizen, but the result of someone else's *non*-arrival at the courthouse building across the street. OJ Simpson had failed to show up for his arraignment following the accusation that he'd murdered his wife, Nicole, and her friend Ron Goldman, and a whole circus of strange events was about to unfold that day.

While I was now writing in my new office on a daily basis, my acting career was still vaguely plodding along. I did a run of seven episodes, across a couple of seasons, on the hit sitcom *Mad About You*. When they were originally casting the roles of Paul Reiser's and Helen Hunt's neighbours, I auditioned for the part of the husband. They decided to read actors and actresses in pairs, and I was paired with Pamela Stephenson, whom I'd loved in *Not the Nine O'Clock News* before leaving England. But, to be honest, neither of us was very good. I think she was already done with the acting profession, because soon afterwards she became a sex therapist—which was an interesting career move. We deservedly didn't get the parts, and my old friend Paxton Whitehead, along with Judy Geeson—best known from the film *To Sir, With Love*—were cast, which made sense both age-wise and casting-wise. But I guess they liked me enough to call my agent a few weeks later and offer me a nice guest role on the show, which I enjoyed doing. Although, I have to confess, Helen Hunt mystified me slightly. After my first day, she ran across the studio parking lot to stop me as I was getting into my car and told me how good she thought I was in the part. I thanked her and appreciated that she'd gone out of her way to tell me that. The next day, when I came in for work, I smiled when I saw her and said good morning. But she looked at me blankly for a moment, then walked right past me. And it continued like that: one day she'd laugh at something you said in conversation like it was the funniest thing she'd ever heard, and the next day she'd blank you. I don't think there was ever anything sinister at all behind it, but I had no idea what to make of it at the time and I still don't.

A few months later, I got a call from the new show runner, who told me Paxton couldn't commit to continuing in the role of the neighbor because he wanted to do more theatre work, and he asked me to take over the part. It would be the same character, with the same name and the same wife, played by Judy Geeson . . . who also happened to be—like Paxton—a fair number of years older than me. It seemed bizarre. Did they think their millions of viewers wouldn't notice? They told me not to worry because they'd age me up by greying my hair, but I still accepted the job with some trepidation. And my trepidation turned into whatever is more trepidatious than trepidation when, after I'd taped a couple of episodes in my new role on the show, I read an interview with Helen Hunt in a popular entertainment magazine. When asked if she had any pet peeves as an actor, she replied: "Yes, when people recast a role with a different actor instead of creating a new role." *Ouch!* I completely agreed with her, by the way, but I don't think I ever felt particularly comfortable on that set again.

Before the twentieth century was over, I helped save the world. More specifically, as the head of the rest of the world's armed forces, I helped prevent it being destroyed by an alien invasion in

Independence Day . . . which became the second film I'd been in that was the highest-grossing film of its year. For some reason, I performed my heroics from under an open tent in a Middle Eastern desert, while the Americans did theirs in a rather more showy and frankly immodest air battle. Anyway, it was my pleasure and you're quite welcome.

Around this time, I also shot a couple of things in the Hollywood studios that had been built by Charlie Chaplin. I don't even remember what those projects were, but I do remember thinking how weird it was that my grandfather—whom I never met because he died before I was born—would also have been working in this same space about sixty years earlier if he hadn't taken his father's advice to forego a Hollywood career with Chaplin because the movie business was a "passing fad." It was a highly romantic notion to imagine that I was picking up a loose thread that had been left dangling in my family history two generations before me.

For a number of years in the 1990s, Margaret and I would go to Martin Short's annual Christmas party in Pacific Palisades. They weren't particularly big affairs, but they were ridiculously star-studded and one of the most notorious Hollywood parties of the holiday season. Although I believe we were the only people who were "below the line," as they say in show business. One morning, after one of these parties, I wrote down the names of as many of the guests as I could remember. In no particular order of billing, this is the list:

Sid Sheinberg
Steven Spielberg
Kate Capshaw
Martin Short
Billy Crystal
Phil Hartman
Harry Shearer
Chris Guest
Jamie Lee Curtis

Dan Aykroyd

Donna Dixon

Christine Lahti

Mark Johnson

Marc Shaiman

Sally Field

Bernadette Peters

Tom Hanks

Rita Wilson

Catherine O'Hara

Kurt Russell

Goldie Hawn

Nora Ephron

Nick Pileggi

Harold Ramis

Eugene Levy

Joe Flaherty

Dave Thomas

Charles Shyer

Nancy Meyers

Michael Shamberg

Larry Kasden

I'm sure I missed a few, but how's that for some first-rate, heavy-duty, try-and-beat-that name-dropping? Those parties were always fun, although it really became more of a show than a party over the years. The impromptu performances that sprang up towards the end of the evening eventually became the main focus of the party itself, and people would get together for weeks beforehand to rehearse. Marty and Nancy Short were great hosts, and Marty, being a born showman, was in his element, taking his place centre stage as master of ceremonies. But the takeaway for me every year was which new Hollywood player was making their debut, who drank too much and made a fool of themselves (never me, I'm glad to say), and what amusing snippets of conversations you might overhear. One brief one that stands out because it was so dry and off-the-cuff was when (the late and great) Phil Hartman greeted Steve Martin, one of the biggest comedy film stars of that era, with the line:

"Hey, Steve, what's up? You working much these days?"

While we're on the subject of shameless name-dropping: I did a film in the mid-1990s that was almost certainly the most star-studded piece of celluloid I've ever been involved in . . . and, even more certainly, it was one of the worst. The cast included Ryan O'Neal, Billy Bob Thornton, Jackie Chan, Sylvester Stallone, Whoopi Goldberg, Eric Idle, Coolio, Chuck D, Sandra Bernhard, Cherie Lunghi, Harvey Weinstein, Naomi Campbell, Robert Evans, Robert Shapiro, Larry King, Dominick Dunne, Billy Barty, Norman Jewison, and many, many more. It was called *An Alan Smithee Film*, written by Joe Eszterhas and directed by Arthur Hiller. The film was essentially a two-hour-long sketch that was an inside joke about the film industry. Its title came from the Hollywood tradition of a director using the name Alan Smithee when he or she wanted to take their name off a film because it was either so bad or not the cut of the film they wanted to release. I had seventeen short scenes with Eric Idle and supermodel Naomi Campbell, so, I thought, how bad could it be?

Eric was playing the title role of a director whose real name is *actually* Alan Smithee. He eventually has a nervous breakdown, and Naomi and I played his carers in the mental facility he ends up in. I was excited to work with Eric because Monty Python had been a massive comedy influence on me, growing up. And I was slightly nervous about working with Naomi Campbell because I'd heard she was "difficult." But that was put to rest on the very first day when she walked into the makeup trailer, where I was getting attended to, and screamed out:

"Bloody 'ell, you look just like Gary fuckin' Oldman!"

I didn't really know what to say to that, but it didn't matter because she embraced me and continued chatting on as if we were old friends.

The week's shoot was extremely enjoyable, doing our little bits and pieces to try and make the scenes at least entertaining, if not funny. And there was something hilariously incongruous about the whole experience: Eric Idle, Naomi Campbell, and myself, being directed by the man who made *Love Story*, in a lunatic asylum. Eric and I soon discovered we had a lot in common—having been sent off to boarding school at a very young age, a love of football and cricket, both also writers, and our acting roots in sketch comedy. Moreover, we made each other laugh—even if the script didn't—and by the time the film was over we'd become friends. And it's been a wonderful and treasured friendship that has endured ever since.

I've lost count of the many amazing dinner parties that Eric and his fabulous wife, Tania, have hosted at their house over the years. They're often filled with well-known faces from the worlds of music and show business, and even, once, a member of the British royal family. And, of course, lots of comedians . . . Steve Martin, Billy Connolly, Garry Shandling, Sacha Baron Cohen, Drew Carey, Kevin Nealon, Robin Williams, Eddie Izzard, and on and on. The evenings often end up with people like Dave Stewart or Jeff Lynne grabbing guitars and songs being sung. The first time I ever went over to Eric and Tania's for dinner, one of the other guests was Peter Asher, who had once been part of the singing duo Peter and Gordon, who'd had a massive hit single in 1964 called "A World Without Love." It was the first single I ever bought as a child and I must have played it hundreds of times because I loved it so much. When I told Peter this, he immediately picked up his guitar and said, "Then you must have your own performance." And he then proceeded to sing the whole song for my benefit. On another night, Ringo Starr was there and people started gathering in the living room after dinner to sing some stuff. Ringo was one of the last people to make his way in from the dining room after the songs had begun and it just so happened they were starting up a Beatles song. Someone called out to him: "Hey, Ringo, you wanna join in?" To which he replied, poker-faced:

"No, I think it'll be better without me."

It was totally insane. But no more insane than the Saturday afternoon ping-pong tournament I played in at Eric's house with country singer Clint Black, comedian Kevin Nealon, Eric, and the novelist Salman Rushdie, who was in hiding from Islamic extremists at the time because of the fatwa placed on him after he'd written *The Satanic Verses*. Fortunately, they didn't find him indulging in the decadent Western pastime of playing table tennis in the Hollywood Hills and we all survived.

Eric and Tania Idle at their Provence home.

Most summers, I usually spend at least a couple of weeks in the south of France, where Eric has had a second home since the early 1970s. One summer, he invited his Provence neighbor James Dyson, of vacuum-cleaner fame, over for dinner. Before he arrived, Eric told me about the new place Dyson had just bought which sounded spectacular—an old château with a vineyard, an Olympic-size swimming pool, a tennis court, and even a helipad—and he said he'd try and get us a return invitation so I could see the place for myself. When Dyson arrived, he brought along his latest invention to show us . . . in top secret because it hadn't yet been patented. It turned out to be the prototype for his bladeless fan. I began to imagine what it must have been like when Henry Ford said to some people in Detroit, Michigan: "Oh, by the way, before dinner, let me show you this new mechanical contraption I've come up with that will replace the horse as a means of transportation."

Anyway, halfway through dinner, Eric said to Dyson, who's a fanatical tennis player:

"Have you been playing much tennis, James?"

Dyson replied that sadly he hadn't because his sons hadn't come down to France yet. Seizing the moment, Eric then declared:

"You know, Jim's a very good tennis player. Maybe he'll give you a game."

Now there were a couple of fairly big problems with this. Firstly, I'm *not* a very good tennis player, or even a *slightly* good one, because I play only about once every ten years. And, secondly, Eric's not-so-subtle invitation-fishing actually worked and James Dyson asked us to come over to his place the following week, saying that he and I could play tennis before dinner. I was happy enough that Eric had succeeded in getting us our invitation but, in doing so, he'd totally pimped me out under flagrantly false pretences!

The next week, we all went over to the Dyson mega-estate, which was like Downton Abbey in Provence. The minute we arrived, an eager James Dyson said that he and I should go and play tennis while the others had some pre-dinner cocktails. And it was every bit as bad as I'd feared it would be. Actually, it was *worse*. He beat me 6–0 in the first set, with me barely winning a point off him. He was as polite and gentlemanly as could be, but the set was over in a flash: the tennis version of premature ejaculation, except there was no sign of any kind of climax from me. I know he'd intended to play a couple of sets, but he very wisely suggested we go and join the others for dinner after that disastrous first one.

He then showed me the pool house—which was bigger than most people's houses—and said I could have a shower there if I wanted.

It was a semi-outdoor shower and he must have read my mind because he quickly added that the others were all inside, so not to worry about being seen. So I stripped off, had my shower, and was just emerging to get my towel when around the corner came the entire dinner party—sans Dyson himself, who was presumably having his own shower somewhere—as Mrs. Dyson gave them a guided tour of the estate. I suspect that getting an impromptu viewing of my cock and balls wasn't listed in the official brochure.

With James Dyson after humiliating myself at his Provence estate.

Going back to *An Alan Smithee Film*, the film itself was a complete mess . . . a multi-vehicle fatal pile-up of a movie. And, in an irony to end all ironies, Joe Eszterhas took over the editing and Arthur Hiller took his name off it, so *An Alan Smithee Film* actually *became* an Alan Smithee film. The studio tried to take the double curse off it by releasing it under the title *An Alan Smithee Film: Burn Hollywood Burn*, but it didn't stop it getting ten Razzie Award nominations (not a good thing, for those of you who don't know what the Razzies are), winning five of them, and achieving a further dishonour three years later of being the winner of The Worst Movie of the Decade.

And, of the seventeen scenes Naomi Campbell, Eric, and I had together, only *one* ended up in the final version of the movie.

I've never been so grateful to have ended up on the cutting room floor.

19

BATS AND BALLS

One of the perks of being an actor is that you can find yourself invited to participate in certain sporting events you have absolutely no right to be involved in. Within a few weeks of arriving in LA in the mid-1980s, I'd found a football team of renegade expat Brits to play in called The Exiles, which also included Rod Stewart. This was a team I *did* just about qualify to be involved in, but in one game Rod and I both jumped for the same aerial ball and, as we landed, his head hit my knee. As we got to our feet he said:

"You alright, mate?"

I replied that I was fine, but then added that he *wasn't*.

"How d'you mean?" he said, with a large cut above his eye and blood pouring down his face that he hadn't seemed to notice.

"Your eye's totally fucked," I told him, possibly using the incorrect medical terminology.

Once he realised the severity of it, he took himself off to a hospital. The next day, I was astonished to be told by friends in England that the story of me splitting Rod Stewart's face open, like a prize boxer, in a football game in California was all over the tabloids. I felt terrible about it but, a couple of days later, I showed up for evening training with the team and there was Rod, all ready to go.

"My mum says I'm not allowed to play with you any more," he said to me with a grin.

I laughed, but I was more intrigued by his eyebrow, which showed absolutely no signs of the gash my knee had inflicted.

"What happened?" I asked in amazement.

"Went to Alana's plastic surgeon," he said. "Fixed it up a treat."

I don't know who his ex-wife's surgeon is, but if you ever need emergency plastic surgery, I can highly recommend him or her because, within forty-eight hours, there wasn't a trace of the heinous wound I'd inflicted. Although, now that I think of it, I'd like to add a caveat and indemnify myself against any legal action if you get a buttock lift or tummy tuck from that surgeon and it goes badly awry.

**The Exiles football team, with me and Rod Stewart
inexplicably holding our private parts.**

Along with Rod, I was invited play in a one-off charity match in Pacific Palisades. Also playing were Hamish Stuart from the Average White Band, Cheech Marin, and various other names from the worlds of entertainment and football. But, for me, the biggest thrill was playing against a former Crystal Palace player called Peter Wall, who was a hero of mine when I was growing up. Shortly after kickoff, when I found he was designated to mark me, he smiled and said:

"Take it easy on me, mate, I'm old now."

But he needn't have worried. Although he was a dozen years older than me, he could still play a bit and I ended up having to ask *him* to take it easy on *me*.

The most bizarre sporting event I took part in was a cricket match in the summer of 1999, when I was asked to play for an LA entertainment industry team against the visiting Lord's Taverners from England, which has always been made up of a mixture of former professional cricketers and showbiz personalities. Although I'd continued to play football since leaving school, playing cricket was never really my thing. In fact, it's fair to say I'm even worse at it than I am at tennis. So much so that I played for the fourth XI at school in a team that was nicknamed "The Relics." We were the lost boys of cricket and, even among those other wretched misfits, I was so dreadful at batting I was always put in at number eleven (which is the last person in a team to bat, if you don't know cricket). I was actually so dreadful I never made it into double figures for runs scored in a game. After school, I sensibly never played again . . . until 1999 in Los Angeles, by which time I was in my mid-forties.

I showed up at the very nice cricket ground in Encino with some apprehension. Which became a shitload more apprehension when I saw who was playing for the Lord's Taverners. The showbiz names like David Essex, Nicholas Parsons, Robert Powell, and Tim Rice didn't worry me at all. But the list of top ex-professional cricketers *did* . . . Robin Hobbs, John Price, John Snow, John Emburey, Brian Close, Roland Butcher, Chris Broad, and Mike Denness, who was captain of Kent and England and another hero of mine growing up. Our team was due to bat first, so I immediately put in my request to bat at number eleven, which was duly granted. Since it was a limited overs game and we had a few decent players, with any luck I would never have to bat and I could relax and watch the rest of team do their thing for a couple of hours while I had a beer and a sandwich in the pavilion. I can't remember who was batting number one for our team, but I do remember that Patrick Stewart was batting number two. However, just as I sat down to enjoy my sandwich, I learned he'd been caught short and gone to the bathroom and was nowhere to be seen. The umpires were getting impatient, with the visiting team already out on the field, and unfortunately I was sitting beside our captain, who promptly turned to me and said:

"Quick! Get your pads on, Jim!"

I tried to object, but he was having none of it, so I *very* reluctantly put on pads, gloves, and a box to protect my family jewels, and before I knew it I was walking out to the wicket alongside our number one batsman.

My batting partner would, of course, be facing the first ball, and when I saw who was opening the bowling for the opposition I nearly soiled my cricket whites then and there. It was John Snow, whom I'd watched play for England hundreds of times, and he terrified me—even watching on the other side of a television screen—because, as described in the program for our game that day, he was "one of England's great fast bowlers with 202 test wickets in 49 matches." But even more terrifying was the fact that his reputation as an international man of danger was well documented. His Wikipedia page describes him as being "England's most formidable fast bowler," who "was involved in several on-field incidents stemming from his aggressive, short-pitched bowling and was disciplined by both Sussex and England." I was literally shaking as he thundered past me to deliver his first ball to my fellow batsman. Even though he was not bowling at the pace he'd delivered in his prime, he was still very, *very* fucking fast. Certainly faster than anything I'd seen playing for "The Relics" at school twenty-five years earlier. The number one batsman took a swing at the ball and missed, unsurprisingly. But, on the second ball from John Snow, he managed to get an edge on it and the ball dribbled away for a single. Which was my worst nightmare come true . . . because I now had to face the bowling of the mighty John Snow—who, incidentally, seemed to be taking this game *way* too seriously. As I took my position in front of the wicket, shaking in terror and with the distant chuckles of people who knew me in the pavilion, I didn't care if I had the indignity of being bowled out on the first ball—a golden duck, as it's called—as long as I didn't get hit with it and lose all my teeth or suffer a brain injury that would render me a vegetable for the rest of my days.

John Snow started his run-up, which was much too long for a supposedly friendly game, and hurled the ball towards me. I vaguely remember seeing something coming towards me and took a valiant, but absurdly late, swing at it . . . and completely missed. Fortunately it had been so hard and fast that the ball bounced over the stumps and into the wicket-keeper's gloves behind me. Now I could hear Brian Close—another former captain of England and hero of my youth—sniggering in the slips, the positions next to the wicket-keeper. Close was the youngest person to play for England and was known as one of the toughest, most fearless men ever to play the game.

"Bit rusty?" he said to me in his thick Yorkshire accent.

"Haven't played since school, actually" I replied, pathetically trying to save face in advance.

And then I waited for the next ball, hoping this would all be over quickly and painlessly. Again, I barely saw what was hurled at me and I swung my bat . . . and again I missed by a mile and the ball sailed past the wicket into the wicket-keeper's gloves. Now Brian Close and other players nearby were clearing their throats and looking embarrassed on my behalf. But I'd survived two balls, so in my mind I'd already won. Any further indignity from here on could be bravely borne. The third ball from Mr. Snow came and again I swung—more like a baseball slugger than anything resembling a cricketer—but somehow I timed my swing a bit better and I connected with the ball. At first I had no idea where it had gone, but then I saw it had slithered away between two fielders and I had to run. What a victory . . . I'd not only scored a run off John Snow, but now I wouldn't have to face him for the next ball! Except I *did*, because my fellow batsman decided we could get *two* runs, so I was back facing the bowling again. I ignored the laughter coming from the pavilion and the muttering and shaking of heads from the players around me, who all knew I was utterly useless but had somehow freakishly managed to score two runs off their star bowler.

Meanwhile, John Snow did *not* look happy. And the next ball was delivered with even more ferocity . . . and this time, it flew off my bat and up into the air. I was surely going to be caught and my nightmare would finally be over. But no . . . the fielder dropped the ball, and my life—as a batsman, at any rate—was miraculously still intact. And there was only one ball left to face before the over was complete, so, if I could survive it, I'd have a welcome respite at the non-batter's end. By this point, John Snow looked ready to commit a homicide and, sure enough, the next ball was *very* fast and *very* short and intended to bounce up towards my head . . . but it didn't bounce as intended, and I—as if I'd been touched on the shoulder by the patron saint of cricket—did something I'd only ever seen professional players do: I knelt on one knee and swept the ball aside, with the technique and timing of a world-class batsman . . . and it went swiftly to the boundary for four runs! As the applause rang out in the ground, I stood there, acutely aware that I had just *acted* being a cricketer, and a rather good one at that. Even the opposing team nodded with approval, and I heard Brian Close say:

"Bloody hell, that was a helluva good shot."

As the fielding team reshuffled their positions for a new over, I saw that the new bowler was John Emburey, who was described in the match program as having played "64 Tests for England as the country's leading off-spinner, taking 147 wickets." But I could breathe easy for at least one ball, at the non-batting end, and bask in my glory . . . six runs in the first over against John bloody Snow! It couldn't get any better, whatever happened now. Well, as it did happen, it could and it did. I survived another half dozen overs, slashing, slicing, and hacking away like a man possessed—some okay shots, some missed shots, some lucky shots, and some appalling shots. I was dropped a couple more times and lived a totally charmed life before I was finally caught by David Essex. As I walked back to the pavilion, I was elated that I'd managed to score an incredible (for me) twenty-five runs! It was the finest batting performance of my life by a country mile, and I was even applauded off the field by an amused Lord's Taverners team, who I assume had concluded that I was the luckiest bad cricketer they'd ever seen.

After that, I vowed never, *ever* to consider setting foot on a cricket field again. I'd clearly peaked, far and away beyond my wildest expectations, and needed to quit while I was infinitely ahead. But when someone asked me, a decade later, if I'd play in a game to celebrate the newly created "BritWeek" in Los Angeles, I stupidly relented. Ten years on, I still had the sweet smell of cricketing success in my nostrils and I was even so buoyed by my fleeting triumph all those years before that I agreed to bat in the middle of the order. It was a more light-hearted affair this time, with lots of joking and ribbing. My friend Ross King, the TV entertainment reporter, went in to bat before me, and I gave him a lot of grief for wearing a huge masked helmet for extra protection. Being a Scotsman, he was potentially qualified to be the second worst player on the team after me, and he soon confirmed he was because he was out on his first ball. As he returned to the pavilion and I headed out to bat, he offered me his helmet, but I waved him aside with a macho shrug and continued to the wicket, knowing I simply had to survive a single ball so as not to get the worst score on our team. And I did survive it. And another ball, which I confidently dispatched for two runs. I was back in the groove, clearly a late bloomer in the world of cricket. And then came the third ball, which I got my bat to . . . but unfortunately diverted only as far as my face. I felt a sharp pain on my cheekbone, but the umpire examined it and concluded there was no discernible damage, which I was happy about because I was due to start shooting a movie in Spokane the following week. He let me continue, but my nerve had been broken and I was bowled out soon afterwards.

My face was still sore after the game, but I felt fine and it looked okay. However, when I got up the following morning my cheek was so swollen I looked like the Elephant Man, and I also had an enormous black eye. I called the director of the film, who asked if the eye was swollen completely shut, and I was happy to report that it wasn't. His verdict was that a lot of makeup and shooting me from certain angles would probably solve the problem. Which is pretty much what any director might say to me on any film, injury or no injury. As it turned out, he was right about hiding the black eye with makeup, but, when I saw the film a year or so later, it was very obvious my face was oddly misshapen in the first few scenes I shot. The film was called *Falling Up*, and the only two things about shooting it that stand out for me now are (1) a very weird scene I had with Snoop Dogg, who was extremely stoned (for real, I mean), and (2) that I liked Mimi Rogers, who was playing my wife. I'd feared the worst because I knew she'd been heavily involved in Scientology. I wasn't sure if she still was, but I did know she'd been responsible for recruiting Tom Cruise into the whole nonsense when they were together. However, she was splendidly irreverent and very smart and silly and not at all what I expected her—or any current or former Scientologist—to be.

Over the years, I've also played in a couple of charity football games at the Home Depot Center—as the Los Angeles Galaxy's stadium was known at the time—and a couple at Selhurst Park, home of my beloved Crystal Palace. They all featured show business and pop music celebrities and recently retired footballers. All I can say is that playing against Vinnie Jones was quite scary, and playing alongside former captain of France, Frank Leboeuf, was a delight because his talent was so contagious he somehow managed to make everyone around him on his team look a hundred times better than they really were.

The last time I played at Selhurst Park, I took a penalty against former Crystal Palace, Manchester City, and Watford goalkeeper Perry Suckling. Just as I was about to start my run-up, he rushed out of his goal, yelling:

"Hey, ref, the ball's not on the penalty spot!"

Of course, it was pure gamesmanship and, after checking, the referee okayed where the ball was and waved him back to his goal-line. I took a deep breath, then ran up and stroked the ball just inside his left-hand post, sending the hapless Suckling the wrong way. I had finally—at the tender age of sixty-one—scored a goal in the ground I'd always dreamed of playing in when I was a child!

And I don't care if some know-it-all football fan tells you that this is the same Crystal Palace goalkeeper who once let in nine goals in a record 9–0 defeat against Liverpool because nothing will stop me from relishing that moment.

Nothing, I tell you.

20

DOUBLE DUTIES

Before the twentieth century was over, I did an episode of the HBO miniseries *From the Earth to the Moon*, which was directed by Tom Hanks. It was outstanding television, and both Tom and the show deservedly won a lot of awards. Tom has a reputation for being one of the nice guys in show business, and he is. So nice, in fact, it's sickening. I've run into him a few times since then socially and he was just as nice as he was in the workplace. It makes you want to try and find some dark hidden scandal about him just to tarnish all the endless niceness. The trouble is, even if you found out he likes to bite the heads off bunnies or tip over children in wheelchairs, you'd instinctively assume they must have deserved it because Tom is so interminably bloody *nice*. The other thing about him is that he puts to rest the stupid myth that all film and TV stars have a certain charisma and that as soon as they walk into a room everyone takes notice of them. Nothing could be further from the truth with Tom. Even with his very recognisable face, he can walk into a room and blend in without being noticed. He's remarkably ordinary looking, which is partly why he's so great at playing ordinary people who do extraordinary things.

After helping launch Gemini 8 into space and just about getting it back down again in one piece, I pitched my actor-director-producer friend Mel Smith an idea for a British sitcom about two Brits, one a struggling actor and the other a wannabe writer (so basically me, divided in half), moving to LA and, as two total outsiders, trying desperately—and I mean *really* desperately—to make it in

Hollywood. I knew TV shows about show business were traditionally a tough sell, but I thought what might be funny and relatable was seeing two deeply untalented people having aspirations way beyond their abilities, while nobly—and often not so nobly—continuing in the face of overwhelming adversity. Or something like that. Anyway, Mel liked the idea, which was called *Too Much Sun*, and wanted to develop it with his company, Talkback. So Margaret and I got a pitch together and the next time we were in London we pitched it to the BBC, who commissioned a first season after we shot a test pilot with the very wonderful Hugh Bonneville and Mark Addy in the lead roles.

And *that's* how I *finally* made it into the BBC!

But, not to put too much of a damper on it, it was only as a writer-producer. And, given that things had recently been rather quiet on the performing front, I was beginning to suspect my acting career had been terminated without mutual consent. But then I got a call out of the blue from Eugene Levy. After the success of the film he and Christopher Guest had done called *Waiting for Guffman*, they were about to do another largely improvised comedy in the same documentary style about a dog show. And I say "documentary style" because Chris gets apoplectic when he hears people call his films "mockumentaries," maintaining that they're not "mocking" anything. Anyway, Eugene told me in the call that he'd suggested me to Chris for a role in it and he wondered if I'd go in to meet him and Chris at their Castle Rock office.

So I went in a few days later and it was one of the most painfully awkward meetings I've ever been party to. Both Eugene and Chris are . . . how shall I say . . . "socially uncomfortable." They opened up the proceedings by telling me there were the roles of two TV commentators at the fictitious dog show and one of them would be Fred Willard and they thought it might be good if the other one was a straight-laced Brit, to contrast with Fred's bull-in-a-china-shop "ignorant American" character. But that was pretty much all they said. And so, to compensate, I filled all the awkward silences by babbling about nothing of any consequence. And I was met with occasional nods and monosyllabic replies. Finally, to mitigate any further damage, I handed Chris my demo reel and got the hell out of there before the going got any worse.

As I was driving home, going over in my head all the numerous other, better ways I could have handled the meeting, I got a call from Chris offering me the role. I was delighted to accept it and be in a film that would feature some of the best and funniest improvisers on the planet—and I'm not exaggerating when I say that about Chris's troupe of actors. On the other hand, there was the buttock-clenching reality that I hadn't really done any improvisation since drama school and that was . . . well . . . pretty shit, to be honest. But an even bigger hurdle soon emerged. The week Chris wanted me to be in Vancouver to shoot *Best in Show*, I was supposed to be in London shooting the fifth episode of *Too Much Sun*. It looked very much as though I'd have to forego doing the Chris Guest movie, but then a potentially workable solution emerged. The BBC agreed to let me, after the read-through on Monday morning, give my notes and then fly to Vancouver. But they needed me back in London by Friday morning to see the run-through of *Too Much Sun* in the afternoon and the taping of the show in front of an audience in the evening. At the other end, Chris was fine with shooting all the dog show commentator scenes in three days. It was *extremely* tight, but potentially workable.

So on that Monday morning of the fifth episode week of *Too Much Sun*, I attended the read-through at the BBC, gave my notes, and then rushed off to Heathrow airport. Eleven hours later I was in Vancouver having dinner with Chris and Eugene and meeting Fred Willard for the first time. Fred and I were told we could have Tuesday to relax and we'd do all our scenes on Wednesday and Thursday. I was happy to get a day to recover and also pleased that my mandate from Chris was, as the straight man of the commentating duo, primarily to be authoritative and knowledgeable about dogs. The pressure of having to be funny was off, which was a relief. But, conversely, the pressure to remember all the stuff from the American Kennel Club book—a stunningly tedious and monumentally thick encyclopaedia that I'd trudged through every night before bedtime while working on *Too Much Sun*—was exponentially increased.

So Tuesday came and went. But, in the evening, I was told they were behind schedule and Fred and I would now be shooting on Thursday instead. So I had another day off. But on Wednesday night I was told they were *still* behind, and they asked if I minded shooting on Friday. At which point I had to politely remind everyone that I needed to leave on Thursday evening to be back in London by Friday morning. And so it came to be that Fred and I shot all our stuff in one day on the Thursday. Given that we're in pretty much the whole last half-hour of the film, it may well be the most amount of screen time that's ever been shot in a single day. But, for a number of reasons— mostly due to magnificent Fred—the partnership worked. I think still being jet-lagged actually worked in my favour in portraying the con- fused and bemused straight man, Trevor Beckwith, opposite Fred's mind-numbingly stupid and hilarious character, Buck Laughlin. His performance was utterly inspired, and I realised on the spot that working with him was going to be like improvising with a rambunc- tious chimpanzee with absolutely no sense of decorum or bound- aries. I knew that his behaving in an unspeakably inappropriate manner would get a sizeable number of laughs, so my task became how to react or respond to whatever he said in a way that might get us even *more* laughs—and, of course, without laughing myself, which was the hardest part. I've been told that our scenes in the film have since become something of a classic to comedy aficionados, and I'm often asked how I managed to keep a straight face. The truth is, I didn't and you can occasionally see me trying not laugh. But I got away with it because it made sense that my character is somewhat amused at first by Fred's off-the-wall comments, but, as the scenes progress, becomes increasingly less so until I finally end up sticking the knife in, very politely, when he makes yet another terrible joke and I respond with the throwaway line:

"Yes, I remember you said that last year."

The biggest challenge in shooting those scenes was the fact that we did them all in a completely empty stadium, with just a few extras placed strategically behind us to make it look like the place was full. And what we were actually commentating on was either (a) some dog show footage that had already been shot that Fred and I would watch before the cameras rolled on us, or (b) a specific event or segment of the dog show that Chris would describe to us verbally so we could then respond on camera. As a director, Chris is slightly more animated than he is away from the set, but he still conducts proceedings with a calm, measured, and relatively impassive demeanour. If you manage to make him smile or laugh during a particular scene, you've almost certainly hit the jackpot, and whatever you did or said has a decent chance of ending up in the movie.

With Fred at an anniversary screening of *Best In Show*.

Fred and I became friends after *Best in Show* and I also worked with him again several more times. Sadly, he passed away at the age of eighty-six while I was writing this book, and the world has without a doubt lost one of the greatest comedy actors of recent times. I miss him terribly and I have to confess it was a slightly unnerving experience seeing a photo of the two of us in *Best in Show* at the top of many of his obituaries when he died. But I know Fred would have been highly amused by my discomfort at seeing *my* face on *his* obituary, and that in and of itself makes me smile.

Apart from learning how to play a straight man during this period of double duty, I also got another lesson in the ever-ongoing school of show business. *Too Much Sun* had been a couple of years in the making and had taken up a huge amount of my time and energy. Going off for three days to do *Best in Show* was a tiny blip on the radar in comparison. But today it's only *Best in Show* that anyone remembers. Alex Jennings, Mark Addy, Lee Majors (yes, *that* Lee Majors), and Nigel Lindsay were all very good in *Too Much Sun* and the show got decent viewer ratings. But a British sitcom set in America was either way ahead of its time (less likely) or caught with its pants down in no-man's-land (more likely). The critics weren't sure either. One major newspaper said it was "the freshest, most original comedy of the year" and another said it was "possibly a new low point in television comedy."

Looking back at it now, I'd say they both had a valid argument. And at least nobody said it was boring.

21

KISSING 8,000 ARSES

L ike a lot of men, I originally became a sports fan because when I was growing up it was a safe place to transfer and release all my emotions. Emotions which I'm sure—as a Brit being raised at a time when psychological therapy wasn't commonplace—were probably even more repressed than those of other young males of my species. Football became an escape and a safe haven from the real world. None of my family shared my passion for the sport, and it was with some reluctance that my father took me to my first ever Crystal Palace game. He didn't like being in crowds and so it was quite a sacrifice on his behalf, but it was day I'll never forget . . . even though the game ended up as a 0–0 draw. It was a brief and cherished moment of father-and-son bonding for me because it was the only game I ever went to with him. After that, I think he felt he'd done his bit and he could see it was safe enough for me to go on my own. As a teenager, I'd sometimes go to games with my friends Martin and Maurice Worsdall, who lived just down the street from me in Bessels Green, but just as often I'd go alone. In that sense, football became a place of refuge for me from the everyday world . . . as baseball did later on when I first came to America.

While I was working on *Too Much Sun*, my beloved Crystal Palace Football Club went into administration. Administration is when a club gets into so much financial trouble that an independent accountant administrator is appointed to sell off the assets to keep the club afloat while trying to find someone to buy the club and inject new capital into it. If no one is found, the next step is liquidation. And, in this instance, it looked very much as though the more-than-a-century-old club was about to go out of existence altogether unless something very urgent was done. Since I'd spent an alarmingly large portion of my life caring far too much about the eleven players in Crystal Palace shirts who run around every week kicking an inflated sheep's bladder (well, originally they did in the nineteenth century), I really didn't fancy the outcome of not having this familiar weekly escape from what passes as my real world, whether in person or by following games from afar in North America.

So I got in touch with a fellow fan called Richard House, a lawyer I'd exchanged pleasantries with on the fans' main internet bulletin board, and invited him and some other more vocal members of the message board to a meeting at the flat I'd rented for the duration of *Too Much Sun*. Someone at the meeting suggested I also get in touch with a guy called Paul Newman (no, not *that* Paul Newman) who was the sports editor at *The Independent* newspaper and had also been talking about the idea of fans getting together to do something. So Richard, Paul, and I met before the next Palace game, and we ended up deciding to form a Crystal Palace Supporters' Trust with the purpose of trying to raise enough money and/or exert enough pressure on the financial powers-that-be to save our club.

We had another meeting in a lounge at the club's ground after the next game and invited dozens of other willing volunteers to attend, along with the team's manager, Steve Coppell. He was extremely supportive and offered to help us do anything possible to save the club. Which he did, by miraculously scratching enough wins out of the remaining patchwork team of players (that hadn't been sold off) to avoid relegation at the end of the season (which, for non-football people, means demotion into the division below). Steve was also very vocal and active in his public support of the Trust. For our part, we raised a million pounds in loans and another quarter of a million in bucket donations in a very short space of time. And eventually we found a buyer for the club and helped facilitate the sale. He turned out to be an absolute cock of a human being and ten years later had run the club into the ground again, but that's a whole other story for a whole other football-related book. I'm just glad to say that, in spite of him, it all ended happily and the club is now experiencing an extended halcyon era in its long history.

Meanwhile, our structure for the Supporters' Trust became the industry standard for football fans in the UK and across Europe. And our launch brochure—with my blatantly manipulative appeal to people's emotions to dig into their pockets and give, give, give!—even made its way into the English Football Hall of Fame. Which somewhat makes up for me not yet having a star on the Hollywood Walk of Fame. Although I believe anyone can get one of those if you're prepared to fork out $50,000. But that does seem like an awful lot of money just to have gaggles of bemused tourists look down at you and say, "Who the fuck is that?" as someone's dog takes a massive dump on you. But I fear I'm veering off topic now.

My principal role in the Supporters' Trust was as a front man and spokesman, whenever I was in England. On one occasion, I flew in to Heathrow from LA and made my way straight to the club's stadium, Selhurst Park, in South London just in time for the 3:00 p.m. kick off. Paul Newman had written a speech for comedian Sean Hughes to appeal to the fans at half-time for donations, but when I arrived, he informed me that Sean was so overcome with nerves that someone else would have to do it. Having said that, he then smiled and thrust the speech into my hands. As tired and jet-lagged as I was, I tried to familiarize myself with it during the first half of the game, but I knew I had a big problem: the match was against Manchester City, who were top of the league and looking very likely to get promoted back into the Premier League, so one entire side of the ground had been yielded to their fans, which was a surefire recipe for an impending disaster. So, when half-time came and a cordless mic was thrust into my hand as I was escorted to the centre of the pitch, I felt like a calf being led into a slaughterhouse.

Fortunately, I still had just about enough of my wits about me to know what I had to do to have any possible chance of averting the looming catastrophe that would be witnessed by 21,000 people... the biggest live audience of my life. As I took up my position in the centre circle, the Manchester City fans were already singing "Who are ya? Who are ya?" in unison and making jerking-off gestures, as if they had some uncanny psychic insight into what I did in my spare time. So, swallowing all my pride and my lifelong football allegiance, I turned to face them and I said:

"I'd like to welcome every Manchester City fan here today. I hope your team gets promoted this year and that you beat Manchester United both home and away in the Premier League next season!"

There was a moment of rather stunned silence before the whole stand exploded with a massive roar, followed by a thunderous round of applause. Yes, it was utterly and deplorably shameless on my part . . . but it absolutely worked and I was able to do my whole speech to the Palace fans completely uninterrupted.

I also believe I may have set a world record that day—kissing eight thousand Mancunian arses (or asses if you're American) in under ten seconds— but I haven't checked *The Guinness Book of Records* to confirm it.

22

AH, HA, HA, HA, STAYIN' ALIVE!

A part from being a terrific film, *Best in Show* reminded a few people that I was still alive and introduced me to others who never knew that I was in the first place. Consequently, a steady stream of film and TV roles started to come my way.

I did an episode of the megahit show *Friends*, playing the boyfriend of Chandler's mother (Morgan Fairchild). At that time, the six main actors in *Friends* were making three-quarters of a million dollars per episode, but I made a bit less (translation: a *huge* amount less).

Friends with Morgan Fairchild, Christina Pickles, and Elliott Gould.

In general, I found the three women, including Lisa whom I already knew from *Mad About You* days, slightly guarded and self-contained, but the three guys were extremely welcoming and very pleasant company. But the real joy was being part of a quartet of seasoned actors (translation: *much* older actors) who got to hang out that week. There was Elliott Gould, who not many years before had been one of the biggest film stars in Hollywood; Christina Pickles, who had done so much great stage and screen work; and Morgan Fairchild, who was a popular TV star in the 1980s. None of us had more than a couple of scenes each, so it was all very relaxed and it felt a bit like we were at a real wedding reception, having a nice weeklong chat. Only without any real booze or wedding cake.

I also began a recurring role on *The Drew Carey Show*, another very successful sitcom, though much sillier and more off-the-wall. Drew's character worked in a department store called Winfred-Lauder, which was managed by Craig Ferguson's character, Nigel Wick. I played the owner of the store, Lord Mercer. Most of my scenes were with either Drew or Craig, and I loved them both. Drew was always delightfully upbeat and Craig was hilariously disgruntled most of the time. Craig was so "over" doing the series at that point and wanted to move on to other things, which of course he ended up doing very successfully, but I enjoyed his very anarchic, couldn't-give-a-fuck approach to working on the show. There was one episode, at the end of the season, that Drew and the producers wanted to do completely improvised. Craig took me aside on day one that week and said he had huge misgivings about the director's ability to get anything good from the actors in the way of improvisation. Our characters were fairly peripheral to the episode's main storyline, and Craig declared it his ambition for us to be cut out of it completely. Drew, having loved *Best in Show*, kept consulting me all week about how we'd worked on the Christopher Guest movies, and I'd tell him. But I soon discovered Craig was right and we were in deep trouble when, about ten seconds into the first scene, the director yelled, "*Cut!*" and then proceeded to tell the actors that what they were doing was all wrong. In other words, the complete antithesis of improvisation. I remember Craig shooting me an "I told you so" look, and we made ourselves as scarce as possible for the rest of the week. And he got his wish; neither of us ended up appearing in that episode.

The next film I did was *Austin Powers in Goldmember*, playing a tiny role as the headmaster of the spy school. I worked a total of about six hours on the film and never met Mike Myers, so I was amused by the wonderful showbiz flattery of a card I got a few weeks later, accompanying the cast-and-crew gift of an Austin Powers hockey jersey. The card read: "I couldn't have done it without you. Mike." In my case, that seemed highly implausible. Years later, I did actually meet him when I went to see the last ever Monty Python live show at The O2 Arena in London. When I was backstage afterwards, a security guy came up and asked me if I was Jim. When I said I was, he told me he'd escort me, and I assumed he meant to the greenroom to meet up with Eric and the other Pythons. He then led me through a labyrinth of passageways, down an elevator, and finally to a bar area where Mike Myers was waiting.

"Here you go," he said to Mike, then left.

Mike Myers looked at me blankly and I looked at him blankly, neither of us having any idea why I'd been brought to see him. He smiled and said: "Hi, I'm Mike."

And I smiled and said: "Hi, I'm Jim."

And then we shook hands and I left. I never found out what the hell that was about, but he seemed like a nice enough guy.

The second Christopher Guest film I did was *A Mighty Wind*, in which I played Leonard Crabbe, a catheter salesman and model-train fanatic who's married to Mickey, Catherine O'Hara's character. My research for that involved visiting some model train shops in Los Angeles and getting a lot of catheters and other urinary medical samples sent to me, which definitely intrigued our mailman. My first scene was with Catherine, whose character had invited her ex-husband, played by Eugene Levy, to lunch. I consumed a bucket-load of Thai soup while we were shooting the scene, so I didn't feel particularly hungry when we broke for lunch and I went to my trailer instead. I lay down, intending to take a short nap, but was back on my feet within seconds as I felt some very ominous rumblings. I made it just in time to my bathroom, where I spent the entire lunch hour sitting on the toilet with projectile diarrhoea. Fortunately, the deluge was over by the time we were called back to set and I finished the scene without any problems—or any more soup.

While we're on the subject of bodily functions, I was quite proud of myself for coming up with one particular speech in the scene. As our three characters tried to make polite conversation over lunch, I offered up this contribution to the proceedings, with Eugene's and Catherine's characters listening and looking on in horror:

LEONARD CRABBE: I'm in the bladder management industry. I sell catheters . . . It's a growth industry really because one in three people over 60 either have a flaccid or a spastic bladder, so in a sense every 13.5 seconds a new incontinent is born, as it were. If people like you and I have what they call "leakage problems" . . . it can be running, playing tennis, laughing, sneezing, anything. I mean, good old constipation, you know . . . you have impacted faecal mass in your rectum and you find that pushing on your bladder, you can have all sorts of problems.

A speech which Shakespeare himself would surely have been proud of. And it's only a few lines short of a sonnet.

Another scene I remember well from that film shoot was a party scene, where all the cast members were divided into pairs or small groups for little snippets of conversation. I was paired up with Jennifer Coolidge, whose character had nothing at all in common with mine, which is always a good equation for some awkward comedy. She'd shown up on her first day and said to Chris that she had two different voices she was thinking of doing for her character named Amber Cole. She then proceeded to give him samples of two extremely silly voices and asked him which one he preferred. He looked at her in his customary deadpan manner and said:

"First one."

And then he walked away. Such was the trust between the director and his troupe, it was all the discussion that was needed. It was an extravagantly strange foreign accent that you could never attribute to a specific country. And I think the short scene Jennifer and I did together produced one of the best lines of improvisation I've ever heard. This is how it went:

LEONARD CRABBE (JIM): I'm a model train enthusiast.

AMBER COLE (JENNIFER): Oh, that's great.

LEONARD CRABBE: Yes, I've got a whole layout in my basement. It's very much a big passion for me.

AMBER COLE: Yes, thank god for model trains.

LEONARD CRABBE: Oh, absolutely.

AMBER COLE: You know, if they didn't have the model train, they wouldn't have gotten the idea for the big trains.

That last line of hers is, in my humble and unsolicited opinion, a piece of inspired comic genius.

Before doing A *Mighty Wind*, I went on a health kick for a couple of months, which included stopping drinking alcohol. Don't ask me why, it just seemed like a good idea at the time. But, when the film was done, I decided to continue not drinking indefinitely because... well, again, it just seemed like a good idea at the time. It was an interesting experience (translation: not fun at all) because I love the occasional beer or, more often, a couple of glasses of wine with dinner. People say you lose weight when you stop drinking, but I didn't. People also say you sleep better, but I didn't. But what it *did* do was force me to deal with things more head-on, without a diversionary shield. And one of those things was the unmistakable fact that my marriage was not, by this point, a happy one and was becoming increasingly toxic. And so—despite it being the hardest decision I've ever had to make—I knew that, after being together for seventeen years, Margaret and I had to separate for the happiness and wellbeing of our daughter and both of us.

Getting divorced is a notoriously difficult and stressful time for almost everyone who has ever experienced it. For me, the hardest thing to deal with was the sense of failure. It broke my heart to see my daughter have to adapt to living in two separate households and to not be able to provide her with the secure single-family upbringing I'd had . . . although, in a strange parallel, that security had ended for me when I was sent away to boarding school at the same age Ally was at the time of the divorce. I felt an immense sense of shame at having failed her in that respect, even though the more rational part of me knew that in the long term it would be a better and happier path to follow.

I also knew it was going to be a massive sea change in my own life that I'd have to come to terms with. I thought I'd finally arrived at where I'd set out to be, personally and professionally, but I hadn't. I knew that homes and families aren't ever things that are set in stone, but I now had to accept the cold, hard reality that—to mis-paraphrase the U2 song—I still hadn't found everything I was looking for.

23

MONTREAL MADNESS

I f you've managed to make it this far into the book, you can probably tell that, while I'm perfectly happy to impart arbitrary opinions and trivial gossip, I'm not generally in the habit of dishing the dirt on my fellow performers. But I feel that if my effusive praise for most actors I've worked with is to be believed, it might need some kind of perspective and context. Which is why, when the pointless fad began on Facebook of people posting a list of ten bands and asking their friends which was the one they'd never seen in concert (how the hell should I know and why would I care?), I decided to turn it on its head and do something I thought was a bit more interesting. So I posted this:

Okay, then, Facebook. 10 people I've worked with as an actor. 9 I really liked and
1 was a complete ****.

1. Michael Caine

2. Angela Lansbury

3. Anthony Hopkins

4. Sharon Stone

5. Tom Hanks

6. Morgan Fairchild

7. Sacha Baron Cohen

8. Naomi Campbell

9. Kevin Hart

10. Faye Dunaway

Yes, of course it was deeply immature and unnecessary, but if you can't be deeply immature and unnecessary on Facebook, where the hell *can* you be? I got quite a large number of comments on this post, mostly people making their guesses, and after a couple of days I started eliminating names every twenty-four hours, creating a kind of cheesy, social media reality show. The first one was this:

First elimination: Anyone who thinks that Angela Lansbury is a **** should seek some psychological counselling. She is one of the most gracious and classy people you could meet.

Which can't be said of a certain friend of mine, by the way, who, when I told him I was doing an episode of *Murder She Wrote* with Angela Lansbury, replied:
"So did you bang her?"
Anyway, swiftly moving on:

Elimination number 2: Tom Hanks? Seriously???... Shame on those who picked him, unless you were joking.

Which they may well have been. And then, the next day:

Third elimination: Morgan Fairchild is smart, engaging, and far more down-to-earth than you'd imagine.

I've no idea what people imagined actually, but it was true. Anyway, continuing:

Elimination number 4: (Sir) Anthony Hopkins bounded into my trailer on my first day and said: "Hello, I'm Anthony and I'm so happy you're doing this film!" From that moment on, he behaved as if we'd known each other for years. Honest, inquisitive, and endlessly charming.

Not quite sure why I put the "Sir" in parentheses there. I certainly wasn't trying to be disrespectful.

And the next day:

Elimination number 5: Sacha B-C is smart, kind, generous, and as fun to improvise with as anyone I've worked with.

And the next:

Elimination number 6: Kevin Hart. Although I couldn't understand half of his off-camera banter.

Which is true, I couldn't. As nice as he was, I've never felt so white or English in my life. Moving on:

Elimination number 7: Naomi Campbell.

Who I've already written about in this book, so no more elaboration needed.

Elimination number 8: Michael Caine. Very surprised anyone picked (Sir) Michael Caine. What you see was absolutely what you got in my experience. The main reason I wanted to do the film was because he'd been an idol of mine growing up (and he had to call me "sir" in our scene!). He was all and everything I expected and wanted. He never played the star card for a second and made me feel like we were both just regular actors in the trenches doing a job together. Likes to laugh too. Sometimes you CAN meet your heroes and not be disappointed.

Again, no idea why I put brackets around his honorary title. The film I mentioned, by the way, is *The Prestige*, directed by Orson Welles lookalike Chris Nolan, which I'm in for all of about two minutes.

By now, a week into this whole thing, my Facebook friends were becoming understandably restless and someone finally wrote:

Time to dish, mister.

So I cut to the chase, without waiting the statutory twenty-four hours:

And so, the 9th (and final) elimination... A number of years ago, I was asked to take part in a reading of "Antony and Cleopatra" by a director friend who was considering mounting a production of the play. Having not done any Shakespeare since drama school, I was a bit hesitant. When he told me what part I'd be playing I was even more hesitant: it was the role of Mark Antony. As my sphincter tightened by the second, I then asked who'd be reading Cleopatra and he said: "Faye Dunaway". I think I laughed out loud at the improbability of it all, but never being one to avoid a chance to fail spectacularly, I agreed to do it. So the entire cast is all sitting in a circle reading the play and, in the first scene I had with her, I start my first speech and she physically throws herself on top of me, acting her heart out... and it all suddenly became a VERY "staged" reading, rather than a casual one. And that's the way it was for the next two and a half hours, with the rest of the cast watching and participating with open-mouthed incredulity. Luckily, my eyesight back then was better than it is now, so I somehow managed to get through the play and read all my lines with a full arm extension and an iconic movie star groping and caressing me in various stages of entanglement. So... yes, she's as mad as a box of frogs. But she was also wonderfully committed, energetic, and—through it all—both appealingly strong, warm, and vulnerable both as the character and as a person. The production never materialised (thank god), but it could never have lived up to the marvellous insanity of that reading. In my, admittedly short, experience with Ms. Dunaway, she certainly left an impression (literally), but she definitely wasn't a ****.

And so, by a process of elimination and without me expressly having to say it, I'd revealed who the offending person was. By the way, I did a final tally of the votes of people who actually bothered to guess and here are the results:

In last place, with absolutely no votes at all, was Morgan Fairchild (kind of a no-brainer).

In ninth place, with one vote, was Anthony Hopkins (spoiled ballot, I suspect).

In joint seventh place, with two votes apiece, were Kevin Hart and Tom Hanks (four people clearly not taking it seriously).

In joint fourth place, with three votes each, were Sacha Baron Cohen, Michael Caine, and Sharon Stone (six shots in the dark and three in broad daylight).

In third place, with four votes, was Angela Lansbury (some people *really* not taking it seriously or banking on a huge surprise twist).

In second place, with seven votes, was Naomi Campbell (a decent guess, to be fair, but wrong).

And in first place, the person whom eleven people believed was a ****, was . . . Faye Dunaway (clearly the bookies' favourite).

Which only goes to prove that most of the people are wrong most of the time. And all of us should probably not waste our time participating in this sort of nonsense on Facebook.

So why was Sharon Stone the exception among this venerable list of celebrities? Well, since you've come this far with me, I shall tell you. I wrote a film called A *Different Loyalty*, based on the true story of British spy Kim Philby's defection to Russia in the 1960s and his wife Eleanor's decision, against all advice, to choose love over politics and join him in Moscow. It was a script my agent at the time liked a lot, but told me would "never get made in a million years." Thankfully, it wasn't a million years and it did get made. But not so thankfully—given its epic nature and the settings of Beirut, London, New York, and Moscow—the film's budget of $13 million was way too small. Rupert Everett was cast as the Philby character and Sharon Stone as his wife. As someone far unkinder than me commented at the time:

"I see you've cast the two biggest queens in show business."

But I'd never ever stoop to saying anything so horribly demeaning and politically incorrect.

I'd heard ominous stories about Sharon Stone but, as I've already related with other examples, such stories are as often as not disproven by personal experience. And I have to confess the reason she and I didn't get off to the best of starts might have been a *teeny weeny* bit my fault. My first meeting with her was in a Montreal hotel after I'd been traveling for about twenty hours, without any sleep, from another set. When I finally got to Canada, all I wanted to do was crash but the director insisted that Sharon wanted to get together to give me some notes on the script. When I arrived at the hotel she was staying in, I called the director to say I'd arrived and he asked if I could hang on for a minute because Sharon needed to talk to him about some stuff. So I sat in the lobby and waited . . . and waited . . . and waited. By the time he called back, I was fast asleep but I quickly pulled myself together and went up to her room. Rupert Everett soon joined us and she started going through her notes.

At one point, she turned a page of the script and said very emphatically: "Oh, and of course I can't *possibly* say this line."

"What line's that?" I asked.

"This one," she replied, and she read it out. I can't remember what the line was, but it was something very short and completely innocuous like "I'm sure you do," and when she read it out loud the others all looked as confused as I did.

"Why can't you say that?" I asked.

To which she snorted, as if I were an imbecile who'd been living under a rock for the last few decades: "Because I said that in *Basic Instinct*. It's one of the best-known lines in film history."

Now I don't claim to have an encyclopaedic knowledge of film history, but I'd seen that movie not *that* long before, and I certainly didn't remember that line. I looked at the director, and, judging by the expression on his face, it was news to him too. And then I made a fatal error . . . because, when I looked at Rupert Everett, we had one of those moments where you make eye contact with a relative stranger and you know the other person is on the verge of bursting out laughing. Well, he's clearly a man of far more self-control than I, because he *didn't* laugh out loud, but I *did*. Okay, more of an exhausted smirk than an out-loud laugh, but whatever it was, it wasn't particularly well disguised. I tried to bury my head in the script and wipe the smile from my face as I wrote the note down, but Dame Stone had seen. And, from then on, our relationship never recovered.

When I showed up on set a couple of days later to shoot a scene that I was in with her, she pretended she didn't know who I was. Maybe she wasn't pretending and she really didn't remember me from forty-eight hours earlier but, even if she didn't—which would be pretty weird—when she did figure out who I was, she wanted absolutely nothing to do with me. As you can imagine, since I was shooting a film with her for the next couple of months that I'd written, and was executive producing, and playing a supporting role in, it meant I had a slight problem on my hands. So, for the best part of two months, I did my resolute best to avoid her. However, it didn't prevent me witnessing her—the same woman who had a poster of the Dalai Lama in her trailer, incidentally—scolding her bemused and tongue-tied toddler son for not knowing what to say when presented with a cell phone.

"Talk to your daddy!" she chastised him sternly. "He's called all the way from home to talk to you!" Finally, the poor child mumbled something into the phone.

And it didn't prevent me witnessing her stop in the middle of a scene when she'd forgotten a line and, shamelessly passing the buck, turn to an extra and shout:

"Don't ever look at me when I'm acting!"

And it didn't prevent her overhearing me answer a question that a Canadian actress had asked me about a British pronunciation she needed help with, at which point she shouted to the director:

"The writer's giving notes to the actors! I want him off the set!"

Fast-forward another couple of years and I was at a dinner party with a friend who's a well-known British actor and who'd also done a film with Sharon Stone. When her name came up, he also referred to her as a ****. Which was my immediate cue to ask him:

"On a scale of one to ten, how much of a **** would you say she was?"

Without a millisecond of hesitation, he replied:

"Eleven."

And he then proceeded to tell me about how an even better-known American film star had been so disgusted by her treatment of the director of a film he was starring in with her that he went to her trailer, pinned her up against the wall, and said:

"If you *ever* fucking talk to the director like that again, I'll walk off this film and I'll tell everyone exactly why!"

Apparently, she was as meek as a kitten after that, which suggests she might just be a bully rather than a diva. I'd tell you the names of the British actor and the American film star, but it's really up to them, not me, if they want to declare publicly to the world—and without asterisks—that they think Sharon Stone is a ****.

By comparison, Rupert Everett, who had his own reputation of being "difficult," was an angel to work with. As chronicled later in his excellent memoir *Red Carpets and Other Banana Skins*, he also apparently had his issues with Ms. Stone. He described her, in no uncertain terms, as "utterly unhinged." Incidentally, in the same book, he describes some other problems with the film: (a) its ever-shrinking budget, (b) having to shoot in Montreal for tax reasons, and (c) some of the "flat, overwritten dialogue" in the script. He was absolutely right about (a) and (b), which nobody could dispute. And, much as I'd like to take issue with (c), I have to hold my hand up and admit he was right on that one too. In hindsight, some of the dialogue I wrote was indeed "flat" and "over-written." Although, that said, let me also state for the record that I've appeared in many productions where the dialogue has been flat or overwritten, and it's been solved either by the actors elevating it or the director judiciously editing it in post-production! But unfortunately, neither really happened in A *Different Loyalty*, and, in director Marek Kanievska's case, he even admitted to me while we were shooting that he wanted to be a ski instructor rather than a film director! He got his wish, too, because he never directed anything again and, according to Wikipedia, has spent the last two decades as "a full-time traveller and photographer, indulging his love of kite surfing, paragliding, paramotoring, and other extreme outdoor activities in various locations all over the world." And who could blame him? That sounds *far* less stressful than making movies with Sharon Stone.

As a footnote to A *Different Loyalty*, and to add insult to injury, the producers of the film are the only people (that I know about, anyway) in show business who have ever stolen money from me. Just before we were about to start shooting, the Canadian producer came to me and asked if I could do him a big favour. He said that some of the film's financing had been delayed, so would I mind deferring $50,000 of my writing fee, which was due to be paid at the start of principal photography? Thinking this would only mean a delay of a few months at most, I agreed and signed an amendment to my contract that allowed them to pay me the deferred amount when the film was delivered to Lionsgate, who were distributing it. But I never got that $50,000. For the next couple of years my lawyer tried to make them pay up, but he had no legal jurisdiction in Canada. The Writers Guild also tried but, because the production company was cunningly dissolved after the film was delivered, there was no entity to sue. Since then, if anyone has ever asked me to defer any kind of salary payment—which, to be fair, is extremely rare—they get a very short two-word answer.

By a strange turn of fate (because I've only ever worked there twice in my life), I found myself back in Montreal a few months later to do another film called *See This Movie*. It was an independent film with a minuscule budget of less than half a million dollars, and the producers were Chris and Paul Weitz, who'd recently made *American Pie* and *About a Boy*. The other four actors who made up the principal cast were a real joy to work with: Seth Meyers, John Cho, Jessalyn Gilsig, and Jessica Paré. My character was a jaded and amoral bullshitter who was only interested in getting drunk and laid. However, being bisexual as well as an accomplished bullshitter, he manages to seduce all four of the other main characters in the course of the movie. It's one my favorite roles that I've ever played and, in my humble opinion, one of my best performances on screen—in a film that I'm still able to enjoy watching.

The scene where I had to kiss Seth Meyers was a first for both of us, being the manliest of manly heterosexual macho men. But a few shots of alcohol loosened us up and we just went for it. Although, there was no tongue action, so I suppose neither of us can really call ourselves method actors.

Seducing Seth Meyers in *See This Movie.*

24

A RAFTER OF TURKEYS

When New Line released a film called *The Man* in 2005, starring Samuel L. Jackson and Eugene Levy, I learned the value of resuscitating deceased scripts that you'd long since put on a shelf or buried in a drawer without a formal wake or funeral. Why did I learn that? Because I'd written the first draft of *The Man* a full **fifteen years** before. It had been optioned a number of times, and all kinds of rewrites had been done: with the two main roles being two men . . . then two women . . . then two black characters . . . then a man and woman . . . and then two Argentinian pink fairy armadillos (okay, I made that last one up). Although Margaret and I ended up with both writing and producing credits on the film, we had very little to do with it being made, except being able to help facilitate Eugene Levy being cast as one of the leads. The director, who shall remain nameless (because I can't actually remember his name or be bothered to look it up), brought in his own rewrite guy who basically eliminated every scene in the script that was remotely memorable and replaced a lot of the dialogue with fart jokes, dick jokes, and needless profanity. Now don't get me wrong, I'm as partial to fart jokes, dick jokes, and needless profanity as the next guy, but I also happen to believe they should at least be (a) somewhat rationed and (b) moderately *funny*.

When I went to the premiere, I watched the film with a strange detachment. I didn't think it was terrible, and the story and the characters seemed familiar, but it was like watching a film you'd stumbled on by accident after walking into the wrong movie theatre. I suppose the fact that one of the biggest celebrities at the premiere was retired baseball player José Canseco (who was wearing a see-through shirt) tells you all you need to know. Although, as an Oakland A's fan for four decades, I will say that he was a very exciting baseball player in his time.

That year, 2005, was also when the statutory three years between Christopher Guest films had elapsed and the whole ensemble was reconvened—with the notable addition of Ricky Gervais.

Ricky is a notorious giggler with a highly infectious laugh, and in my first scene with him I'm afraid I couldn't resist the temptation of making him corpse ("crack up," in American parlance), which was a bit like shooting fish in a barrel. He could barely get a word out in the first few takes because he was laughing so much. I felt slightly guilty the next day because it was his first ever film role, and I apologised to him. But he wouldn't have any of it. He laughed even more maniacally and said I did exactly what he'd have done to someone joining the cast who was known to be a "corpser."

With Jennifer Coolidge, Chris Moynihan, and Jane Lynch at at the Toronto Film Festival.

The film premiered at the Toronto Film Festival, and a small group of us were flown up there in a private plane, which didn't suck. The audience seemed to like the movie well enough, but, despite some outstanding performances and very funny moments, the subject matter was almost certainly too rarefied for a wider filmgoing audience. I also think the mixed critical reception it received was what led to Chris's subsequent ten-year hiatus from filmmaking.

Almost every actor, if they've been around a while, will have been in a really bad movie. But in the space of little more than a year between 2007 and 2008, I somehow managed to be in *three*. This trio of celluloid classics were *Epic Movie*, *Meet the Spartans*, and *Who's Your Caddy?*

Epic Movie and *Meet the Spartans* were both parody films in the vein of *The Naked Gun* and *Airplane*, but not as healthy a vein . . . more like a blocked artery. Lovely directors—and great comedic actors, including Jennifer Coolidge, Kal Penn, Fred Willard, Sean Maguire, Diedrich Bader, Ike Barinholtz, and Crista Flanagan—but geared fairly and squarely at thirteen-year-old boys. Both movies were savaged by the critics but cleaned up at the box office. I believe each of them was the number-one-grossing movie on its opening weekend. In *Epic Movie*, I did my best Ian McKellen impersonation from *X-Men* and had a giant magnet on my head the whole time, and that's probably all you need to know.

For *Meet the Spartans*, I got to wear a very silly beard and do a scene with a very naked Carmen Electra, which was nice . . . even if her credulity-defying flawless body was more than a slight distraction. And to round it off, though I say it myself, I also did a rather decent Simon Cowell impersonation in the second role I played in that movie. Although I'm not sure that's necessarily something to brag about.

My dubious versatility on display in *Meet The Spartans*.

Who's Your Caddy? was another story altogether. Intended as a *Caddyshack* with a racial twist—rich, very street black guy joins stuck-up, very white, waspy golf club—it was an absolute monster of a crazy experience from start to finish. The rapper and hip-hop singer Big Boi was cast in the lead, and Jeffrey Jones and I were the club's president and manager respectively. There were some very good character actors in the movie: Sherri Shepherd, Finesse Mitchell, Tony Cox, James Avery, Terry Crews, and Faizon Love. But there were also a lot of complete fucking lunatics: bodybuilders, stand-up comedians, even more rappers, and Andy Milonakis. The net result was that it turned into more of a freak show than a film. And there was a *lot* of drinking and partying and drugs—although, thankfully, drugs have never been my thing. We were based in Aiken, South Carolina, and I finally had to move out of the hotel we were staying in because I couldn't get any sleep. The partying went on every night, all night, and the hotel was run by a lovely British guy of

Indian descent who was so thrilled to have a film cast and crew at his hotel that there were no rules whatsoever.

I have no idea how the director, Don Michael Paul, didn't have a nervous breakdown . . . or several nervous breakdowns. Jeffrey Jones and I would show up on set at our call time and sit for hours, waiting for the other cast members to dribble in whenever they felt like it. In Big Boi's case, on one occasion it was *forty-eight hours later* because he'd gone to Vegas to do something or other without bothering to tell anyone. But I think the worst offender was a former professional wrester who was addicted to painkillers and alcohol and pretty much anything else he could get his hands on. I'm not sure I ever had a conversation with him, on or off set, when he was even remotely sober.

Not surprisingly, the film died a death at the box office. It was nominated for only one Razzie, shockingly, but it did win the Women Film Critics Circle Award for Most Offensive Male Character . . . which wasn't me, incidentally.

Big Boi and Tamala Jones on the set of *Who's Your Caddy?*

The film has since been rehabilitated somewhat because Bill Clinton declared in an interview that it was his favourite comedy. Which possibly tells you more about the taste and judgement of the former president than about the film itself. But I have to admit, when I watched it again recently, it did make me laugh out loud a number of times. It's absolutely, off-the-charts nuts and completely shameless, but it's never dull.

The final memory I have of working on *Who's Your Caddy?* was being on a golf course, and everyone trying with no small amount of desperation to shoot a scene in a snowstorm. The story was set in the summer, but we'd gone over so long because of all the delays and the no-shows and the other numerous forays into the descent of madness that we were now well beyond summer . . . and autumn . . . and into a very dark winter. Waiting for breaks in the falling snow—and hoping the sun would come out for just a few minutes so we could shoot a few seconds of film—encapsulated the entire experience of working on that film. And, while doing so, the lines from Shakespeare's *Richard III* rang in my ears with a whole new meaning:

Now is the winter of our discontent
Made glorious summer by this sun. . .

If we ever managed to see it again.

25

SNAKES, SPIES, AND SAUSAGES

T he standard minimum shooting day in the film and television world is twelve hours. So it's always nice to come home and sleep in your own bed after a long day of filming (i.e., about eleven hours of sitting around and one hour of actual acting). But if you're shooting on location, it's a hotel bed you have to get accustomed to. There are some locations that have become very commonplace, depending on who's offering the best tax rebates. Toronto, Vancouver, Georgia, and Louisiana have been the most prominent for the last couple of decades. And there are other places I've been on location that are less common and more interesting, like Madrid, South Carolina, Montreal, Hawaii, New York, and San Francisco.

And then, in an entire category of its own, there is Romania.

After the success of the first couple of Harry Potter films, Twentieth Century Fox decided they wanted to create their own franchise of megahit movies, based on a series of children's fantasy books written by Susan Cooper called *The Dark Is Rising.* I was cast as one of the four "immortals"—a character called Old George— and when I discovered we would be shooting for three months in Romania, I was quite excited because I'd never been to Eastern Europe. So, after stopping off in London for wardrobe fittings, I found myself in Bucharest.

Soon after I arrived, I met the three actors playing the other immortals: Ian McShane, Frances Conroy, James Cosmo, and the villain in the movie, Chris Eccleston.

With Francis Conroy, James Cosmo, and Ian McShane outside our trailers.

It proved to be a major bonus that we all got along very well throughout the three months of filming. Ian McShane, who James Cosmo and I soon nicknamed "Mad Dog," was in his mid-sixties and a pent-up bundle of manic, furious, and often amusing energy. He'd been completely sober for many years by that point in time, and one couldn't help wondering how utterly insane it must have been to work with him back in his drinking days. Frannie Conroy was the exact opposite: as gentle, quiet-spoken, and polite a soul as you'll ever meet. Although, her endless concern about all the feral dogs in Romania (and there were thousands) occasionally tested everyone's patience. Every morning on the way to the set, she'd want the driver of the cast's minivan to pull over every few minutes to feed some stray dogs on the side of the road. At the end of the shoot, she even ended up adopting a whole slew of them and bringing them back to the United States.

Frannie rescuing more dogs at the film studios in Bucharest.

Chris Eccleston, on the other hand, was more of a prickly sort of fellow. Four "I" words spring to mind in describing Chris; he was intense and intractable, but always interested and interesting. And, surprisingly for a Manchester United supporter, he was consistently very good company. Coincidentally, one day on set, when we were all talking about football, I learned that Ian McShane's father actually played for Manchester United in the early 1950s, which is why Mad Dog also supported "the Red Devils."

Eccleston outside his trailer, trying to pretend he's an intellectual.

James Cosmo's character and my character were a double act in the film, sometimes heroic and at other times providing comic relief. I'm not sure that "Cos"—as I rather unimaginatively nicknamed him—and I could have come from more different backgrounds: the mean streets of Glasgow, Scotland (him), and the leafy, upper-middle-class English environs of Bessels Green, Kent (me). But, for whatever reason, we immediately made each other laugh and it was man-love at first sight.

Cos, Mad Dog McShane, and Chris Eccleston would all go back home to England at every opportunity during the shoot, but with LA being so much farther away, I was pretty much stuck in Romania. So why did everyone want to get out of Romania at the first opportunity? Well, primarily because—apart from the quite smart Athénée Palace Hilton hotel where we were staying—Bucharest was, by and large, extremely depressing. It didn't help that, on the night we arrived, our dialect coach was beaten up in a nearby park in a homophobic assault by a gang of shaved-head thugs. And it didn't help that a lot of the architecture of the city was a bleak reminder of the dark days of communism under the repressive Ceaușescu regime. And it didn't help that on our first day of shooting, some of us saw a woman's dead body, which had been hit by a bus, lying in the road as we were being driven to the set. And, even though I'm more of a simple peasant-food eater than a sophisticated "foodie," it didn't help that the food on the set and in most restaurants veered from the barely edible to the truly disgusting. Although, it was big hit with the feral dogs Frannie Conway fed it to.

We did finally find an Italian restaurant near the hotel that wasn't too bad and another decent place that was, rather surprisingly, an Indian restaurant. And, when we found out that the Indian place also delivered, we started ordering lunch from them from the studio we were shooting at, which was forty-five minutes outside Bucharest. McShane would call up and order for about ten of us, and we'd all chip in for the food and a taxi to bring it out. It sounds like an extreme measure, but we'd pleaded with production to get us a decent caterer—even an *okay* one would do—but they couldn't seem to find one. As a producer, I've come to learn that food on the set of a movie or TV show is absolutely crucial. Most crews and casts will put up with almost anything if they're fed well, but morale can very quickly plummet if the food is bad. And the food on the set of *The Dark Is Rising* was excruciatingly bad.

One breakfast on location, we were served a ten-inch, pinkish-brown sausage that looked a bit like a saveloy or a raw hot dog and smelled like a toilet at a petrol station. It was comically obscene and revolting. Nobody dared eat theirs, so most of us either threw it away or left it on the plate. But I had more creative plans, and I put mine into a plastic water bottle and took it with me to the set.

We were shooting a religious service scene that day in a church in Transylvania, which was supposed to be a church in an English village rather than Dracula country. Cos and I knew we were going to get bored out of our minds sitting at the back of the church for hours with very little to do in the scene, so we devised a game to try and stay sane. We amused ourselves the entire day by secretly planting the extremely nasty sausage in people's pockets or elsewhere on their person and seeing how long it took before they got the very unpleasant surprise of discovering it. As everyone began to catch on and the phallic food folly moved around the set like a hot potato, Cos and I behaved like two juvenile delinquents, doubling up with laughter as actor after actor let out a shriek—sometimes in the middle of a scene—when they found it.

We got the normally unflappable and ever-ebullient John Benjamin Hickey so many times he was almost reduced to a maniacal wreck. But the coup de grâce was when I secured it in the brim of a large hat Frances Conroy was wearing. We were crying with laughter as the beautifully serene and elegant Frannie acted her heart out at the front of the church, with the sausage visible to the whole cast and several dozen extras sitting behind her. The director couldn't figure out why he had a whole church full of people unable to keep a straight face, and it was only when he did a panning shot around

Frannie that he—and she—finally caught on and the jig was up. It was unquestionably one of the most childish things I've ever done on a set. And that's saying something coming from someone who, when playing Prince Charles a decade earlier, released so much explosive flatulence during a scene that it necessitated an early lunch call so the entire cast and crew could compose themselves. But, on this occasion, it was welcome comic relief from the general grimness of shooting in the Eastern bloc.

Trying to maintain a modicum of dignity while Cos loses his on the set of *The Dark Is Rising*.

Being stuck together for the best part of three months in Romania made the cast of that film a pretty tight and close-knit family, which was one major positive for me about the whole experience, especially having just gone through a divorce. I'm also eternally grateful to Cos for helping me overcome one of my biggest fears. There was a scene—which I'd been very nervous about since I'd first read the script—in which he and I, fighting for the force of good against dark and villainous powers, become buried in a massive pit of snakes. I'm very slightly terrified of snakes, to put it mildly, so after I heard it wasn't going to be done with CGI but with *real* snakes, my blood pressure would spike every time I thought about doing the scene. A couple of weeks before we were due to shoot it, the director explained how it would work on the day. There would be a large tank filled with lots of wriggling serpents—*five hundred* of them, to be exact—of all shapes, sizes, and colours. Cos and I would be required to insert our heads and torsos into the bottom of this container and eventually emerge at the top of the pile of snakes . . . at which point—if we were still alive—we would then have a brief exchange of dialogue to deliver. I was repeatedly assured that the snakes, which had been imported with their handler from Poland, were all nonvenomous. But I kept wondering how they could know for *sure*. I mean, what if they'd made just *one* mistake? Luckily, Cos didn't share my ophidiophobia (yes, I looked it up), and every time I brought it up, which was a lot, he'd reassure me that we'd be okay. But then Ian McShane would always drop in a remark like:

"Listen, Piddock, you've had a pretty nice life, so if it all ends here you've not been short-changed."

Which wasn't particularly helpful.

The day we had to shoot the scene did not start well. When I arrived, I was told that one of the two enormous pythons had died because the temperature in the studio was wrong, which angered me from an animal rights perspective and didn't fill me with a lot of confidence from an actor's perspective. Cosmo and I took our places beneath the tank and when the moment came and the director called, "Action!" Cos grabbed my arm for emotional support and we inserted our heads into the pit of hell. As our heads emerged through the pile of squirming snakes, I saw a couple of snake heads a few centimetres from my eyes, *with their forked tongues flicking right at me!* At this point, I remembered I had only one good eye (thanks to the botched squint-correction operation when I was three years old), so now I'm thinking, *Jesus Christ, if one of those tongues touches my good eyeball, I'm going to be legally blind!* Rigid with fear, I turned towards Cosmo, with both of us up to our chins in snakes, and he gave me a big smile before he said his line and I just about managed to get my response out before I heard the director shout, "Cut!"

There's something incredibly exhilarating about overcoming a major phobia, and I felt elated after we'd finished the scene and were both still alive. Someone in the makeup department gave me a Polaroid they'd taken of me with my head sticking up through the snakes, and that, I'm afraid, is the only record I have of it because the whole section of that particular scene was cut from the movie.

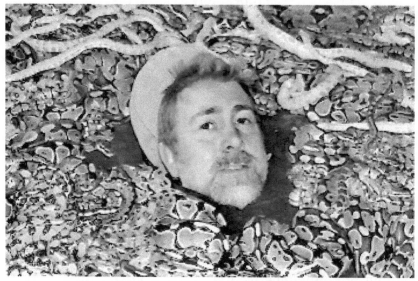

Buried in snakes and trying not to soil myself.

During the filming of The Dark Is Rising, I did manage to escape once for a long weekend in London for my birthday. On the flight back to Romania, I got talking to a woman sitting next to me. She was visiting her husband, who worked for Credit Suisse Bank and, despite his Eastern-European-sounding name—Vadim Benyatov—was a US citizen. She told me that, a few months before, he'd been arrested and charged with espionage in connection with the privatisation of an energy company, which had been orchestrated by the previous government. After spending months in jail, he had been released on the condition that he not leave the country before his trial, and it just so happened that he was also staying at the Athénée Palace hotel. She gave me his number and asked me to call him sometime because she thought he'd love to have some company over dinner after she'd gone back to the UK.

I was intrigued because I've always been a fan of Cold War spy stories, and this one sounded particularly extraordinary given that the Cold War had ended sixteen years earlier. And so, a week later, her husband and I went out for a meal at the nearby fairly decent Italian restaurant. As we left the hotel, two very cliché black-suited secret policemen followed us extremely indiscreetly to the restaurant, and they watched and waited the whole time we were there. As we ate, Vadim told me how he thought the entire case against him was all about the new government's political grandstanding against corruption and actually had nothing to do with him. All the bank's documents for the privatisation of the energy company, which he'd handled, had been marked "Private and Confidential," but the archaic 1968 Communist law being used to charge him considered *private and confidential* to mean "the passing of a state secret." We had an enjoyable time at dinner and, at the end of the evening, I suggested we meet again sometime. But he shook his head and said that, while he'd very much enjoyed our conversation, it would be too dangerous . . . because if the guys following him thought we were having regular contact, they'd start investigating whether I was a foreign agent and I might also be arrested. Despite being amused by the idea that I, as a spy, had been cast in a children's fantasy-adventure film as my "cover," what he said also sent a chill down my spine.

Over the next few years, I kept an eye on his case from afar. After years of delays, he was finally found guilty and sentenced to ten years in jail. It was later reduced to four and a half years by an appeals court, but by then he'd already managed to flee the country somehow and get back to London . . . and eventually to his home country, the US.

The other unusual encounter I had in Bucharest happened one evening when I arrived back at the hotel after a long day of shooting. I popped into the bar for a quick nightcap and some of the crew were already there having a late dinner. I wasn't hungry so I sank onto a nearby couch to have a glass of wine and watched as some of the crew reluctantly engaged with a loud American, who was sitting at the bar and clearly well into his cups. He looked like the archetypal American businessman abroad: short back and sides, moustache, conservatively dressed, and a little overweight. Our crew guys politely answered his questions about what they were doing in Bucharest, before dispersing to their rooms as soon as they could.

I decided to do the same but, as I was going, a loud voice bellowed at me from the bar: "So are you with those guys too?"

I replied that I was and started to leave again. But then he shouted: "Y'know, I'm also in show business."

My heart sank as I turned back to him.

"What d'you do on this movie?" he asked me.

I told him I was an actor and his face lit up as he insisted I let him buy me a drink. I thanked him but said I was tired after working all day. But he became even more insistent, and so—being very British and not wanting this to develop into an unpleasant scene—I somewhat nervously agreed. He beckoned me over and, pulling up a stool for me, told the barman to get me another of whatever I was drinking. My wine came quickly because there was nobody else left in the bar by now and, as we clinked glasses, he repeated that he was also "in show business." Forcing a smile, I politely picked up his very obvious cue and asked him what he did.

"I'm a director," he said. "I'm doing a film here too."

And, just as I'm thinking hard-core East European porn, he adds: "I'm also a writer."

I nodded and said I was a writer too. And then, certain I'd live to regret it, I asked him what sort of things he'd written.

To which he replied: "I wrote a film called *Taxi Driver*."

And then he held out his hand and told me his name was Paul Schrader.

So, despite my secret shame at having so miserably misjudged this particular book by its cover, I found myself talking with a legend in the film world, who *very* much wanted to talk the night away with me for the next few hours. And the more he drank, the more I became the best person he'd "ever met in show business." He told me all about the time he was so down on his luck in New York he was forced to live in his car for several months. And how he'd been angry and suicidal, but a friend encouraged him to write about his experiences and that was how *Taxi Driver* was born. And we talked about his directing career and how he'd also worked with George C. Scott and we laughed about how George always wore less clothes the more drunk he was. And he related a story about how, while he was directing George in *Hardcore*, George holed up in his trailer, drinking profusely, and refused to come out. And how he had to negotiate with the cantankerous movie star, who was wearing nothing but his boxers, to continue with the movie. And he told me all about the film he was about to shoot and that there was a perfect role for me and would I be in it? I thanked him but said I couldn't because I still had a few weeks left on *The Dark Is Rising*. But he insisted, saying he *knew* I was a fantastic actor and I *had* to do the film and we could work the two schedules out. We finally parted company in the wee hours of the morning and I was very grateful I didn't have to work the next day.

I got up late the next morning and struggled to the elevator to head down and get some lunch. When it came and the doors opened, there was Paul Schrader, looking ten times worse than I felt. I said hello and he nodded and grunted and I began to wonder if he even remembered who I was.

So, to find out, I said: "Good talking to you last night."

He nodded mournfully as we descended and muttered: "I was really drunk."

When we arrived at the lobby, we shook hands and I never saw or heard from him again.

26

A POO ON A TRAIN

On a summer trip back to England, my daughter Ally and I planned a visit to see James Cosmo and his family in Surrey. We arrived at Waterloo station, grabbed some breakfast, and got on the train. We had a few minutes before it was due to leave and the tea I was drinking was already working its magic, so I needed to have my morning evacuation. But, being something of a foreigner in my own land after having lived in America for so many years, I hadn't actually had a poo on a train since I'd left England, so I wasn't sure if there was still a rule that you couldn't use the toilet while it was stationary. Back in the day, when you flushed a train toilet it all just went down onto the track below. I was fairly sure train toilet technology had progressed significantly since then, but just to be sure, I checked with the guard on the platform.

When I got the go-ahead from him, I headed straight to the toilet at the end of our carriage. And I was impressed by the very large, modern-looking, circular-fronted lavatory with electronic buttons. I pushed the Open button . . . waited for the door to glide open . . . went in and pushed the Close button . . . waited for the door to slide closed . . . and then looked down to see a quarter of an inch of water on the floor. At least I *hoped* it was water. But at this point the turtle was almost poking its head out, so I shrugged it off and—just to be safe—rolled the bottom of each trouser leg up to just below my knees so they wouldn't get wet. And then I lowered my trousers, sat down on the toilet, and happily did what I had to do. I needed to have a bit of wipe afterwards, so I stood up and started some rear-guard cleaning action with the toilet paper. However, just as I'm doing this, *the door slides open* . . . and I'm standing there with my trousers pulled down *and* rolled up from my ankles to my knees, a piece of soiled toilet paper in my hand, and my entire meat and two veg on full display to a *very* shocked and immaculately attired man standing outside the door. I was both mortified and very confused . . . until I looked over at the far wall and saw a Lock button that you're supposed to push *after* you push the Close button!

But the problem I now faced was that the toilet compartment was too big for me to reach the buttons from where I was. So this well-dressed man watched me flail around like a whirling dervish as I simultaneously attempted to cover my private parts with one hand and lock the toilet door with a piece of shitty toilet paper in my other hand. And while I was performing this unimpressive circus trick, a sweet little old lady wandered by behind the well-dressed man and made the fatal mistake of turning to see what he was so transfixed and appalled by. And, when she saw, she looked like she was about to have a major coronary. I finally lunged for the Close button and the door finally slid—very slowly, I might add—to a close. And this time I locked it firmly afterwards.

After washing my hands, I emerged very cautiously, praying that neither of these two poor people I'd just badly traumatized were in our carriage. To my relief, they weren't. But when I told Ally what had happened, she was highly—and rather unsympathetically—amused. And when we got to Cosmo's house he laughed so long and hard when he heard the story that I was worried he might do himself a serious injury.

I'm afraid there's no particular moral to this delightfully tasteful tale, but at least it may serve as a useful warning should you ever need to have a poo on a British train.

27

THE TOOTH FAIRY COMETH

I was having dinner one night with Ally, who was eleven years old at the time, and I told her I wanted to create an original movie about Santa Claus. But, as we talked some more about it, I realised that almost every conceivable type of Christmas movie had already been done and it would be extremely difficult to come up with something unique. So I started thinking about similar arenas that hadn't already been mined and I soon settled on the Tooth Fairy. Ally liked the idea a lot, and we talked some more about it and the next day I scribbled down a few rough notes.

Not long afterwards I had a general meeting with a young producer who'd recently worked at Miramax and now had a deal at Paramount. His name was Jason Blum and he's since become the biggest producer of horror movies in the world. He asked me if there were any ideas I was working on and so, off the top of my head, I relayed some of the notes I'd scribbled down about the Tooth Fairy. And he liked the idea a lot and asked me if I could develop it into a pitch. So I went away and wrote a full treatment for a movie called—rather lazily, but also fittingly—*Tooth Fairy*. But, as I wrote it, I became aware of something relatively important: I *didn't actually want to write the screenplay itself*. Partly because I'd already written some family movies, and, though I knew it was a very commercial idea for a film, I wanted to write something in a different genre next. And partly because I also knew there were people out there who could do a much better job than me of writing a mainstream family film like this for a major studio. It helps to know your limitations.

Jason wasn't fazed by this at all when I told him, and we decided to pitch it to some A-list writers who could then write the movie based on my treatment and I'd be an executive producer instead. The first writer we met was a very talented guy who had created one of the most successful American sitcoms in recent history. And he told us a very sobering tale. He said that earlier that year, soon after his hugely successful show had finished airing after ten seasons, he went back to the studio that had made it and pitched them a new series. But they acted as if they'd never met him. He got no sense whatsoever from any of them that he'd created and produced a hit show which had made them billions of dollars. And, to cap it all, they passed on his pitch!

The next people we met were the legendary veteran comedy writing team of Lowell Ganz and Babaloo Mandel, who had written films like *Parenthood, City Slickers, Mr. Saturday Night, A League of Their Own,* and *Fever Pitch.* It soon became clear that their ideas and my treatment were very much in sync, so we asked them to come on board and they accepted. Our first port of call was Paramount, which is where Jason's deal was. The execs were polite, but I could tell they weren't that into it as we pitched it. The second place we went to was Fox and they bought it.

The studio had no problem making a deal with Jason as producer and Ganz and Mandel as writers, but they offered me what amounted to the equivalent of a very small option or "finder's fee." One of the things I've always been acutely aware of is that show business is a composition of two words: *show* and *business.* As an actor, that means knowing, realistically, what your fair market value is as a performer. And, as a writer, knowing realistically what the fair market value is of something you've written. And I knew right away that Fox's initial offer was unacceptable. I'd originated the project, I'd written the film's story, and I'd helped attach two A-list writers, so I gave my agent a figure which I thought *was* acceptable. Actually, I gave him two figures: one for them to buy the underlying material, which was my treatment, and another for my executive producer fee.

The two sums combined came to an amount that was about twenty times what they'd offered me, but I knew I wasn't being greedy. I was only asking for what was in line with what I'd previously been paid and what I thought was a fair market value for my contribution. However, it didn't go down too well with the studio's business affairs department, and my agent was sworn at and ridiculed and belittled, but I wouldn't budge. I honestly believed that *Tooth Fairy* was going to be a big mainstream film and if they didn't want to pay me properly for it, I'd try and find someone who did. The studio's faux outrage and my not-so-faux intransigence lasted a few days before, finally, with a lot of grumbling, they agreed to pay me what I was asking for. And immediately all the acrimonious negotiations were forgotten and everyone went about their business in getting the screenplay written and the film made as if nothing had happened.

As far as studio films go, the development process for *Tooth Fairy* was a relatively swift and painless experience. And, for the first time I could remember, I actually enjoyed being in script meetings and not feeling like every muscle in my body was tensing up as I listened to reams of (sometimes stupid and contradictory) notes. Instead of agonising over how I could possibly do—or even understand—what it was that the executives wanted, I could now just smile politely and turn to Ganz and Mandel and say:

"Sounds great. What do you think, guys?"

Despite this flagrant betrayal of my wordsmith roots, I did occasionally make myself useful by helping the writers find solutions to the studio's (sometimes stupid and contradictory) notes. But it was a very pleasant change not to have to do all the heavy lifting myself.

Inevitably, we had the customary studio-system revolving door of writers after Ganz and Mandel delivered their contractual obligations. Next up were two writers who'd worked on *The Simpsons*, and they came up with the idea that Dwayne "The Rock" Johnson—who was by then attached to the project to play the title role—should be a professional hockey player "enforcer" who knocks people's teeth out for a living, rather than a marketing guy who always plays by the rules. A number of other A-list writers then did revision drafts before it finally landed in the hands of an experienced family film writer called Randi Mayem Singer, who wrote the megahit *Mrs. Doubtfire*. Randi ended up sharing the screenplay credit with Ganz and Mandel and Josh Sternin and Jeffrey Ventimilia, and I was awarded an exclusive "Story By" credit by the Writers Guild, which rather oddly meant that I was the only person connected to the film (and I mean literally the *only* person) who ever received a fee (though a very small one) when Fox made a low-budget *Tooth Fairy 2* sequel with Larry the Cable Guy. I heard it was unwatchable, but I can't confirm that because I've never watched it.

I visited the set of *Tooth Fairy* up in Vancouver for a couple of days, and someone asked me what I did on the film. When I told them I was an executive producer, they asked me what that entailed and I told them it can vary on different films, but on this one it entailed me visiting the set for a couple of days and telling people I was the executive producer if they asked me what I was doing there. I hadn't met Dwayne Johnson up to this point, but when I arrived on the set he gathered all the cast and crew and introduced me as "the man responsible for everybody being here today." I'd heard Dwayne was one of the good guys in show business, but that was far and above the call of duty. And I'm glad to say he ended up being very charming and funny in the film. There are also some lovely performances from Ashley Judd, Julie Andrews, Stephen Merchant, Billy Crystal, and Seth MacFarlane. I would have been in the film too if they'd have let me. I wanted to play one of the fairies in Tooth Fairy Land, but I was told by the studio that there were already "too many old British fairies in the movie." I knew I had three slam-dunk discrimination lawsuits against them right there . . . but, being a forgiving sort, I decided to let it go!

Tooth Fairy cost $48 million and made about $130 million at the box office worldwide. That's not a massive blockbuster hit but, with all the ancillary markets of DVD, pay TV, etc., it still meant it was a highly profitable film and has now been watched by millions of people all over the world. By the way, I know what you're thinking, but no . . . writers never *ever* NEVER see any net profits from a film, even if it makes a trillion squillion gazillion dollars. Throughout the hundred plus years of Hollywood history, "creative studio accounting" has always made sure of that. Writers can get very well paid, without question, and the residuals can be very lucrative too, but actors, writers, and directors never *ever* NEVER see a dime of net profits. *Gross* profits, yes, but good luck getting a piece of that pie if you're not a megastar with a great lawyer.

More importantly, though, it was a genuinely wonderful feeling going onto that set in Vancouver and knowing that the simple idea I'd had, chatting with my daughter over dinner one night, had resulted in hundreds of people being employed. And even now, more than a decade later, it's a lovely feeling knowing that millions of viewers all over the world have enjoyed the manifestation of that simple idea.

28

JUDDSTER AND THE WOODMAN

Table reads are something I'm very ambivalent about. Which is a polite way of saying I like them only marginally better than auditions. A table read is a necessary part of the job on multi-camera sitcoms on the first day of rehearsals, but on films or single camera TV shows it isn't. Sometimes on those shows they ask if you're available to do a table read before the job starts, and most experienced actors, if they're being honest, will reveal the dirty little inside secret that I'm going to tell you right now: we get our agents to say we're unavailable. Why? Firstly, because the readings are unpaid and, secondly, because all producers (except me) can be notoriously fickle. So, if for some reason they don't like what you do at the reading, there's always a possibility you can be replaced. If you've already auditioned for the role, obviously the chances are they're going to like what you do, but, if you've been hired with a straight offer, a table read leaves a small window open for them to change their minds and hire someone else.

There's another type of table read which is for a film in development that either is *definitely* going to happen or might *possibly* happen depending on how the reading goes. I used to do a lot of those, but I kept finding that if it went well, the people I was doing a favour for would end up casting a better-known "name" actor to do the role in the movie itself. It finally got to a point where I became a prima donna about it and said to my agent that I'd only do these readings if he could get it in writing that I'd be guaranteed the role if the film got made (good luck with that one, Jimbo). But then, of course, all that goes out the window when someone you know asks you to do a table read and you don't want to piss them off or insult them by saying no.

One of these happened when a casting director I knew and trusted asked me if I would read a role in a new film that Judd Apatow was going to produce as a spin-off from *Forgetting Sarah Marshall*, highlighting Russell Brand's character and to be directed by the same director (Nick Stoller), called *Get Him to the Greek*. What also persuaded me to abandon all my high-minded principles and prima-donna flouncing was that I'd be reading the role of Russell Brand's father, and, although I was a wee bit young for it, it was a very nice part. And at the very star-studded reading, though I say it myself, I think I did it justice. I even tried a few improvised lines that got big laughs. So when I was asked to read the same role again at a *second* table read, I felt confident that the role was mine. Particularly as almost all the other supporting roles had been recast, and the very delightful Jonah Hill told me I'd stolen the show at the first reading. (He also asked me politely not to improvise a fat joke about his character, as it was a sore subject for him, but that's another story.) After the second reading, which also went well, I waited by the phone (not literally, figure of speech) for an offer . . . but it never came. As disappointed as I was, I knew that the harsh reality was they'd cast someone older and/or better known than me. And I was right on both counts. It was my old friend Colm Meaney.

Luckily, Judd Apatow and Nick Stoller are decent enough people to have felt bad about it (as well they should), so they offered me a cameo role, telling me I could improvise and play with it as much as I liked. I ended up taking the small consolation prize because (a) I liked both of them and (b) it was scheduled to shoot in London right after I was due to finish a vacation in France, so the timing was perfect and it would pay for the vacation!

That summer fell even more nicely into place—and, god knows, this happens so rarely—when I was offered a role with a couple of scenes in a Woody Allen movie, which would shoot in London right *before* the vacation in France. Win-win-win!

Working on the Woody Allen film (*You Will Meet a Tall Dark Stranger*) was a brief but pleasant experience. I've already mentioned how wonderful and fun Anthony Hopkins is. I also liked Celia Imrie, who played my wife, and Gemma Jones, who played Anthony Hopkins's ex-wife. But mostly I was intrigued to see how Woody Allen worked. First of all, he seemed *very* old, pale, and frail—even though he was around the same age as Anthony Hopkins, who was brimming with energy and vibrancy. You barely noticed Woody as he shuffled around the set, almost anonymously, and when he wanted to talk to you he did it in a very quiet, barely audible voice. But he also didn't pull any punches. I think I was spared because, fortunately, he seemed relatively satisfied with what I was doing. But he wasn't nearly so easygoing, or even tactful, with Celia Imrie and Anthony Hopkins if he thought what they were doing on camera was too theatrical.

Sadly, Woody Allen's reputation has now been tarnished by the sexual abuse accusations against him by certain members of his family. I can only say that I have no intention of weighing in on that particular subject because only the people who were directly involved can possibly know the real truth, and I'm not remotely interested in expressing an opinion on who should or should not be believed in such a controversial and inflammatory family dispute.

A couple of years later, I was asked again by Judd Apatow and Nick Stoller to do a table read. And, like Charlie Brown when Lucy holds the football, I fell for it again. This time, it was the part of Emily Blunt's father in *The Five-Year Engagement*, which Nick had written with Jason Segel, who was to play the romantic lead opposite Emily. But this time I also had a strong gut feeling I'd end up playing the role when the film got made. And I was right. Playing my ex-wife, and Emily's mother, in the film was two-time Oscar nominee Jacki Weaver. And Jason's parents were played by Mimi Kennedy and David Paymer, who'd also both had Oscar nominations. I felt a bit left out on the Oscar nomination front, but I was happy to be playing in the sandbox with such exalted company. Also in the cast were Chris

Pratt, Alison Brie, Dakota Johnson, Rhys Ifans, Mindy Kaling, Chris Parnell, and Kevin Hart. So it was quite a line-up.

We shot in the summer of 2011 and I had two spells on the film. The first was for two weeks in Ann Arbor, Michigan, and the second was a couple more weeks in San Francisco and the Napa Valley, separated by a nice break of seven weeks in the middle. Which was perfect because I'd recently finished extensive work on a house I'd bought in the Hollywood Hills and I could relax by the pool and catch up on a lot of reading. Living the dream, baby!

Shooting the film itself was as much fun as I've had doing anything, and it was another wonderful surrogate family to be a part of. I loved Jacki Weaver, and we laughed our way through the entire shoot. Mimi Kennedy and David Paymer were also really great to work with and hang out with. And Jason Segel was as amiable as I'd remembered from doing a TV pilot with him years before. And I can't say enough about how much I adored Emily Blunt. On my first day on the film, we had a scene together in a hospital cafeteria, in which my character—a roguish philanderer from the north of England, who has a different new Asian girlfriend in every scene—tries to tell his daughter that, in years past, he gave her mother a sexually transmitted disease. Throughout the scene, I was eating a bear claw donut that had a lot of glazing on it, and Nick had asked me to improvise a line at some point about how the crusty, oozing piece of food I was eating somehow reminded me of the gonorrhea I'd given Emily's mother (classy, huh?). It ended up being a huge mistake on the director's part because Emily and I already had, from the minute we began the scene (and for the duration of the whole movie) one of those inexplicable acting dynamics where we couldn't look each other in the eye, not even for a second, because we (well, she, mostly) would immediately start laughing. And, once I'd see her go, I'd lose it myself. We did finally manage to get through that first scene (sort of), and we had a grand time doing so, but it was a hell of a struggle. Naturally the whole scene ended up being cut, but fortunately I have a copy of some of the outtakes from it, and they still amuse me when I watch them.

**With Emily Blunt, Alison Brie, and Jacki Weaver
on the set of *The Five Year Engagement*.**

During the hiatus I had in the middle of *The Five-Year Engagement*, I had a catch-up dinner with Ann Cusack—sister of actors John and Joan—whom I'd worked with about fifteen years earlier on a film called *Multiplicity*, directed by Harold Ramis and starring Michael Keaton. We'd got along well working on the film and had kept very loosely in touch over the years. We had a lovely time at dinner and, at some point, the subject of Catalina Island came up. I'd been there almost every year when Ally was young, but Ann had never been and asked me if I'd accompany her sometime and be her tour guide. So, a couple of weeks later, we went off on a beautiful summer's day to the charming little island twenty-two miles off the coast of California. And, for the duration of the journey there and back and all our time on the island, we laughed and talked and laughed some more. At the end of the fourteen-hour excursion, when I said good-night before heading home, we had our first kiss. And we've been together, very happily, ever since. At the time, I was fifty-five years old and Annie was just a few years younger. So I guess the moral of this particular story is that you're never too old to fall in love again. Unless you're in your nineties and it's with someone in their twenties. Then it's just creepy.

Incidentally, the immensely bright and talented Harold Ramis—who sadly departed from this planet prematurely—was already a good friend by the time we worked together on the film where I first met Annie. I'll always forgive him for letting me get away with what was probably one of the worst, over-the-top performances I've ever given in a movie because, in addition to casting me in the role, he also gave me some invaluable advice—a life tip which he himself lived by and which I shall now pass on to you, dear readers, to apply in whatever field you happen to have chosen or aspire to work in. He said, "Look around whatever room you find yourself in, and if you think you're not the smartest person in that room, then go and sit next to the person who is."

Wise words indeed.

29

A FINGER UP MY NOSE

My actress friend Kate Burton once said to me: "Voice-overs are a gift from the show business gods." And she's right. From the time in New York when I did my first voice-over as the spokesman for Virgin Atlantic's first-ever radio campaign, I've loved doing them. It's quick, stress-free, and, in terms of dollars per hours worked, one of the best-paying acting jobs there is. But best of all . . . you can show up in shorts and a T-shirt! Also, voice-over actors—and, by that, I mean people who mostly *only* do voice-overs—are a different breed. They're generally less competitive and needy. Which I guess makes sense. On-camera actors need to be seen *and* heard, whereas voice-over actors only need to be heard, so they're probably half as egotistical. Although, if they insist on talking to you outside of work in a Donald Duck voice, it can get annoying.

When I first started doing voice-overs in New York, I only ever did commercials. The most lucrative and easiest of these was a Panasonic spot for TV, in which all I had to say was, "Panasonic. Just slightly ahead of our time." I must have read the line about fifty times, but for that half-hour's work I earned as much as I made in the whole seven-month run of *Present Laughter* on Broadway.

I managed to corner three small markets in voice-over commercials. The first was as a John Cleese soundalike, which for many years was a very popular request. The second was as a (usually hushed) golf-style commentator. And the third was a Richard Attenborough nature documentary–style narrator.

Oddly, one of the most memorable voice-over jobs I've done was memorable for all the wrong reasons. I'd auditioned for it, along with a lot of other actors, and my agent told me a couple of days later that I'd booked it. So I showed up at the studio and went into the booth, where the familiar copy was positioned on a music stand. After all the pleasantries had been exchanged with the agency reps, the clients, and the engineer—who were all watching me in the booth through a glass window—I did my first take. I thought it was pretty good, but there was a look of confusion among everyone in the booth. They talked among themselves for a few moments, and then the director pressed a button so he could talk to me:

"I wonder if you could do it a bit more like you did in the audition," he said.

This threw me slightly because I thought that's exactly what I had done. So I did a second take, and again there were some looks of consternation and some very serious discussions before the director pressed the Talk button again.

"Okay, Jim, we're just gonna play you back what you recorded in the audition."

And they played it back. And now it was me who had a look of consternation.

"Ah, okay," I said. "I think I know what the problem is." They all looked relieved . . . until I told them what it was.

"That's not my voice," I said.

And it wasn't. It was an English accent, but that was about the only similarity because it was a considerably older and much deeper voice than mine. Now there were some more frantic and earnest conversations behind the glass, until finally the director pushed the Talk button again.

"Okay, it seems there was a bit of a screw-up because you were either right before or after the guy we chose on the tape, and the names got mixed up. But we've all decided we're very happy with your voice. In fact, we like your voice very much. So let's just go ahead and do it."

And so I did it, doing several takes, all the time knowing exactly what the outcome would be. And, sure enough, when I finally heard the commercial on the radio, they'd rerecorded it with the guy they originally wanted, which made perfect sense. But I still love that I got paid a nice fat recording fee for being hired by mistake.

The most ridiculous voice-over copy I was ever given to audition for was this:

LINES:

Get Ready for Anything.

Get Ready for Anything. You're Up.

Get in there.

Get in there. You're Up.

Be ready for anything.

Be ready for anything. You're Up. Prepare for anything.

Prepare for anything. You're Up.

This was for a TV commercial, so bear in mind there could have been some dazzlingly exciting visuals to accompany the copy. But even assuming this—which is a very big assumption—this copy is pretty extraordinary, unless you believe mindless repetition is the key to all sales. And what was with all the capital letters on certain words? Below this copy, on the same page, were the voice "specs." And here's where the advertising agency really pulled out all the stops:

SPECS:

Range of male voices from current and hip, to pseudo-heroic, to odd and quirky. Brits are okay. We need someone who can simply deliver a straight line with personality. A character actor should be able to do it, or a comedian.

And then, my favourite voice-over acting instruction of all time:

The line speaks to being ready for anything.

No shit . . . it only says it *six* times in a row! But where the advertising agency really expanded their seemingly limitless creative horizons was in the "examples of celeb voices."

EXAMPLES OF CELEB VOICES:
Rob Drydek, Christopher "Big Black" Boykin
Daniel Tosh, Andy Samberg
Tracy Morgan, Zach Gallifonakas
Chris Parnel, Jack Mcbrayer
Chris Rock, George Takei
Powers Boothe, Tom Baker
Matt Lucas, Russell Brand
Keanu Reeves, John Lithgow
Seth Rogan, John DiMaggio
James Franco, Michael Cerra
Jonah Hill, Cee Lo Green
Malcolm McDowel, Larry Kenney

I think they pretty much covered all their bases there. Although Gilbert Gottfried was an obvious omission. And they'd also managed to misspell the names of Rob Dyrdek, Zach Galifianakis, Chris Parnell, Michael Cera, Seth Rogen, and Malcolm McDowell. And capital letters were clearly now optional when it came to Jack McBrayer. And CeeLo Green acquired an uncalled-for gap between his "Cee" and his "Lo." I can't remember if I got that job or not. Probably not, due to a flagrantly bad attitude.

Incidentally, one thing you don't want to see when you read for a voice-over job is your name anywhere on the copy. If "Jim Piddock" is named as the prototype, or they say they're looking for a "Jim Piddock type of voice," there is absolutely *zero* chance of Jim Piddock actually getting the job. Don't ask me why, but you can ask any other actor if this weird voice-over casting quirk is true and I'm sure they'll confirm it. One time, when I was named on the script as their prototype, I even asked my agent to tell the advertising agency that I wouldn't read for the job, but that if they wanted to offer it to me then I'd be happy to do it. My agent never heard back.

The most enjoyable voice-over job I've done is one that landed in my lap completely out of the blue. I received a call one morning from a number I didn't recognise and, when I picked up the phone, I heard a voice that I also didn't recognise:

"Is this Jim?"

"Yes," I answered, a little cautiously.

"Hi, this is Ethan Coen," the voice came back with. And, just as I was beginning to try and guess which of my friends was playing this oddly obscure prank on me, the voice continued, "Joel and I are releasing a director's cut DVD of *Blood Simple*, and we hate director's commentaries, so we want to do one from a fictitious character called Kenneth Loring, who's supposedly the artistic director of a film restoration company called Forever Young Films. It's pretty nuts, but we thought you'd be perfect."

Once I'd established that this was the real Ethan Coen (not easy, as there are no obvious security questions to ask like: "What's your mother's maiden name?"), he sent me the script. It was completely nuts, and I loved it. Soon afterwards, Ethan and I spent two full days together in a studio in Santa Monica, recording the inspired ninety-minute monologue he'd written to accompany the film. It starts out very straight at first, but then you gradually become aware that Kenneth Loring is perhaps not all he's cracked up to be as he tells you that a scene you're watching was actually acted in reverse, as well as upside down, to sync the headlights of a passing car. He also claims that a (very obviously) real dog is animatronic . . . that the sweat on the actors' faces is "movie sweat," gathered from the flanks of palomino horses . . . that Fred Astaire and Rosemary Clooney were originally supposed to star in the film . . . and so on and so on. By the end, the commentary on the film has been totally abandoned and he's screaming about the times he was punched by Nick Nolte and attacked with a stiletto heel by screenwriter Ruth Prawer Jhabvala. The script was completely bananas and genuinely hilarious.

I ran into Ethan and Joel Coen at a party a couple of years later, and they bounded over to me excitedly.

"You'll never guess what happened!" said Ethan. "We got a furious letter from someone who rented the director's cut DVD. They were outraged that it was a bootleg copy with a ridiculous commentary by some British idiot who didn't know *anything* about our work, and we should find out who he is and make sure he's prosecuted to the full extent of the law!"

"That was *exactly* the reaction we wanted!" added Joel, who was equally as enthusiastic.

After a few years of doing commercial voice-overs, I started doing some animation ones as well. My first was a TV series based on *The Lion King* in which I played Zazu, the role that Rowan Atkinson had originated in the film. Although I can do a pretty good voice match to him, I'm not nearly as nasally, so I ended up having to do every session we recorded with one finger stuck up my nose. I alternated nostrils on each take to prevent a permanent deformity, and I'm happy to say both nostrils shrank back to their normal size within a few weeks. Since then, I've been lucky enough to do a whole slew of animation roles over the years, including seemingly endless versions of *Batman*, in which I've played Alfred Pennyworth among numerous other characters in the city of Gotham.

The entertainment industry is constantly changing and, since I've been in Los Angeles, there have been as many seismic shifts in the business as in the land the city is built on. One of the first of these was the emergence of video games. And one game I did was called *Metal Gear Solid 3: Snake Eater*, which subsequently got expanded into two more *Metal Gear Solid* games, so the makers essentially got three games for the price of one when we recorded it. I voiced the character of Major Zero, which was one of the principal roles. I don't play video games myself, so I don't know much about *Metal Gear Solid* other than what fans of it tell me (and, god *knows*, there are plenty of them), but I do know it ended up being hugely successful, won numerous awards, and made a shedload of money.

I was happy it did well, but, over time, I did have pause for thought when I learned that the game and all its spin-offs had made a profit of not just millions of dollars, but *billions*. But none of the actors made a cent more than what they were originally paid, which I can assure you wasn't a massive amount. So, a few years later, when the makers of the game asked if I'd do the same role in a new *Metal Gear Solid* game, I figured they'd make up for the first time and pay us all a bit better. But I figured wrong. They offered me *one-third of the amount I'd been paid before!* My agent told them very politely that I'd be happy to reprise the role, but they'd actually have to pay *more* than I got the first time, not less. Their response was that they'd make a special exception for me and offer me *half* of what I got the last time. Their rationale was that, even though I was a much better known on-camera actor than I had been when I did the first game, *nobody would see my face*. Really??? People wouldn't see my face in a video game *voice-over*? Who'd have thought?

My instructions to my agent about how we should respond to this second offer were slightly less than polite. Speaking on my behalf, I believe the words *ass, shove, game, video, up,* and *your* were used in some order.

30

"I KNOW YOU FROM SOMEWHERE!"

When I was young, like most kids, I was rather impressed by famous people and loved to get autographs . . . mostly from football or cricket players, but sometimes actors too. But, years later, when I first began to get people asking *me* for an autograph, it felt strange. In some ways, it was a fantasy come true . . . but, at the same time, it made me acutely aware of what an insanely odd ritual it is. I suppose, like selfies, it's about having some piece of evidence that you've had an interaction with a person you consider to be well-known or successful in some way. Although that, in itself, is kind of weird, not to mention illogical. Will it really make your own life any different because you've got a photo of yourself with a professional sports player or an actor or a politician or a mass murderer? I suppose you could argue it's just capturing an out-of-the-ordinary moment in your life because it's not every day that you meet someone you might admire, or already know of, but have never met in person. I don't know. It still seems like it would be a difficult phenomenon to explain to a visitor from another planet.

I first encountered the whole autograph experience from the other side of the pen in New York when I was doing Broadway shows and there would be people waiting outside the stage door before and after the performances. Later, after I started doing TV and films, there would be letters sent to my agent. Sometimes they would contain a blank card to sign, or a photo—often one I had never seen before because it was a still image they'd freeze-framed on their TV or computer. For a long time, I always signed these because I felt duty-bound to respond if someone had gone to that much trouble. But then I began to get more and more requests, from all over the world, and they started to ring more and more hollow. There were still some obviously genuine ones, but a lot seemed like very generic letters: "You've always been my favourite actor," but with no reference to anything I'd ever done. Or they wanted multiple cards signed. It was then I learned that there's a whole industry of selling autographs for profit online and it soured me a bit to the whole rigmarole. So now I'm a bit more selective. Although, if somebody has paid for a stamped, self-addressed envelope and included it with their written request, I'll always oblige.

Having said all that, there was one letter I kept that had followed an initial approach from a fan by email. And I kept it because (a) I believe it was from a real fan—if not of me specifically, then of a show I'd been in, (b) it was very sweet and earnest, and (c) I didn't know whether to laugh or cry when I read it. This was the letter from Paul in Indiana, which was accompanied by still photos of me in the show he loved that he wanted me to sign:

Dear Mr. Piddock, thank you for agreeing to sign my items for me. I am a HUGE fan of the show LOST. I even made the journey from Indiana to Oahu last year and spent days looking for where they filmed the show. I finally located the place close to Pipeline, but a local told me that filming for Season 1 had just finished. I did manage to find a make-up trailer still in the lot—and that was very exciting for me. Just to have been that close to where such a fabulous show was filmed meant a lot to me. I rummaged through the jungle and surrounding areas hoping to find a memento or souvenir (like a LOST script) or something like that, but all I found were empty soda cans and trash, which I did carry off and place in the dumpster. I did sit on the beach and enjoy the ocean breeze from what I think is the same beach where the show is filmed. I have decided to try and collect autographs from all those people involved in this show. I designed these nice little cards for each episode and I would be very grateful if you wouldn't mind signing them for me. I also include a blank index card, and if you wouldn't mind signing it as well.

Sometimes one of the 2 get damaged, but at least I would still have your autograph. I am trying to save enough money to make it back to Oahu before this season wraps, but I don't know if that will happen. Thank you again for your involvement in the show. Many Mahalo's. Sincerely, Paul.

Even though it might seem unintentionally amusing, there's something extremely touching about his solitary and singular determination to connect with the show he loves so much. Especially because, judging by the spelling and grammar in the letter, he's clearly a well-educated man. So I was more than happy—and even honoured—to sign anything and everything he sent me, with or without a stamped self-addressed envelope.

In terms of getting recognised in public and people approaching me, my relative anonymity as a character actor and spectacularly mediocre acting career means I've generally (and very fortunately) had a nice balance. It happens frequently enough to be reminded now and again that what I do for a living does actually entertain people—which is always welcome—and it never happens so frequently that it ever becomes intrusive or a problem. Sometimes it's people who recognise you from a specific role, especially if it's recently been shown on TV or in a movie theatre. But, if not that, they often seem to know I'm British before I've opened my mouth. So if nothing else, at least I've succeeded in becoming a professional Englishman. Mostly, though, I get a lot of people who look at me longer than any stranger should and, if they catch my eye, they'll say:

"You look really familiar. I know you from *somewhere!*"

Unless I do actually know them, I usually then shrug and mumble with enormous humility:

"I'm an actor, so maybe it's that?"

And then they'll usually nod and say: "I knew it!"

After that, they either remember what they recognise me from or they'll ask me what I've been in, which is a conversation that an actor never wants to get into because it means you can end up reciting whatever you can remember from your resume that you think they might have seen, which is like searching for a needle in a haystack and infinitely less exciting. One of my favourite encounters, though, was when a woman said the familiar line to me in a supermarket:

"I know you from *somewhere!*"

So I smiled politely and mumbled my usual humble refrain: "It might be because I'm an actor."

But she immediately came back with: "No, it's definitely not *that*."

And she said it with such conviction it made me laugh out loud. Especially as she continued stubbornly trying to figure it out where she knew me from, with me offering no help other than continuing to laugh.

But my favourite recognition event of all time was connected to something that was also extremely painful. I've had kidney stones a couple of times in my life, and it's the most excruciating agony I've ever experienced (if you don't include seeing James Woods or Scott Baio trying to get political on Twitter). The last time was a few years ago. They managed to get the stone out and put a stent in my ureter to make sure urine could flow from my kidney to my bladder. By the way, just typing that sentence made me wince. A few days later, I went to the urologist's office, where he—without giving me any kind of anaesthetic, I might add—stuck an extremely unpleasant-looking medical implement up my penis to pull the stent out. So there I am, lying on an examination table and exposed to the world, while he and his nurse are performing this delicate and painful removal procedure. And then, just as the urologist inserts the implement of torture up my John Thomas and I'm crying out in agony, the nurse blurts out:

"Oh my god . . . you were in *Best in Show!*"

I managed to nod bravely through my tears as she continued on, saying how much she *loved* the movie, but all I could think was, *What the hell was it about a metal rod being stuck up my cock that reminded you I was in a film about a dog show?!*

On the other side of the equation, I'm not brilliant at recognising celebrities myself. When I went to the Aspen Comedy Festival, where a film I was in was being screened, the Festival sent a minivan to the airport to pick me and another person up. As we were being driven to our hotel, we had a lovely chat and I assumed he must be an actor because he looked familiar. But I was too embarrassed to ask his name, so I asked him what film he had at the festival. He said he didn't have one, but was a journalist covering the festival for TV.

"Of course," I said. "I knew I'd seen your face before. I'm so sorry, what's your name?"

For some unknown reason, I thought that asking a familiar-looking person his name is less embarrassing with a journalist than with an actor. But, when he told me, I realised it wasn't.

"It's Anderson Cooper," he said.

However, in another instance—at a wedding in upstate New York—I knew very much who I was being introduced to because at the time Bill Murray was one of the best-known film stars in America. So when he said, "Hi, I'm Bill Murray," and I replied, "I'm sorry, I didn't catch the last name," I was just being a dick.

I should perhaps add that I didn't do that when I was introduced to Vice President George H.W. Bush at the Kennedy Center when I was a young actor.

I'm not *that* much of a dick.

31

IDLE PLEASURES

A fter my father died when I was in my early twenties, I've been blessed with some wonderful friendships in my life with some slightly older, slightly paternal mentors: my half-uncle, Peter Egan . . . my actor friend, Paxton Whitehead . . . my first literary agent, Bob Wunsch . . . and, most enduringly of all, Eric Idle. Over the years since Eric and I first became friends on the set of the amusingly shambolic *An Alan Smithee Film*, we've worked together a number of times. One of the first things I did with him was a cameo in *The Rutles 2: Can't Buy Me Lunch*, in which I played Troy Nixon, the young gay lover of the Rutles manager, Leggy Mountbatten. It was an utterly shameless performance but I blame Eric, who'll always encourage me in these matters.

The next Idle project I was involved in was a series of readings, starting at Eric's house in Los Angeles and ending in a conference room in New York, of a musical he was working on called *Spamalot*, based on the film *Monty Python and the Holy Grail*. Since I'd grown up watching Python avidly, I could slide into most of the parts with ease.

Also involved in the readings were Tim Curry, David Hyde Pierce, and Hank Azaria. As the project continued to be developed, with Mike Nichols on board as director, it was pretty much a given that I'd be involved in the show if it came to fruition. However, when it did come to fruition, unfortunately the timing was terrible. It was very soon after my divorce and I didn't want to uproot my life, or my daughter's life, any more than it already had been. I knew I couldn't leave LA and go to Chicago and New York for fourteen months. I needed to put roots down in my new home and spend time with Ally, so I had to take a pass on the show and on a return to Broadway.

Before *Spamalot*, Eric had written a film called *The Remains of the Piano*, which was a splendidly silly spoof of award-seeking Merchant Ivory–type films. It had been in development at Miramax but never got made, so Eric renamed it *What About Dick?* and adapted it into what he called "a motion picture for radio." Which, in reality, meant a play that was to be read onstage as if it were being done for radio. I mean old-school radio, complete with live sound effects created on stage with tins, a sandbox, and various other old-fashioned sound tricks. The Ricardo Montalbán Theatre in Hollywood was booked for a couple of nights by producer Arnold Engleman, and Eric assembled a stellar, once-in-a-lifetime cast: Billy Connolly, Tim Curry, Eddie Izzard, Jane Leeves, Emily Mortimer, Tracey Ullman, Eric himself, and little old me. The show sold out within minutes, and, each night, people were lining up around the block for no-show seats. I shared a dressing room with Eddie Izzard, whom I'd met briefly before, and it soon became clear we had more in common that just being in this mad theatrical event together . . . we were both rabid Crystal Palace Football Club fans. Eddie and I have stayed in regular touch ever since and, very often end up watching Palace games together whenever we're both in England at the same time.

Another person who was already a pal by then is Emily Mortimer, along with her equally as wonderful and talented husband, Alessandro Nivola. Alessandro became a regular football teammate of mine in the BAFTA team, but my favourite story about these two lovely people is when they came to dinner when I was living in Studio City. We had a great evening, which finally came to an end soon after midnight (which is extremely late by Hollywood social standards).

As they both left the house and we all said our goodbyes on the front porch, Emily declared very politely: "Thank you for a lovely evening, but I'm really glad to be outside."

To which I quickly replied: "I'm so sorry, was it too hot in the house? I could have turned the air-conditioning up."

"No, no," she reassured me in her perfectly demure manner and beautifully elegant English accent. "I've just needed to fart really badly for the last couple of hours."

What About Dick? was a rip-roaring success, and the audiences were as in awe of the incredible cast on stage as I was being on it with them. There were so many memorable moments, but I think it's fair to say that Billy Connolly probably stole the show with his hilariously incoherent police detective with a very unfortunate speech impediment. Billy is almost certainly the most naturally funny person I've ever met. He can tell a story at a dinner party or in a restaurant and you never want it to end. And he paid me one of the greatest compliments I've ever received as an actor when we were doing the show. I'm far too modest to repeat it here, but suffice to say it still warms the cockles of my heart when I remember it. As does every time I get a text or email from him celebrating Crystal Palace's latest win. He's a lifelong Glasgow Celtic fan, but when he first moved to London as a young comedian he'd sometimes go and watch Palace games because he "just liked the name of the club—it sounded so *exotic!*"

With Eddie Izzard, Emily Mortimer, Tim Curry, Jane Leeves, Billy Connolly, Eric Idle, and musical director John Dupre after a performance of the 2007 version of *What About Dick?*

A few years later, the once-in-a-lifetime show became twice-in-a-lifetime as we performed *What About Dick?* again at the larger Orpheum theatre in downtown LA for four nights. This time, Russell Brand was added to the cast, but we lost Emily Mortimer who wasn't available and was replaced by Sophie Winkleman. I'd just played Sophie's father on the hit TV show *Two and a Half Men* and thought she'd be an excellent replacement, so I recommended her to Eric and it turned out she was. I'd also worked with Russell before, albeit briefly, on *Get Him to the Greek*. I know he's a bit "Marmite" for most people (which, for non-British readers, means you either love him or you hate him), but up close and personal, Russell is more than likeable. A few years ago, I was asked to contribute something about him for a "world's most eligible bachelors" article *Town and Country* magazine were doing, and this is a slice of what I wrote:

Russell Brand is a narcissistic, preening, puerile, hyperactive, attention-seeking fame whore . . . but I love him. Partly because he's the first person to tell you all of the above, but mostly because that's only the half of it. First and foremost, Russell is a comedian. And, like the very best comedians, he's brutally honest and also a seeker, constantly questioning the world we live in with high-octane comic streams of consciousness and a dazzling verbal facility. . .

. . . But Russell is also a walking, talking contradiction. Who else can express such smart, eloquent, and humorous thoughts, using the most grandiose and antiquated language, yet in the broadest and crudest of Essex/Cockney accents? And who else can be so openly self-involved and suffer from such obvious ADHD, yet be so consistently focused and engaged in one-on-one conversations about raising children (mine), kicking heroin addiction (his), and the importance of finding spiritual enlightenment (mostly him)? . . .

. . . Russell is a larger-than-life, splendidly contradictory concoction of part *enfant provocateur*, part Buddhist, and part so many other things. And when I look around and see how many dishonest, uncaring, fear-based assholes are out there, I can't help thinking we need more Russell Brands in the world.

For the second incarnation of *What About Dick?* I shared a dressing room with Tim Curry, whom I'd also worked with before and knew quite well socially. Tim is probably best known for *The Rocky Horror Picture Show*, but the whole body of work in his long career is mightily impressive. I loved being his dressing-room roomie for the main reason that he has a distinctly unique sense of humour which is droll, wickedly cutting, and slightly campy all at the same time. Even his grumpy rants (and there were a few!) made me laugh out loud. Unfortunately, not long after we did that second run of *Dick*, Tim had a serious stroke. But when I visited him to have dinner and catch up, despite being in the early stages of his rehab and still physically restricted, his wit and humour were no less droll, cutting, and campy.

With Russell Brand and Sophie Winkleman now aboard on *Dick* at the Orpheum, the show was also filmed for posterity and can currently be found on Netflix, should you wish to watch a stellar cast of British comic persons delivering a lot of excellent double entendres in very extravagant costumes for a couple of hours.

Backstage with Billy C. before *What About Dick?*

The fortieth anniversary of the birth of Monty Python was in 2009, and Eric wanted to direct a show to celebrate it. He cast a younger generation of performers doing all the best and most durable sketches in a show called *An Evening Without Monty Python*. The cast of Alan Tudyk, Jane Leeves, Rick Holmes, Jeff Davis, and myself did the show for two weeks in LA and then a week on Broadway, which was my first time back on the Great White Way in almost twenty-five years.

On stage with Alan Tudyk in *An Evening Without Monty Python*, photo credit to Gilbert Smith.

We did pretty reasonable business at the box office, but the level of fanaticism from people who bought tickets was astounding. The response from the audience, many of whom were dressed as Python sketch characters, was incredible, and the crowds outside the stage door seeking autographs and selfies were so large you'd have thought we were the original Pythons. It was a reminder of just how big a phenomenon Monty Python was, if that was the scale of the reception for what was essentially a tribute band.

Getting in touch with my feminine side in *An Evening Without Monty Python*, **photo credit to Gilbert Smith**

Eric also sent an unusual writing opportunity my way at one point, although it was something of a poisoned chalice. He was friends with Lauren Hutton, who is generally considered to have been the world's first ever "supermodel." She'd approached Eric about co-writing her autobiography, and he politely declined but pointed her in my direction. I'd already met Lauren a few times and, while I liked her a lot, she's also as crazy as a soup sandwich. We ended up meeting a few times and she sent me a pile of photos and scribblings but, despite dancing around the project for a few months, I knew it was never going to happen. That said, Lauren was incredibly sweet about offering her time to give some professional tips to Ally, who was a teenager at the time and was showing some interest in modelling. But, in typical Lauren fashion, at the same time she took me aside and said:

"If I had a choice between letting my daughter be a model or taking her outside and shooting her in the head, I'd shoot her in the head."

I'm happy to say I didn't have to do either because Ally soon lost interest in modelling and I could let her get back to being a teenager without a portfolio.

32

THE TIME I NEARLY SNUFFED IT

There's something I have a bigger fear of than snakes, and that's death. I could be wrong, but I think death is very overrated. More simply put, I'm not a fan of it and never have been. Which apparently means I'm a thanatophobic. If you already knew that word, either you are one yourself, or you have a far better vocabulary than I do and I salute you. If you didn't know the word, then you can add "educational" to all the other dubious benefits of reading this book.

In my early fifties, an annoying medical issue that I'd managed to live with as an inconvenience was getting so annoying and inconvenient I finally decided to do something about it. About a decade before, I'd had a strange episode while I was in my office, writing away happily, and my heart suddenly started palpitating outrageously. I think we've all experienced that for a few seconds from time to time, but this time it didn't stop. After about half an hour, I finally called a cardiologist friend in Santa Monica and he said he'd see me right away. I was pretty sure the symptoms weren't those of a heart attack, so I drove myself over there and right away he diagnosed that I had atrial fibrillation. Which, for those of you who don't know, is like having hiccups of the heart. The electrical impulses go kind of haywire and your heart rate then decides to go all over the place . . . up and down . . . from normal to double normal . . . and everywhere in between. It's a common condition for people in their seventies and eighties, but less so for someone who was barely forty at the time. Although I've been told it's also quite common in young athletes.

My doctor friend prescribed some medication, and eventually, after a couple of hours, it stopped. I did some tests the following week and learned there was nothing wrong with the heart itself, it was just an electrical issue. I played "wait and see" for the next couple of years, changing medications a couple of times and learning how to deal with it when it happened, which was about once or twice a month and lasting a couple of hours at most. My only major concern was that it would happen when I was performing, but mostly it was just an inconvenience if I was doing something socially because I felt light-headed and distracted and all I'd want to do is sit down somewhere and be quiet . . . although I'm sure there are a few people who wish I'd do that more often anyway.

Over the years it started to happen more predictably: an hour or two after exercising, or if I drank too much caffeine or alcohol, or when I was traveling. I was told that the only surefire remedy was to have an ablation operation, which is where they go into your groin with a very thin electrical wire, then guide the tip of the wire up through a vein and then—passing through the middle of your heart with it—cauterise around all four veins going in and out of the heart to create scar tissue, which then prevents the electrical currents taking the wrong path. It had become quite routine surgery by that time, but the thought of any operation involving such a vital organ seemed mildly terrifying. However, I was told that the operation had about a ninety percent success rate in solving the problem. Although I liked those numbers, I also wanted know what the odds were of something going *wrong*. And I was informed that the chances of that were about one in a thousand. When I then enquired what the "one" meant, it was explained to me that there were very rare instances where a patient's heart had been punctured and they'd died or the operation had induced a stroke, which is why they give patients a blood thinner before it. Well, you could count me out right there . . . however good the odds were. Hearing that, I decided I could live with it being an inconvenience and stay on medication instead.

But over the course of the next ten years, the relatively infrequent inconvenience progressed to a point where it was happening every other day and for much longer spells. So, finally, I summoned up all my courage (which wasn't a lot, it has to be said) and decided to get the operation done. I opted for an electrophysiologist (another fancy word you can feel free to throw about at your convenience) at Cedars-Sinai hospital in West Hollywood. When I did all my pre-op tests a couple of days beforehand, they told me not to worry in the slightest because ablations today are like taking out tonsils. So, by the time I went into the hospital, I was feeling pretty reassured. Funnily enough, the thing I found most scary about it all was the thought that once you go under the general anaesthetic that could be it . . . you might never wake up again. Which I know is illogical because if it's something you wouldn't even know about, why be scared of it? But I was, and I still am, so there.

Anyway, I *did* wake up after the anaesthetic. But the problem was that it was rather sooner than expected. And can I just say for the record that the seven words you don't ever want to hear your surgeon say to you when you wake up from a general anaesthetic are: "I am afraid there was a complication."

After being told that, I was immediately aware that I had a very heavy feeling in my chest . . . although I wasn't in any pain. And then, when I looked down at my chest, I saw a tube coming out of it leading to a plastic bag that was filled with blood. Now I don't pretend to be a medical expert, but I had a pretty good idea that that wasn't a very good thing.

Fortunately, I don't remember a lot of the next two or three days because the main reason I wasn't feeling any pain was that I was on an extremely strong cocktail of painkillers. And with good reason, I soon learned. What had happened was that the septum that divides the chambers in my heart was tougher than a usual patient's and, in the effort to pierce it to get from one side of the heart to the other, the cauterising wire had pierced the lining of the heart and my pericardial sac had filled with blood. At this point, I probably don't need to tell you that this is *definitely* not a good thing. In fact, it's a very bad thing. So they immediately had to postpone the operation, then drain the pericardial sac and try to stop the bleeding, which wasn't super easy because of the blood thinner I'd been given pre-op. Apparently, as I lay in intensive care, there was a lot of concern about the bleeding not stopping and the hole not sealing up because if it didn't . . . well, let's just say you probably wouldn't be reading this book right now.

But I'm happy to say it all turned out okay in the end. As an added bonus, my daughter, Ally, informed me before I was sent home that I was infinitely funnier in my heavily drugged-up state than I am normally. Sadly, I don't remember anything I said during that time . . . except for a long and misanthropic rant I had about how intensive care units are the noisiest places in the world and the worst possible venue for getting any sleep because you get woken up every couple of hours to have your vital signs taken and get more medication pumped into you. I'm sure the hardworking nurses and doctors found it absolutely hilarious.

When I got home, I felt about ninety years old. I couldn't get out of a chair or cross a room without feeling out of breath. At one point, I had to walk to the end of the street to mail a letter—no more than two hundred feet—and it took me an aeon. I felt like I'd run a marathon afterwards.

Fortunately, within a week I was much better. And a few months later, figuring lightning couldn't strike twice, I went back to the hospital for another attempt at getting the ablation done. It all went swimmingly well the second time, and within a couple of weeks I felt as fit as a fiddle. And, as soon as I'd come off the blood thinners, I was able to play football again every week.

Over the next couple of years, I did notice that I sometimes felt a bit light-headed when I exercised and I was also aware that my heart rate didn't always go back down to its resting rate for an hour or two afterwards. So I went back to the electrophysiologist, who determined that I now had something called atrial flutter, which was less problematic than atrial fibrillation but would nevertheless require another ablation operation. So I got that one done, and my surgeon told me afterwards he'd also treated *another* form of arrhythmia he'd found when he was digging about in my atrial regions, the name of which I can't even remember.

But now—almost a decade later—I'm cautiously optimistic that I've run out of arrhythmias for one lifetime.

Incidentally, while we're on the subject of hospitals, a screenwriter friend once told me a story about how, in the late 1980s, he'd had a spell in a Los Angeles hospital for a series of tests because he'd been experiencing terrible headaches and dizziness. My friend, who had long hair and a beard at the time, was lying in his bed in his hospital gown and felt the urgent need to use the bathroom. I guess there wasn't one connected to his room, so he had to go to one down the hall. Feeling a bit unsteady on his feet, he grabbed a long stick that he'd been using to get around and went off to relieve himself. But, coming back, he mistook someone else's room for his own and walked into it . . . and it just so happened that in the bed of *that* room was Gary Busey, the well-known actor, who was recovering from a near-fatal motorcycle accident and staring at this stranger in his room with wide-eyed confusion. My friend raised his stick apologetically and, turning around, went back out again to find his own room.

A few months later, after my friend's tests had proven negative and the headaches and dizzy spells had gone away, he happened to read a magazine article interview in which Gary Busey claimed that, after his near-death experience, he found religion when he saw Jesus in the hospital he was taken to, and he'd since become a devout Christian. And my friend couldn't help but wonder if that vision of Jesus might not *perhaps* have been himself—with long hair and a beard, in a white gown and carrying a staff—entering the wrong room after a much-needed pee.

Whether this was the case or not, I imagine many religious conversions have been based on considerably less.

33

MAKING SHIT UP

Somewhere in between Christopher Guest movies, Chris called me and asked if I wanted to do a series of five short films he was going to direct and appear in for the National Geographic Channel, to promote their upcoming series about Stonehenge. He was going to play Nigel Tufnel, his mind-numbingly stupid heavy-metal rocker character from *This Is Spinal Tap*, and I would play a National Geographic Channel interviewer who—unlike Nigel, who knows nothing about the subject—is very well informed. All the pieces would be improvised and I knew we'd have fun doing it. And we did. There was one riff we came up with that I particularly liked:

INTERVIEWER (JIM): Do you think the builders of Stonehenge played music?

NIGEL TUFNEL (CHRIS): Build-*er*.

INTERVIEWER: Build-*er*?

NIGEL TUFNEL: Yeah. One man.

INTERVIEWER: One man built Stonehenge?

NIGEL TUFNEL: One man, yeah. You see, again it goes against this new theory of thousands of people and all that.

INTERVIEWER: (INCREDULOUS) Do you know exactly *how* Stonehenge was actually built? Or when? And what are your actual theories, then, on its origins?

NIGEL TUFNEL: Well, you know, they have a new film apparently, the National Geographic people.

INTERVIEWER: Correct.

NIGEL TUFNEL: Yeah.

INTERVIEWER: This film is based on probably the largest archeological dig in modern times, so it isn't really just another theory, it's a lot more than that. Would that change your views at all, knowing that?

NIGEL TUFNEL: Well, yes and no.

INTERVIEWER: "Yes" being . . . ?

NIGEL TUFNEL: There's no "yes," I'd say "no."

INTERVIEWER: So more "no" than "yes"?

NIGEL TUFNEL: Yes, I'd say—

INTERVIEWER: So it's "no" and "no"?

NIGEL TUFNEL: It's really just "no." There's not "no" and "no," it's just "no."

INTERVIEWER: (AFTER A BEAT) Do you ever watch the National Geographic Channel, by any chance?

NIGEL TUFNEL: (LONG PAUSE) Yes and no.

INTERVIEWER: Again, is that "no" or a—

NIGEL TUFNEL: It's a "no."

INTERVIEWER: It's a "no."

NIGEL TUFNEL: It's not 'cause it's not good. It's hard to follow. They should do puppet shows.

Interviewing *Spinal Tap's* Nigel Tufnel for *National Geographic*.

I guess I was forging a reputation for playing interviewers in improvised comedy pieces because I also had a request to play a BBC interviewer in Sacha Baron Cohen's film *The Dictator*, which was shooting in New York. I'd never met Sacha before, but I thought he was one of the best and funniest satirists of our age and so fearless he must have balls of graphene (which is 200 times stronger than steel—I just looked it up). I don't know what I was expecting when I first met him but he was incredibly gracious, telling me how grateful he was that I was doing this day on the film. And, by the way, "day" is an exaggeration. We got into costume, he played himself a tape of the accent he was doing in the movie to get into character, and we rolled. No script, nothing, just some questions I'd scribbled down in the makeup chair. And we kept going for about an hour or so, pretty much nonstop, starting with stuff like this:

INTERVIEWER (JIM): General Colonel Aladdin . . .

GENERAL ALADEEN (SACHA): Aladeen.

INTERVIEWER: General Colonel Aladeen, there are various reports of various human rights violations in your country, which—

GENERAL ALADEEN: This is silly! I am the president of Wadiya's commission on human rights. If there were ever any such violations, I would pick up the phone and call myself.

INTERVIEWER: But you just denying it to yourself doesn't actually alter the fact that there were human rights violations. How does this address the issue?

GENERAL ALADEEN: It does address the facts because of the situation

INTERVIEWER: There are also various allegations that you have had elderly women stripped naked and tied to wild oxen.

GENERAL ALADEEN: (CHUCKLES DISMISSIVELY, THEN NODS) That was true.

As silly and nonsensical as that might read, it's actually—like most of what Sacha does—a very accurate satire of the way autocratic leaders deal with the press, creating their own reality and not even bothering trying to hide their obvious corruption and crimes.

I was able to take my "interviewer" character a bit further when I did two *Human Safari* documentaries for Bravo. One was shot in Sturgis, South Dakota, where I explored the annual motorcycle rally—in which, among other things, I attended an illegal drag race . . . covered a bare-knuckle boxing match . . . interviewed some elderly biker nudists . . . and, finally, was inducted into a motorcycle gang.

Human Safari **in Sturgis.**

The other was shot in Las Vegas—in which, among other things, I slow-danced with Carrot Top, was persuaded (reluctantly, of course) by a very well-endowed porn star to "motorboat" her, talked Mickey and Minnie Mouse into taking off their heads, and attended a very drunken bachelorette party.

Apart from the intros and tag lines, the shows were completely unscripted and challenging in a different way than fictional improvisation because I was interviewing real people on the street and not accomplished comic actors with great improvisational skills. It was also interesting to be playing a role that—with one exception—I'd studiously avoided playing during my whole career: *myself*. And, after decades of hiding behind characters, I found it surprisingly liberating just being me for a change. It only took five plus decades to feel comfortable enough to do that, but there you are.

While we're talking about Las Vegas, I don't mind admitting that it's probably my least favourite city in America. To me it seems tasteless, fake, seedy, depressing, soulless, corrupt, and just plain ugly. And those are its best qualities. People say, "Yeah, but it's fun if you just go in for a couple of days and get out." A couple of *minutes*, maybe. And, as far as I'm concerned, what happens in Vegas *shouldn't* stay in Vegas . . . it should never happen at all. Which explains why, shortly after I'd shot *Human Safari* in Las Vegas, I wasn't exactly doing cartwheels about having to go back there several more times that same year. The reason being that I was cast as Kevin Hart's butler in the film *Think Like a Man Too*. They wanted an older straight man/younger wild man dynamic, somewhat in the same vein of *Arthur* with Dudley Moore and John Gielgud. The director, Tim Story, was great about allowing us to go wherever Kevin and I wanted to in our scenes, as long as what we improvised wasn't so obscene that it would need to be cut (some of it was and did need to be), so it became as pleasurable an experience as I've had in Vegas.

With Kevin Hart on the set of *Think Like A Man Too*.

We were all staying and shooting at Caesars Palace, so at least I could roll out of bed and head straight to the set. Although I'm making that sound a lot easier than it was because Caesars is a massive complex and, despite having a pretty good sense of direction, I was always getting lost between my room and where we were supposed to be shooting and I frequently ended up wandering, like a confused traveller, through a maze of slot machines and morbidly obese people on mobility scooters and repeatedly calling the first assistant director to try and guide me to my destination. But, all in all, the only time I remember wishing I was somewhere else was when we did an outdoor night shoot. I hate night shoots anyway because after midnight my brain pretty much ceases to function. But this wasn't just any night shoot. It was a wedding scene, in a temperature of over thirty-eight degrees Celsius (one hundred degrees Fahrenheit), and I had few, if any, lines in the scene (as far as I can remember) and I had to stand throughout it in a wool tuxedo with a waistcoat. Luckily it was my last day on that section of the shoot, so at least I knew I was going home to LA the following afternoon.

When I left for the airport the next day, it was forty-eight degrees Celsius (one hundred eighteen degrees Fahrenheit) in the shade. Driving past all the giant billboards for where to buy guns or hire a personal injury lawyer (one thing leads to another, I guess), I thanked my lucky stars that I was getting out of Sin City in one piece—my body, mind, and dignity relatively unscathed—and I couldn't get on the plane back to LA fast enough.

34

BE MY GUEST

One Sunday afternoon in 2010, I drove up to see my TV reporter friend Ross King, who'd recently moved up into the Hollywood Hills near the Hollywood sign. Driving up the narrow, winding streets to get there, I saw a "For Sale—Open House" sign at the other end of his street and decided to stop off and take a look at it. I wasn't thinking of moving from the Sherman Oaks house I'd lived in for more than six years, but I love looking at open houses and this one seemed like it might be interesting.

From the outside, you couldn't tell anything because it was surrounded by a fifteen-foot, stucco wall covered with thick creeping fig, and you had no idea what was behind it. But, walking into the property, I was amazed. There was a fairly modest 1930s English-style house on two and a half levels. It was in a state of some disrepair but situated on a sizeable property with a long swimming pool and a magnificent two-hundred-year-old oak tree standing beside the house. There were trees everywhere on the periphery, which gave the house more privacy than it needed because the whole property sat on the crest of the ridge between Beachwood and Bronson Canyons, so nobody could see you anyway. In fact, all the trees did was partially block the spectacular views of downtown LA, Griffith Park (including the magnificent Observatory), and the Hollywood sign.

Inside the house, it was a really strange hodgepodge. The owner, an exile from Chicago in his early eighties, had great taste but it was an odd blend of original early-1930s features and things he'd added when he'd bought it in the 1970s. But there was a very impressive large, wood-panelled study with a vaulted ceiling that he'd added on a dozen years before. As I walked around, I knew it needed loads of work, but I also knew it was the most original house I'd ever seen in California and that it was oozing with character and potential. After viewing the two very large but rather rickety decks off the living room and study, I then discovered the icing on the cake: at the back of the house, beneath the kitchen, was a small ten-foot-by-ten-foot British pub. It was completely authentic, down to the bad, very worn tartan carpet. And it even *smelt* like a country pub, thanks to the creosote that was used in the 1930s to coat the undersides of a building's wooden foundation beams.

The house had been on the market for a few months, but because home sales were still slow after the financial crash, and because it needed so much work, it hadn't sold. I put in an offer that was a fair bit lower than the asking price, and, after some haggling, a price was accepted. For years, I'd joked about wanting to live in a house at the top of a big hill because I'd always wanted to look down on people, and now I'd found it! And I got a surprise bonus, too, very soon after I'd bought it. I had decided to add on a new wing where the decrepit garage was currently (just about) standing. And when I climbed onto the roof of the garage to see what the views would look like from where I wanted the new master bedroom to be, I could now see over a row of trees at the front of the property, and there was a direct view of the Pacific Ocean and—on the horizon—Catalina Island.

Soon after I'd finished the addition and remodel on my dream house, Chris Guest called me and said he wanted to meet for lunch to discuss an idea he'd been thinking about. So we met at Hugo's restaurant in West Hollywood and he told me about some recent research he'd done into his family tree. But, more importantly, it had led him to wonder if it might be possible to do a film about people's obsession with ancestry, as evidenced by TV shows like *Who Do You Think You Are?* and websites like Ancestry.com. He asked me if I thought the idea had any legs and my immediate response was that I liked the concept very much—particularly as I'd spent most of my life searching for the meaning and manifestation of my own family, immediate and otherwise—but I didn't think it was a film. I thought it had to be a TV series because exploring a family tree isn't a singular story . . . by its nature, it would be episodic and have different branches and characters, all snaking off in many directions. Chris had never done a TV series, but he mentioned that his wife, Jamie Lee Curtis, had a producer friend named Deborah Oppenheimer, who was currently an executive at NBC Universal International, and had told him that if he ever had an idea for a show to come to her with it. So he decided he'd talk to Deborah and get back to me. And then I didn't hear from him for three months.

In the pub beneath my LA house with British TV presenter and fellow Crystal Palace fan Susanna Reid.

When he did get in touch again, he wanted to have another lunch—which, I was beginning to learn, was a meal he rather liked. So we met again and he asked me if I wanted to get together and see if we could come up with something to take to Deborah. So, a couple of weeks later, we met at his house and started to bash around some ideas and, if nothing else, we laughed a lot. After a couple of hours, we'd come up with a few things that might work and, at the end of the day, Chris said he wanted to think about it some more while I went off to do an acting job.

After I'd done the acting job, we met up again and after that session, we started meeting more regularly—two or three times a week—to develop the idea. Chris did warn me he works at a glacial pace, so I knew it wasn't going to be a fast process. But I tend to work extremely fast, so I thought it would be a good challenge for me not to be in such a damn hurry all the time. Over the course of the next few months, our normal writing day would unfold as follows:

1. At 10:00 or 10:30 a.m., we meet. Either with me having driven to his house in Santa Monica or him having driven to my house, which is about an hour either way.

2. We start the work day with a cup of tea and, for the first hour, talk about the news or what we've been up to since we last saw each other, before one of us finally says: "Okay, lunch?" After laughing at that (it never got old), we slide into some vague form of creativity, saying various things that make us laugh, whether they have anything to do with the show or not. Mostly not. This also often involves us doing a lot of silly voices and characters and me occasionally scribbling something down on a notepad.

3. At least two or three times in the course of the morning, Chris gets distracted by an email or a text on his iPad and then we both spend several minutes looking up things on our smart devices that might have something to do with what we're working on, but usually don't. Oh, and we also talk about English football a lot because we both watch the Premier League every weekend.

4. At 12:30 p.m., Chris suggests lunch for real and we head out to get something to eat, during which we talk about anything and everything *not* connected to what we're working on and try and spot unusual-looking people. While doing this, we always assess the job

done by a fictitious casting director who we pretend is responsible for casting these "extras" at the establishment we're eating in.

5. At 1:30 p.m., we get back to the house and have another cup of tea—or, in Chris's case, coffee—and off we go again, but without a recap of the news or what we've been doing lately since we already know what we've been doing and it certainly doesn't warrant any more scrutiny.

6. At around 4:00 p.m., we start getting punchy and spend the rest of the day coming up with funny names for characters, which often end up becoming obscene—such as "Mr. Prineaux," pronounced "Pricknose." Sometimes, just for a change, we make lists of currently or recently popular expressions and catchphrases that annoy us.

7. At 5:30 p.m., we call it a day. I sometimes mention in passing that we've achieved virtually nothing, and Chris then reminds me he once booked a hotel suite in New York for three days for him and Ricky Gervais to try and write something and, at the end of the three days, they'd written absolutely nothing except a title. Which makes me feel a bit better before we say our goodbyes.

After six months of this punishing routine, I wrote up a summary of what we had, based on all my scribblings. At that point, Chris brought his longtime producer, Karen Murphy, into the mix and we had some teleconference meetings between the executives at NBC Universal International in LA and some of the company's executives in London. Those of us in LA sat on one side of a long conference table, and on the other side of the table—projected onto the blank wall facing us—were the executives in London. A massively superior step up from Zoom and the like, a teleconference call is essentially a virtual meeting, as if you're all literally in the same room, sitting across from each other. Except it doesn't *quite* work the way it should—firstly, because there's a slight time delay, and secondly, because the camera eye-lines are all slightly off, so you're never entirely sure who the person on the other side of the Atlantic is actually speaking to. It might seem like they're looking at Karen or Chris or Deb, but they're asking me a question, or vice versa. So there was an awful lot of people saying, "Sorry, are you talking to me?" during these calls.

Finally, Chris and I flew to London and pitched the show to a couple of broadcasters, and we got interest from both of them and a firm commitment from the BBC, if we could find a US partner. One of the things we were asking for, having already worked on the show for more than six months, was a full first-season commitment and not just a pilot. We also met some actors, and we settled on Chris O'Dowd for the lead role of Tom Chadwick and Tom Bennett as his very lovable but terminally stupid best friend, Pete.

Then we came back to LA and pitched the series to some American broadcasters and we got offers from Netflix and HBO. I was inclined to go with a Netflix-BBC combo platter because Netflix were only just beginning to make their own content and I'm always attracted to getting on board something in its inception, even if it's more of a risk. But Chris's agents were keener on the HBO-BBC combination because HBO was currently at the top of its game. So we signed up to do a first season of the show that was now called *Family Tree* with HBO and the BBC.

After Karen found us some offices at Culver Studios, Chris and I started writing a season of eight episodes and also figuring out what actors might play the other regular roles. We knew we wanted the wonderful actress-ventriloquist Nina Conti to play Chris O'Dowd's sister, because the idea of a character who has a talking monkey puppet on one hand the whole time—which everybody accepts as another character and part of the family—really appealed to us. We also settled on Michael McKean to play the father, and various other members of Chris's film ensemble for various roles in the American-based episodes. Chris wasn't sure what role he wanted to play but finally decided on Dave Chadwick from North Carolina, a mysterious character with a vestigial tail. And we created a character for me called Mr. Pfister, who was Chris O'Dowd's character's eccentric neighbor and confidant in London, and who owned an antique store called Mr. Pfister's Bits and Bobs.

One day, as we were working, Chris said to me: "So what kind of an accent are you going to do for Mr. Pfister?"

I said I wasn't sure, then asked, somewhat rhetorically: "What's the *least* funny accent someone could do in a comedy?"

We discussed this for a while and came to the conclusion that South African, with all its historically racist associations, was the least used and most annoying accent we could think of in a comedy. I'd already used it in *Lethal Weapon* 2, but that part was deliberately written to be unsympathetic and racist—and it was only for one scene.

Then, of course, Chris started egging me on: "Go on then. Say something as Mr. Pfister."

So I did and it made him laugh. And every time after that, when we came to a scene with my character, he'd smile knowingly and nod for me to improvise in that accent. And, before I knew it, it had stuck. So, basically, I chose a South African accent for my character in a television show on a dare.

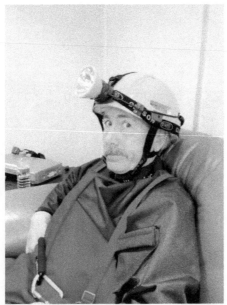

Dressed as Mr. Pfister on the set of *Family Tree*.

The production schedule was atypical for television. We had six weeks' prep in England followed by a four-week shoot. Then it was back to LA for six weeks more prep, followed by another four-week shoot. One of the first questions I was asked by the press when we were filming was: "I'm assuming that writing a show that's largely improvised is much quicker and easier, right?" Nope. *Wrong.* It actually takes a lot longer than scripted material. Why? Partly because Chris likes to work at a glacial pace, but mostly because if you're going to ask the actors to improvise their lines on the day you shoot, you have to do twice as much work to set up the structure and beats of that scene for them, so it achieves what you need it to in telling the story and doesn't get off track. We also add suggestions of lines and jokes and write detailed character biographies for every role, down to details like the names of the schools they went to or what their first pet was called.

At a press junket for *Family Tree* with Chris and Chris.

The reason for having actors improvise their lines on the day is to make sure the dialogue sounds unscripted in true documentary style. But you need to leave as little as possible to chance. The best analogy I can think of is that you're an anal-retentive planning a very long car journey and you work it all out in great detail in advance: all the timings, where to stop for gas, where to stay, when to eat, when to stop and stretch your legs, etc. And then, on the day itself, you let the actors drive the car so they can make the journey theirs.

Although there are no rehearsals, most of the actors read the outlines—or "scriptments," as Chris and I called them for the benefit of contractual obligations—and figure out a number of ways that a scene might go in advance and then come up with some good lines or jokes for themselves. An extreme example would be Fred Willard, who would write copious notes to give himself numerous options and would even bring his own comedy props to the set. I suspect Ed Begley also prepares certain riffs because he also tends to go on extended verbal runs—and if he doesn't figure them out in advance, he's an even greater improviser than I already think he is. In *Family Tree*, we wrote his character, Al Chadwick, as a guy who is very congenial and practical on the surface but gives off subtle hints that suggest he might be rather paranoid and prone to believing in conspiracy theories. Finally, in the last episode of the season, there's a scene where Chris O'Dowd's character, Tom, stumbles on Al's hidden "conspiracy room" in the garage of his house and it all comes out.

This is what Chris and I wrote in the outline:

INT. AL AND KITTY'S GARAGE—NIGHT

There are several tables with detailed MODELS on them . . . JFK'S ASSASSINATION AT DEALEY PLAZA . . . THE FIRST MOON LANDING . . . THE TITANIC HITTING AN ICEBERG.

Tom also notices some NEWSPAPER ARTICLES and PHOTOS pinned up on a CORK BOARD.

As he walks in and takes a closer look at the board, we see an article about MARTIN LUTHER KING . . . an original newspaper story about JACK THE RIPPER . . . a photo of POPE PAUL VI . . . and a NEIL DIAMOND album cover.

He turns sharply as he hears AL'S VOICE

— "I see you've found my little hobby room."

Al is standing in the doorway, dustpan and broom in hand. Tom apologizes and says that he opened the wrong door.

Al tells him it's okay and explains how his interest in conspiracy theories began when he was 14 and he picked up something on his ham radio right after JFK's assassination. He's reticent to elaborate, but:

— "Let's just say that Cuban pilots, the mob, the FBI, the Dallas police, and the CIA all used the airwaves for covert communication in those days."

And this is what Chris O'Dowd and Ed Begley came up with and how the scene played out when it aired:

INT. AL AND KITTY'S GARAGE—NIGHT

Tom turns on the lights and is surprised to see an array of ELABORATE MODELS on work benches. Fascinated, he goes to the first one, which is a street with buildings, trees, and a few cars.

                TOM (CHRIS)
Wow.

He simulates a crash with two of the miniature cars. Doesn't see Al appear behind him in the doorway, staring at him in a slightly sinister fashion.

AL (ED)
I see you've found my special room.

Tom turns back to him, a little guiltily.

TOM
Oh. Yeah, this is great. I mean this is very similar to what I used to do at work. And the detail is so good.

AL
Do you know what you're looking at here?

TOM
Uh . . . no.

AL
This is Dealey Plaza, where JFK was shot in 1963. Exact replica.
(points them out)
Grassy knoll, book depository. With this model, I was able to prove that not only did Oswald not act alone, but I proved how they were able to cover their tracks with all the evidence they left behind. The grassy knoll and the book depository were moved in the middle of the night. Cut into pieces. They took it all down. Moved it to Area 51.

TOM
(nervously)
They moved the grassy knoll?

AL
To Area 51. It's sitting there right now. I have friends who have seen it.

Tom points to another model with a lunar module on a desolate landscape.

TOM

Is that the moon?

AL

That's the moon, all right. Where the supposed lunar landing took place in 1969.

TOM

The "supposed" lunar landing?

AL

Do you really think we had the technology in 1969 to get men on the moon and bring them home? 238,000 miles? Average 221 at perigee, 252 at apogee? A moving target? You think they landed on the moon? No, they were orbiting around the Earth while they did all this on a soundstage. Where? Area 51.

TOM

Oh. Behind the grassy knoll probably.

AL

You ever see the footage of the men on the moon? There's an American flag blowing in the wind on the moon. Oh, wait, there's no wind on the moon because there's no atmosphere. There should be a crater under the LEM. There's no crater. There should be a crater for when they're landing. What about the star field behind them? There's no stars in the background. Why? They're on a soundstage.

TOM

It didn't happen?

AL

We got taken for a ride is what happened.

Tom points at a city skyline on the moon model.

> TOM
> Is that a city on the moon?

> AL
> Well, that's on the dark side of the moon. There are people there. They've been there for thousands of years. There's a whole alien race living there.

Desperately trying to change the subject, Tom picks up an old Neil Diamond LP.

> TOM
> That's a good album.

> AL
> My hero. Neil Diamond. A great singer and a man who knows it all. That's why they wanted to shut him up. Look at this.

He picks up an old newspaper and shows Tom the headline on the front page.

> TOM
> (reads)
> "Neil Diamond Concert Cancelled. Singing Legend Cites Throat Problem."

> AL
> Yeah. Couldn't talk, or they didn't want him to talk?

> TOM
> Probably couldn't talk.

AL

Oh, no. They didn't want him to talk. He knows where all the bodies are buried. About the New World Order, enslavement of the masses, health care for all. He knows.

TOM

Neil Diamond does?

AL

Oh, yeah. And he was ready to sing.

TOM

I like that song "Sweet Caroline."

AL

He knows how it all comes together.

TOM

He's a good guitar player as well.

AL

Yes, he is.

Tom points to another model. It's the Titanic sinking into the ocean.

TOM

Titanic?

AL

Yeah.

TOM

No iceberg there.

AL

Exactly.

And *cut!* Two outstanding comedy improvisers taking the road map and driving the car they've been given at warp speed through that particular leg of the journey. Ed Begley reeled off all that conspiracy nonsense almost without taking a breath, and Chris O'Dowd was happy to ride shotgun, letting Ed take the wheel. But when you watch the scene, Chris gets almost as many laughs reacting to it all. Clever boy.

When *Family Tree* aired, the show garnered a fiercely loyal audience. The series was voted by critics as one of the best new shows of the season in America, and the reviews were mostly superlative. Both the BBC and HBO wanted to do a second season, but the show was ultimately killed by NBC Universal International, who didn't want to continue financing the portion of the budget that HBO and the BBC didn't cover per episode. A number of loyal fans lobbied to get them to change their minds. But, sadly, no amount of campaigning by fans on social media was ever going to change the minds of the people in charge of the purse strings.

An immodest ten-storey billboard for *Family Tree* on Sunset Boulevard.

35

HOW I WROTE FIFTY SHADES OF GREY

S ocial media is an interesting can of worms. Or perhaps I should say a nest of vipers. What started out as an innovative way for us all to connect has somehow managed to divide us in equal or greater measure. I was a big champion of Facebook when it began, but not so much any more. Before it became a haven for data-harvesting abuse and a minefield of dangerous misinformation, an early preview for me of what it might become occurred in 2012. And, though it was harmlessly amusing at the time, it was also a warning shot fired across the bow. When Facebook and Twitter started, I'd sometimes use both forums to try out a joke or share an amusing thought—something I occasionally do have from time to time. So one night on a whim, after a couple of glasses of wine (which I offer as a mitigating circumstance, Your Honour), I posted this on my Facebook page:

Very excited to announce I'll be writing the screenplay for "Fifty Shades Of Grey". I only pitched 49, but still got the gig.

Now I'll be the first to admit that this was at best a below-average David Letterman joke and at worst an above-average Jay Leno joke (or a very good Jimmy Fallon joke). I hadn't actually read *Fifty Shades of Grey*, nor did I intend to, but for some reason in my mildly wine-sodden state I found this an amusing enough line to share with more than a thousand of my closest Facebook friends. It immediately got a number of "likes"—way more than it deserved—and that should have been the end of it. But it wasn't. I went to bed shortly afterwards, so I didn't see any of the numerous comments it also received. But the next day, before I started a writing day with Chris Guest, I saw some of the replies, which made me realise the joke had, if not backfired, not been received *quite* the way I intended:

> *Jim, that is amazing!!!!!!!!!!!!!*
> *I have many friends who will want to use me to get to you. :)*
> *Really? Good for you!*
> *Awesome!*

There were also a number of responses which indicated, thankfully, that maybe half the people who'd read my post hadn't taken it so seriously:

> *Damn - I thought I had that. I must have blown it when I couldn't remember what a vagina was.*
> *And naturally, Jim, you're playing Christian Grey, which makes it a double score.*

But the turning point came in a response, posted after the others, which I hadn't seen by the time I switched my phone off to start work. Someone, demonstrating a talent for very diligent research or a severe addiction to entertainment news, picked up on a story from something called COMINGSOON.NET and posted a link to it. And anyone who clicked on that link would see this:

> *Moviehole is reporting that Jim Piddock has been hired to write the screenplay for* Fifty Shades of Grey, *based on E. L. James' #1 bestseller. The site says: "The Brit, best known as an actor, has written such films as Fox's* Tooth Fairy *starring Dwayne Johnson,* The Man *with Samuel L. Jackson and Eugene Levy, and* A Different Loyalty, *which he also acted in opposite Sharon Stone and Rupert Everett. Universal Pictures and Focus Features announced earlier this week that Mike De Luca and Dana Brunetti will produce the film."*

After that, the comments on my timeline took on a whole new tenor. Most of the people who originally thought it was a joke started apologising and everyone else was now convinced there was conclusive evidence that it was true. As for me, I was blissfully unaware of any of it until Chris and I took a break for lunch and I saw that I had literally *hundreds* of emails, texts, Facebook alerts, Twitter alerts, and phone messages. The story had by then been picked up by more than two hundred news outlets all over the world and gone very, *very* fucking viral. Most of them reported the news as a breaking story, but some offered their own opinions. And, justifiably, most were either surprised, confused, or outraged. Others, however, were not. Such as this, from a website called Books & Review:

"With all his experience, it seems like Piddock might just be the right guy to write the steamy script."

I have no idea what they meant by "his experience." I mean, I've been around the block a few times in both my personal and professional life, but I can honestly say I have no experience in bondage or any other sadomasochistic practices. Put that down to a lack of imagination, if you like, but it's true.

But if Facebook is the Chernobyl of social media, then Twitter is the gulag. And that was where the most venomous responses came. Including, believe it or not, from *American Psycho* author Brett Easton Ellis, who was infuriated—and I mean insult-laden furious—that I'd been chosen over him to write the screenplay. Meanwhile, my manager's phone was ringing off the hook . . . but he had absolutely no idea what the hell anyone was talking about. Eventually, I was forced to make a public statement, explaining my bad joke on Facebook and apologising for any confusion it may have caused. Although, even then, some people wouldn't believe the truth. Six months later, a handful of well-established news outlets were *still* referring to me as "the Fifty Shades of Grey screenwriter." I wish I could say the whole episode fell into the alleged industry truism that "all publicity is good publicity" and it generated a ton of new writing work, but I think in this case there really was such a thing as bad publicity!

I suppose the moral of this particular tale is don't drink and post on Facebook. Or anywhere on social media, for that matter. And a lie really *can* travel halfway around the world while the truth is still putting on its shoes.

Unfortunately, the explosion of the internet as the world's biggest conduit of information means that misinformation and disinformation are also high on the list of its poisoned fruits. The "go-to" entertainment industry website IMDB—The Internet Movie Database—is a perfect example. When it started, it was a comprehensive compilation of the credits of all those who work in the entertainment industry. But then they made the mistake of adding "user ratings" for films and TV shows, which, of course, make a mockery of an allegedly factual "database"—apart from confirming the old saying that opinions are like arseholes because everybody has one.

But far worse than their user ratings is their "STARmeter" ranking system, which gives every person working in the entertainment industry a ranking, supposedly based on the number of hits a person's IMDB webpage gets. This is a clusterfuck of stratospheric proportions for more reasons than I have the space to list here. And what makes it even worse is that casting directors, producers, and directors frequently use these rankings to decide whether they're going to hire someone or not. But, EVEN worse than that is another dirty little inside secret I shall now reveal to you:

The IMDB STARmeter ranking system is rigged.

How do I know this? Well . . . because I've done it myself.

A number of years ago, when I decided to break my boycott of using a publicist to further my career, I had a couple of big projects being released so I hired one. And one of the things I'd heard about, but not believed, was that you could pay a tech-savvy person to manipulate your STARmeter ranking. At the time, mine was somewhere in the top 3,000 to 5,000 range, but by the time the publicist had finished boosting my STARmeter ranking, I was in the top fifty, alongside people like Leonardo DiCaprio and higher than Robert De Niro and Meryl Streep!

When the folks who run IMDB finally figured out people were manipulating the system, they altered the site's algorithms to try and prevent it. But it didn't take long for the hackers to find a way round it. Proof of this came to me, not long ago, when I was acting in a high-profile movie. While we were shooting, I found out that some-one who was an extra in the film for one day—and had just a single speaking-role credit to their name in a low-budget short film—had a higher STARmeter ranking than almost all the major actors in the cast, including a couple of well-known names!

So please, by all means, use IMDB to get your facts and figures because those are mostly right. But make sure you also treat their STARmeter rankings with more salt than all the prehistoric dried-up mega-lakes in Bolivia.

But if I ever wanted conclusive proof that the internet has plunged us all into the deepest realms of insanity, I found it quite recently. After I'd mentioned that I was writing a book to some friends, one of them very kindly but rather prematurely tried to pre-order a copy on Amazon. He didn't find the book because it wasn't yet available, but he alerted me to the fact that he *had* found a "Jim Piddock Wall Hanging Tapestry" for sale. I thought he was joking at first, but when I realized he wasn't, I checked for myself and there indeed was the item in question, available for the princely sum of $17.00, $18.00, or $24.00, depending on the size. Furthermore, the listing assured any potential purchaser that the Jim Piddock tap-estry was "lovely for bedroom aesthetic." There was very little I could do about the company selling the very unusual *objet d'arts*, as the laws on image rights in other countries are very different than those in the United States or Europe (in other words, there aren't any). Apart from finding the whole thing relatively amusing, I also found it extremely baffling. Tom Cruise didn't appear to have a "Wall Hanging Tapestry" dedicated to him, nor did Leonardo DiCaprio, or Brad Pitt, or Matt Damon, or George Clooney. But I *did*? What world were these merchants inhabiting that made them think this might be a profitable venture?

Once I'd shared the Amazon listing with a few friends and we'd all had a good laugh about it, I quickly forgot about it. But then, a few weeks later, someone else alerted me to the fact that there were now several *more* "Jim Piddock Wall Hanging Tapestries." Five in all, to be exact, each with a different photo of me that had been lifted from the internet. Again, my friends and I all had a good laugh about it and that's where I left it. But my infinitely better half, Annie, decided to surprise me (although "shock" might be a better word in this instance) by ordering one and having it sent to me. When it arrived in the mail, it was a truly alarming thing to behold. First of all, it measured 60 x 80 inches, which isn't just large . . . it's fucking enormous. Not Bayeux Tapestry enormous obviously, but it's *really* big: big enough to serve as a bedspread for a queen size bed, although I wouldn't recommend that, as the item feels like it's made of mega-inflammable material.

Since Annie was out of town when this monstrosity arrived, I decided to pin it up on my office wall and take a photo of it for her to enjoy from afar. However, the stool I needed to use to stand on in order to hang it (because it was so damn big) was somewhat unstable and, in the act of hanging myself, it gave way and I hit the ground so hard that I wrenched my shoulder. Hopefully, it's the only recorded "Jim Piddock Wall Hanging Tapestry" injury that's ever occurred. I would assume so, because I can't imagine their sales went beyond the single order that Annie, god bless her, put in. At the time of writing, I regret to say that my shoulder still gives me pain when I turn over in my sleep.

And frankly, I blame the internet.

36

SON OF TEXAS

Sometimes in life you make friendships and you're never quite sure how or why you became friends because it's something you'd never have predicted. One of the more unlikely friendships I've had in my life was with Bill Paxton. Although most people know him as an actor from films like *Aliens*, *The Terminator*, *One False Move*, *Apollo 13*, *Twister*, *Titanic*, etc., and as the central character in the HBO series *Big Love*, my first introduction to Bill was as a director. He'd read a script of mine and was interested in directing it. This was early in the 2000s, shortly after he'd directed his first film, called *Frailty*, an excellent small-budget thriller that he'd also starred in. On the surface, Bill and I were polar opposites. He was born and raised in Texas and very much on the extrovert end of the personality spectrum. I was born and raised in England and rather more on the introvert end of that spectrum. But, for some reason, we got a big kick out of each other.

He was constantly defying what I expected him to be. He seemed at first acquaintance to be a nonintellectual, but he was a huge reader and a connoisseur and collector of art, which is something I know nothing about. He never did end up directing that script of mine, but we'd still stay in touch and meet every so often to talk about doing a project together or just to chew the fat about show business. And finally, a few years ago, I found something else that we both really wanted to work on together. It was a book that had been recommended to me by one of my other unlikely friends, James Cosmo. I loved the book so much that I adapted it on spec, and Cos,

Bill, and I partnered up and optioned it as soon as the rights became available. We came close to getting it made as a limited series for television, but for one reason or another we couldn't get it over the line. Bill had another project he was also keen to direct during that period, but that fell apart at the last minute also, and I think he was getting disillusioned with producing and directing, so he turned his focus back to acting. And in 2016 he got cast as the ageing detective in the TV series *Training Day*, which was based on the film by the same name. It was while he was shooting the first season of the show that I got a call from him out of the blue.

"Hey, buddy, how you doing?" he said.

"I'm great, Bill. And you?"

"Well, I'm doing this new series for CBS and there's a fantastic role in next week's episode that you'd be perfect for. I've told the producers they gotta hire you, so make sure your agent follows up on it."

He then proceeded to describe to me, with much enthusiasm and in great detail, what the part was: *a clinically insane and reclusive former film director who kidnaps prostitutes and keeps them in extravagant dioramas in his basement.* I couldn't help laughing as he described the role and kept saying how *perfect* I was for it. It was classic Bill—you never knew quite what to expect from him. Even though I've played a few villains and weirdos in my time, I don't know of anybody else on the planet who would have immediately thought of me for a role like that. But Bill's outside-the-box and instinctual thinking paid off because, a week later, I was on set with him and playing the part.

So, after years of dancing around various projects, Bill and I finally got to work together on an episode of *Training Day*. And that week and a half, shooting that episode, was an incredibly happy time. Bill was like a wildly enthusiastic child and made me feel so welcome every day. And he got such a kick out of my performance and concluded how *right* he'd been to think of me. He even came to the set when he wasn't scheduled to shoot so we could hang out and talk about work, life, and everything under the sun. We laughed, we reminisced, and one day over lunch—like all men of a certain age—we exchanged medical procedure stories. I told him about my ablations and he told me that when he was growing up he'd had rheumatic fever, which left his heart with a faulty valve. It was a bit of a ticking time bomb, so he knew he needed to get it fixed sooner rather than later but was unsure whether to do it right away.

On the set of *Training Day* with Bill Paxton.

Before I finished the episode, Bill invited me to the episode wrap party he was holding at his apartment in West Hollywood. He'd recently bought it as a place to stay when he was shooting because it was too far to commute to Hollywood from his home in Ojai. It was a great evening. Bill was in outstanding form and I finally got to meet his wife, Louise, whom I'd heard so much about over the years but never met because, though Bill and I were friends, we'd never really socialized. Annie and I immediately adored her as much as I loved Bill. About half way through the evening, he grabbed me and said:

"Listen, buddy, I wanted to give you something."

And he produced a package wrapped in brown paper and string. I opened it up and it was a framed sign he'd had made for ABEL CRIBBS PRODUCTIONS—named after my character in the show and expertly distressed to look like a real antique. It was beyond thoughtful and something no other actor had ever done for me after I appeared on their show. I mean, you might get a cast and crew jacket like everyone else, but this was so specifically personal.

When we left that night, the four us vowed to have dinner in the new year, once Bill had finished shooting the series. I had a text from him a few days later, wishing us a happy Thanksgiving, and then less than three months later, as I fired up my computer one morning, I saw a news story saying he'd died. It turned out he'd decided to get his heart operation sooner rather than later, but he had a stroke on the operating table and passed away a few days after that. I couldn't fathom it. He was only a year older than me and had more energy and enthusiasm for life than most twenty-somethings I know—and he was gone.

His memorial was a heartbreaking affair and I wept openly as his two children talked about their father. It's still hard for me to believe that he's not around any more, but I have a wonderful and everlasting image in my head of him in a short video clip he made for my sixtieth birthday. It was a typically original Paxton-conceived shot with him riding along a path on a bicycle as he wished me a happy birthday, with this added exhortation:

"May the road always rise up to meet you. Stay thirsty, my friend!"

And then he rode off into the distance.

37

BACK HOME

After *Family Tree*, Chris Guest and I wanted to find something else to do together. I'd had an idea for a while about doing a real documentary about football mascots in England, but the relatively small budget I knew I'd have to work with had cooled me off on it. I knew Chris found sports mascots as amusing as I did, so I suggested the prospect of us doing a fictional version. And that was the genesis of the Netflix film *Mascots*.

The film featured most of the regular Guest troupe, plus some great new additions like Sarah Baker, Kerry Godliman, Brad Williams, Zach Woods, and Susan Yeagley. It turned out very nicely and did extremely well for Netflix. And, as with HBO, the people at Netflix were fantastic to deal with from start to finish. Once they'd agreed to make it, they gave us a bigger budget than we'd ever had for any previous Christopher Guest film, and they trusted us enough to leave us alone throughout the whole development and writing process as well as the making of the movie. The film also had a similar structure to *Best in Show*, culminating with a third act international mascots' competition, but instead of dogs there were people dressed up in insane costumes of every imaginable type. Chris decided to reprise his community theatre director character from *Waiting for Guffman*, Corky St. Clair, who was now training Parker Posey's Mississippi born and raised character, Cindi Bouchard's "Alvin the Armadillo," a college basketball mascot. I played Owen Golly (pronounced "Jolly") Sr., a former suburban London football team mascot training his son Owen Jolly Jr., who had taken over his mantle as "Sid the Hedgehog."

Being photobombed on the set of *Mascots* by Chris O'Dowd.

It was great to work again with former *Family Tree* castmate, Tom Bennett, who played my son, as well as act for the first time with Kerry Godliman, who played his wife. And, once the film was edited, I had a blast promoting it with Jane Lynch, Parker Posey, and Susan Yeagley before it debuted at the Toronto Film Festival.

After *Mascots*, I found that, having spent nearly four decades in America, my life was starting to come full circle and I was being pulled back to England a lot more for work and various other things. For a start, a lot of the projects I was working on as a writer were English-based. And for some reason—not by any design on my part—I found myself doing more acting work there. These jobs ranged from the sublime to the ridiculous. The ridiculous was getting cast in the pilot of the E! channel's first attempt to make their own series, which was called *The Royals*. It was extraordinarily trashy but great fun to do, and the show's creator, Mark Schwahn (who also created the hit show *One Tree Hill*), was a really top man. My character wasn't a regular in the show, so I felt safe that I wasn't going to get trapped in something I'd later come to regret. We shot at wonderful locations like Blenheim Palace and stayed in fabulous old village inns. But while I enjoyed doing the show, *watching* it was another matter altogether (please don't hate me for saying that, Mark). Needless to say, it ran for four seasons, so what do I know about popular taste and culture? And, thespian prostitute that I am, when I was asked to return and be in another episode in season two and work with Mark again, I didn't hesitate to say: "Hell, yes!"

Something else that took me back to my homeland was an offer to play a mouthwateringly nice role in the film version of John Niven's cult book *Kill Your Friends*, a wickedly dark comedy-satire about the hedonistic misdoings in the music business, set in the Britpop era of the mid-1990s and starring Nicholas Hoult in the lead role. I played Derek Sommers, the vicious, angry, sadomasochistic (maybe the producers had read all those bogus 5o *Shades of Grey* news stories?), rent-boy-paying queen who was head of the record label that Nicholas Hoult's character worked for.

Sporting a more effete Ricky Gervais look on the set of *Kill Your Friends*.

The film was packed with some of Britain's best young acting talent; and by young, I mean compared to me because I was very much the geriatric on set. But they couldn't have been more pleasant and respectful and I was genuinely impressed by the performances of that cast. I'm also not surprised that a lot of them have already gone on to have very successful careers. Although I'm not sure whatever happened to that James Corden fellow.

Another thing I did back in England was to act as master of ceremonies for a charity comedy event organised by Crystal Palace Football Club at the Fairfield Halls in Croydon. It was an impressive lineup of comedians . . . Holly Walsh, Kevin Day, Mark Steel, and Eddie Izzard . . . all of whom are fervent Palace fans. And the audience was mostly made up of Palace season ticket holders and fans. I'm not a stand-up comedian—and I have never had any desire to be—but I knew I had to do something more than just introduce the acts. So I decided to tell my "poo on a train" story. That was how I opened the show, and it went down pretty well . . . but then I got a bit cocky.

During the interval ("intermission" for American readers) I asked Kevin Day if he thought the audience would have already heard the most concisely rude joke I knew of. I told it to him, and he laughed and said I should go ahead and do it. However, my cunning plan was to put a clever twist on the joke in order to turn it on its head and make it a bit smarter and less disgusting. This joke, by the way, can be adapted to refer to any group of people that you feel is an appropriate target. In this case, because it was an audience of Crystal Palace fans, I decided to make fans of their South London rivals Millwall the butt of the joke. So let me tell you the joke . . . but if you're of a sensitive and delicate disposition or easily offended, you should skip the next couple of lines. For the rest of you, here it is:

"How does a Millwall fan know when his daughter is having her period? . . . His son's dick tastes of shit."

I'm sure some of you have probably heard that joke, or a version of it, before. It's quite horrible, but it's also rather inspired in its ability to be offensive on at least three different levels in such a singularly concise way. However—and more importantly—my oh-so-clever twist after delivering it was to then say:

"I'm really sorry, that was incredibly offensive. I should never have used the word *Millwall* in a joke."

I thought, with some justification, that would make the whole thing more palatable and elevate it—to some degree, at least. So I went out and opened the second half of the show with the joke. But the reaction took me completely by surprise. After delivering the punch line, there were simultaneously five hundred people who let out an audible gasp of horror and five hundred other people who exploded with laughter. I'd never heard an audience reaction like it. And it really threw me. So much that I laughed and said:

"Okay, I guess we now know where the line can be drawn tonight!"

But then I completely forgot to say my oh-so-clever twist about apologising for using the word *Millwall*! So, in essence, all I did was walk onstage and tell a horrifyingly filthy joke. And this is why it's a good thing that I never wanted to be a stand-up comedian.

With Eddie at Wembley, watching Palace play in the 2016 FA Cup Final.

Being back in London also gave me a chance to see more of my mother before she died at the ripe old age of ninety. I did the eulogy at her funeral and recalled two important things she used to say to me when I was young. The first was:

"You can achieve anything you want to if you put your mind to it."

Which is advice I've always tried to follow in my personal and professional life. The second thing she'd say was:

"When vulgarity begins, humour ceases."

Which is advice I've always tried to ignore in my personal and professional life.

Despite that, I'm sure some of my sense of humour comes from her. A few years before she died, when she was starting to suffer from the early symptoms of dementia, I was having a chat with her and she started talking about one of her elderly friends and her concern for him.

"Poor old chap," she said, "he's got that terrible disease where you can't remember things."

And then there was a beat before she added: "What's it called again?"

Incredulous, but amused, I replied: "Alzheimer's."

"Oh, yes, that's it," she said.

And then her face lit up and she laughed—at herself and at the unintentional joke she was still able to grasp. And the fact that we could both enjoy it.

When I visited her in her nursing home about a year before she died, for the first time ever she didn't know who I was. As anyone who has been through the experience of having of a loved one with dementia knows, that's a very tough moment. So when I was back in England a couple of months later for a brief visit, and I'd heard she wasn't recognising anyone or responding much to anything, I wondered whether it would be too painful to go and see her. But I did. And during our fractured conversation, I wasn't quite sure what reality she was in or what she understood. But when I left, and I kissed her goodbye and told her I was heading back to LA the next morning and that I loved her and would miss her, her response floored me.

She said: "That's what make these visits so hard, dear. It's so far away and I always miss you so much when you've gone."

After her death, I finally pulled the trigger on something I'd been thinking about doing for years: I bought a flat in London as a home away from home, back home. Since then, it's been lovely to reconnect even more with my sisters Anne and Caroline, my seven nephews and nieces, and the recent addition of three of their own children . . . my great-nephews and nieces. Over the years, time spent with my biological family has always been fairly consistent, but also somewhat sporadic depending on when I was able to get back to England. So, consequently, I missed out on a lot of important events and gatherings in the passage of time since I'd left for America. But now I believe we're closer than ever, which I'm delighted about.

However, one of the things I've learned in my eternal quest for the meaning of family is that it's a *choice*, not a right. Acute evidence of this became apparent when, shortly after my mother's death, my only (older) brother suddenly announced completely out of the blue that he wanted to have nothing more to do with our two sisters or me, or any of our families. Apart from a relatively minor and insignificant disagreement with my older sister, Anne, about how they should perform their duties as co-executors of our mother's will, it was shocking and totally inexplicable (if indeed that was the reason for his discontent). I've attempted to reach out to him on a number of occasions, but I'm still none the wiser. What's particularly bizarre and mysterious is that he and I have barely had a cross word in our entire lives. But, at a certain point, one has to accept that, whatever the reason for his grievance, it's his to own. And it certainly doesn't dampen the fact that, after a lifetime of searching, I now have four very wonderful families which all complement each other: my immediate family, my biological family, my show business family, and my Crystal Palace family.

And that leads me to another thing I found myself back in London for recently . . . which was to be master of ceremonies for my fellow

Palace supporter and friend Steve Browett's sixtieth birthday party, which he celebrated in grand style. And I say "grand" because he hired the Clapham Grand theatre in London for a night, invited six hundred people, and booked an amazing lineup of performers for the evening: comedians Mark Steel and Al "The Pub Landlord" Murray, the mega-band UB40, and music legend Maxi Jazz.

In the Manchester United boardroom with former Palace player, Mark Bright, and being photobombed by football legends Sir Bobby Charlton and Sir Alex Ferguson in the background between us.

The reason Steve asked me to be emcee was in itself family-related. My great-grandfather, my grandfather, and my great-uncle had all performed at that same theatre when it was a celebrated and esteemed music hall venue. It was a genuinely emotional experience for me to perform on the same stage that so many of my ancestors had appeared on a century before. It definitely felt like a torch had finally been passed on and the connections were complete after I'd picked up that hanging thread left by my grandfather . . . by actually going off to Hollywood to make films and television, then coming back to perform on the same stage as both him and his own father.

And, to everyone's immense relief, I didn't spoil the evening by repeating any stories about having a poo on a train, or telling offensive jokes about Millwall fans.

Master of Ceremonies at the Clapham Grand.

38

WHITHER WOULD YOU GO? (NOT THE END)

A t the time of the writing of this final chapter, for the last two years, the whole planet has been in the grips of the first major global pandemic it's experienced in more than a century. It's been a very testing time for most people. And a tragic time for all those who have lost loved ones to the dreadful virus. For those of us who work in industries that couldn't really function properly until we had some sort of protection against the illness thanks to rigorous testing and double vaccines, the main hardship was having one's life put abruptly on hold for a forced sabbatical. I was fortunate enough to have snuck in a very nice acting role shortly before the shutdown in the Netflix series *The Haunting of Bly Manor*, but another film I was offered, due to start in the spring of 2020, was postponed until October of 2021. And a film I wrote, which I was due to produce and act in, was bumped from the summer of 2020 to the summer of 2021, and then again to the spring of 2022.

These, of course, are minuscule inconveniences compared to the hardships that the majority of the world has endured, but they still presented their own minor challenges. As I'm sure many people discovered, it was initially quite difficult to adjust to a strict stay-at-home routine with no end in sight. But, ultimately, what had once promised to be a busy year workwise turned out to be a productive one in a different way. Since there was no acting I could really do, apart from some voice-overs recorded at home, there was no choice but to focus on writing every day. Which meant I was able to complete this book, which was only half-written when the coronavirus first struck and probably would have remained so if it hadn't struck.

Further silver linings from that first year (plus some) were that I also had time to write a couple of new screenplays, and I also sold (god bless Zoom!) and wrote six episodes of a new TV series for ABC with my old friend and Chris Guest troupe compatriot Don Lake. All of which is of no consequence or importance at all in the grander scheme of world events, except that it did stop me going insane . . . and *that* I am deeply thankful for.

Christmas morning selfie in lockdown with Annie and Ally.

What is important, though—and I've spoken to a number of people who feel the same way—is that it was an unexpected and welcome chance to reset, recharge, and reevaluate everything in one's life. Yes, it was horrible not being able to hug any other loved ones apart from Ally and Annie for a whole year. And, yes, it was frustrating not being able to get back to London and see friends and family there. And, yes, I couldn't wait to travel again, and eat in restaurants again, and go to live sports events again, etc., etc. But, when all is said and done, the truth is Annie and I were remarkably happy in that year (plus some) of isolation, holed up in our hideaway in the Hollywood Hills. And, since neither of us had any interest in getting the deadly virus and we didn't work in essential services, we were very strict about our mask-wearing precautions and social distancing. Apart from going to the doctor for a flu shot at the end of October 2020, and getting my first two COVID vaccinations in January and February 2021, I never went into any building other than our own house after the pandemic was declared. However, I did go for a walk in the hills around us once or twice every day, and, consequently, my only in-person social contact was talking to the neighbours I saw—masked and at a safe distance—on those walks. The only exception was Ally coming over a few times for barbecues on various birthdays and holidays.

By the time things did start to open up again on the acting front, it had been almost two years since I was in front of a camera. Ironically, it was to appear in a supernatural thriller/horror film, which was the same genre as the last thing I'd done (*The Haunting Of Bly Manor*) before the pandemic. Which maybe suggests that, as I get older, my face is more suited to frighten people than to make them laugh. The working title of the film was *The Queen Mary* (and may be the eventual title), and I played the captain of the famous ship in the 1930s. It was a wonderfully nuanced part, both villainous and heroic, and it gave me a chance to do some very fine "beard acting." Almost all my scenes were with a lovely actor named Tim Downie, whose acting roots also began in comedy, and, despite some brutally long and cold night shoots and the numerous hurdles of filming during COVID with a relatively inexperienced crew, the very creative and personable young director, Gary Shore, was a pleasure to work with and he made the whole experience a rewarding one.

However, the film also marked a first for me in a somewhat painful way. About a week before I flew from LA to London for the shoot, I got a kidney stone. I hadn't had one for many years, but I knew what it was the moment the excruciating pain came on in the middle of the night. Annie rushed me to Cedars-Sinai hospital and I was in so much pain that the twenty-five minute drive seemed to take several hours. Anyway, I was scanned, given the requisite painkillers, and released a few hours later, having been told that the stone had either moved into my bladder or that I'd passed it. Sure enough, I was fine the next day and, a few days later, I flew to London to shoot *The Queen Mary*. About a month later, on one of my last days on the film, I was in my trailer between scenes and needed to have a pee. But when I did, I got a very unpleasant pain right below my stomach and the "flow" into the toilet bowl was barely a dribble—and a sharply uncomfortable one at that. I shot one more scene and then had another break in my trailer. And then the same thing happened again. Only this time, as I felt the very unpleasant pain below my stomach and experienced the extremely uncomfortable dribble as I had my pee, there was suddenly an additional searing pain in my *membrum virile* and then an almighty gush . . . and I was immediately peeing with the force and volume of a prize racehorse. It was like a twisted hosepipe had been straightened to allow an almighty flow of built-up water, and—hey, presto—the pain below my stomach and in the Piddock manhood evaporated entirely! When I returned to the set to shoot my next scene and casually told everyone that, after forty-three years as an actor, I'd just done something I'd never done before between scenes—passed a kidney stone—I think the whole cast and crew were genuinely impressed.

Analysing my journey in life thus far, with as much clinical and brutal objectivity as I can, I'd say I've had a decent, but modest journeyman career as an actor. And I've had a very maverick, lucrative, and unusually independent career as a writer. I've certainly been fortunate enough to have experienced a *lot* of things I never remotely expected to when I started out as an actor in children's theatre in England all those years ago. Back then, my ambition was mainly focused on being a working actor on a consistent basis. I honestly didn't expect to find myself starring on Broadway by my mid-twenties. . . or appearing in two major studio box office hits . . . or creating and running my own TV show . . . or conceiving and writing a film that's made over a hundred million dollars . . . or owning a villa with a swimming pool in the Hollywood Hills, etc., etc. On the other hand, there are still a few things left that I'd really like to experience . . . like playing a regular character in a long-running TV series. Given the length and variety of my dual careers in show business, it's actually surprising I haven't done that yet, but I'm very happy to have a goal or two still left to achieve!

At home in the Hollywood Hills, photo credit to Adrian Woolfe.

As a writer, you get used to telling stories with a beginning, a middle, and an end. And even though this book is technically a collection of mostly chronological stories and anecdotes, you might be expecting the whole entity to have that kind of conventional structure. While there's no doubt there is *some* resolution in these pages, I nevertheless apologise if I can't serve up a more climactic third act car chase or exploding fireworks type of ending. I can only offer the humble excuse that I can't . . . for the very simple reason that the sorts of experiences I've shared in these pages are very much ongoing.

So, in lieu of a more traditional or conventional ending, I'll leave you instead with one of the many reflections I've pondered on during the course of these last couple of pandemically-tainted years (and I think I just invented a very 2020/2021 adverb there). I don't know whether you've experienced the same thing, but after the pandemic restrictions were put in place, I began having more lucid dreams than I can ever remember having. And early one morning, about a year ago, when I was in that half-awake, half-asleep state before you get out of bed, while I lay there I began to hear the voice of my late friend Bill Paxton. I think it was for several minutes, but I'm not really sure because I wasn't aware of time. Those of you who believe in such things might speculate that his spirit was talking to me; those of you who don't believe in such things will almost certainly say it was just me talking to myself in my head. And the rest of you may simply believe that someone who hears voices in his head should be institutionalized posthaste. I have no idea which of those reactions is the correct one, but what I will say is that I wrote down everything I heard after I got up that morning. And this is some of what I wrote:

> . . . All of life, who you are, what you achieve, what your relationships are, *everything*, is a choice. Every second of every day, from the minute you're born. It's often not complicated or multiple choices, mostly just A or B. But it defines everything about our personalities and our lives . . .
>
> . . . When you're alive, time is linear and horizontal. Outside of that, time is vertical. Look up or down that tube and you can see everything—past, present, and future—all as one. It doesn't exist as past, present, or future. Just all at the same time, in an instant or an eternity. But while you're living in linear, horizontal time, you can't see all the high and lows, or the victories and defeats, that are to come. So you have to enjoy the moment. It's the only way to experience linear time. And, again, it's a *choice* . . .
>
> . . . It doesn't matter if this is me talking to you or you talking to yourself. It's all the same thing. Just a reflection and a refraction. Like light. Like sound . . .

Thank you for taking the time to listen to me talking to you, by reading this book. And may all your own choices in life be as true to you as I hope mine have been to me.

It's what we are.

ACKNOWLEDGEMENTS

First and foremost, in terms of this book, the person I have to thank the most is Gordon McClellan at DartFrog Books, who believed in it from the moment he first read it (in one sitting, he claims!). I sincerely hope your faith in me and in the book will be repaid a thousandfold, Gordon. I'm also indebted to Katelynn Watkins and Amy Bachelder for their fine editing, proofreading, and project managing skills, Mark Hobbs for the cover design, Amanda O'Connor for her social media marketing and publicity expertise, and the rest of the DartFrog Books team. And I'd like to extend special thanks to Alex Cole, Tom Connolly, Ann Cusack, Felicity Hayes-McCoy, Eric Idle, Taryn Johnston, Ross King, Sophie Lambert, Dan Rutstein, Will Shindler, and Jenny Wood for reading early drafts of the book and offering a lot of very welcome encouragement and advice.

In terms of my life and career, it's hard to know where to begin when trying to remember all the people who have given me encouragement or shown me kindness or helped me in some way. I'm certain there will some people I forget and I'll be kicking myself later because they were such an obvious omission. If you don't see your name in this list below and you think you should have, please let me know and I'll buy you a drink or a cup of coffee to make up for it. That said, in alphabetical order, I'd like to give my eternal thanks to:

Trevor Albert, Phil Alexander, Cindy Ambers, Robert Amram, Beverly Andrews, Tom and Millie Ashworth, Simon Astaire, Hugh and Paula Aynesworth, Bob Balaban, Alan Barnette, Ray Bateup, Ed Begley, Jr., Ian Granville Bell, Jeffrey Bihr, Don and Gerry Bleach, Sue Blu, Jason Blum, David Brady, Caroline Branfoot, Pat Brannon, Steve and Sophie Browett, Kimberly Buccieri, Tony Burns, Kate Burton, Bill Bushnell, Terry Byfield,

Gabriella Capisani, Deb Caponetta, A.J. Carothers, Johnny Chambers, Joe Cohen, Stewart Cohen, Alex Cole, Bill Condon, Billy Connolly, Peter Connolly, James Cosmo, Elaine Craig, Gladys Cross, Yvonne Crossley, Ann Cusack, Jeff Danis, Howard Deutch, Colleen Dewhurst, Suzi Dietz, Chip Diggins, Steve Dontanville, Peter and Myra Egan, Mike Eisenstadt, Craig Emanuel, Julian Farino, Pat Faulstich, Janne Fecht, Mitch Feral, Pat and Lou Feuerstein, Peter Flannery, Neil Fleckman, John Francis, Peter Franklin, Natasha Galloway, Lowell Ganz, Paul Gardner, Kathleen Garrett, Sean Gascoine, Rupert Gavin, Duncan Gibbins, Vanessa Gilbert, Brian Glanville, Mark Gordon, Christopher Guest, Bill Haber, Kathryn Harrold, Vince Hilaire, Debbie Deuble Hill, Tony and Elizabeth Hirsch, Dustin Hoffman, Beth Holmes, Olivia Homan, Richard House, Sheila and Charlie Hume, Erik Hyman, Eric and Tania Idle, Taryn Johnston, Hugh Jolly, Rob Kenneally, Walter Kerwin, Rob King, Ross King, David Kipper, Tom Lacy, Jeffrey Lane, Don Lake, Vera Lake, Katie Law, Peter Layton, Steven Levine, Eugene Levy, David Lewis, Meg Liberman, Colin Lovelace, Graham Ludlow, Babaloo Mandel, Alan Mandell, Darryl Marshak, David Lozell Martin, Archer Mayor, Koni McCurdy, Robin McFarland, Colm Meaney, Karen Medved, Jon Melichar, Eric Michael, James Mitchell, Dudley Moore, Peter Lawrence Morley, Clint Morris, Eric Mottram, Karen Murphy, Chris Neame, John Newman, Paul Newman, Anne Nida, Mike and Adeline Nolan, Paul Norton, Margaret Oberman, Deborah Oppenheimer, Father Stephen Ortiger, Martin Page, Steve Parish, Bill Paxton, Jerry Pavlon-Blum, Paul Pepperman, Sheryl Petersen, Alexandra Piddock, Charles and Celia Piddock, Irving Posalski, John Prince, Richard Proudfoot, Harold Ramis, Richard Reineccius, Judy Rich, Michael Ritchie, Natanya Rose, Dan Rutstein, Mike Ryan, John Sachs, David Salazar, Richard Schmenner, Mark Scroggs, Richard Seyd, Mike Shallbetter, Steven Siebert, Deborah Skelly, Jean Smart, Mel and Pam Smith, Art Spigel, Julian and Barbara Stone, Nick Stoller, Alan Strachan, Bill Straus, Bobby Summerfield, E.W. Swackhamer, Teo Tat, Yale Udoff, Terry Venables, Paul Ventura, Jane Villiers, Dori Weiss, Dan White, Paxton Whitehead, Fred and Mary Willard, Ken Wilson, Jenny Wood, Bob Wunsch, and Laurie Zaks.

ABOUT THE AUTHOR

A s an actor, Jim starred in several Broadway shows in the 1980s, including *Present Laughter*, *Design For Living*, and the original production of *Noises Off*. Since then, he has appeared in numerous movies, such as *Independence Day*, *Lethal Weapon 2*, *The Prestige*, *Best in Show*, *The Five-Year Engagement*, *A Mighty Wind*, *Kill Your Friends*, and Woody Allen's *You Will Meet a Tall Dark Stranger*. He's also been seen in dozens of TV shows, like *Modern Family*, *Mom*, *Two and a Half Men*, *Lost*, *Monk*, *Friends*, *ER*, *Mad About You*, *The Drew Carey Show*, and *Castle*. He was also in the award-winning HBO series *From the Earth to the Moon* and starred in the CBS miniseries *The Women of Windsor*. In 2007 and 2012, Jim secured his reputation as one of the UK's most notable comedic exports when he starred on stage in Hollywood with Russell Brand, Billy Connolly, Tim Curry, Eric Idle, Eddie Izzard, Jane Leeves, Emily Mortimer, Tracey Ullman, and Sophie Winkleman in *What About Dick?*

As a writer/producer, Jim's films include *Tooth Fairy*, *The Man*, and *A Different Loyalty*. With Christopher Guest, he co-wrote and starred in the HBO series *Family Tree* and *Mascots* for Netflix. Production on his film *Frankel* is due to start in 2022 in the UK.

As I mentioned in the introduction, a large percentage of my royalties from this book will be split between these two charities:

BAFTA's US Access for All initiative provides local community programs that help underprivileged students in American high schools through mentoring, scholarships, after-school programs, industry access, hardship funds, and financial aid. The programs champion creativity, opportunity, and social change for all through the transformative power of film, games, and television.

Crystal Palace Football Club's Palace for Life Foundation works with children of all ages in South London, England, to help them make healthy, positive, and safe choices—now and in the future—through football and health programs, education academies, targeted invention, and routes to employment. The foundation's unique position in the community helps inspire individuals to make long-lasting changes to their lives.

What does an author stand to gain by asking for reader feedback? A lot. In fact, what we can gain is so important in the publishing world that they've coined a catchy name for it: "social proof." And without social proof, an author may as well be invisible in this day and age of digital media sharing.

So if you've enjoyed *Caught with My Pants Down and Other Tales from a Life in Hollywood*, please consider giving it some visibility by reviewing it on the sales platform of your choice. Your honest opinion could help potential readers decide whether or not they would enjoy this book, too.